BITTER-SWEET DEMOCRACY?

Bitter-Sweet Democracy?

Analyzing Citizens' Resentment Towards Politics in Belgium

Edited by Louise Knops, Karen Celis,
Virginie Van Ingelgom, Heidi Mercenier, and
François Randour

OpenBook
Publishers

ISBN Paperback: 978-1-80511-290-7
ISBN Hardback: 978-1-80511-291-4
ISBN Digital (PDF): 978-1-80511-292-1
ISBN Digital (EPUB): 978-1-80511-130-6
ISBN HTML: 978-1-80511-295-2

DOI: 10.11647/OBP.0401

Cover design: Jeevanjot Kaur Nagpal

'Cause it's a bittersweet symphony, that's life
Trying to make ends meet, you're a slave to money then you die
I'll take you down the only road I've ever been down
You know the one that takes you to the places where all the veins meet,
    yeah

No change, I can change
I can change, I can change
But I'm here in my mold
I am here in my mold
But I'm a million different people
From one day to the next
I can't change my mold
No, no, no, no, no
(Have you ever been down?)

Well, I've never prayed but tonight I'm on my knees, yeah
I need to hear some sounds that recognize the pain in me, yeah
I let the melody shine, let it cleanse my mind, I feel free now
But the airwaves are clean and there's nobody singin' to me now'

'Bitter-Sweet Democracy' is meant to convey the duality we observe in citizens' resentment towards politics and the mixed picture that is drawn throughout the chapters of this book: feelings of anger, betrayal, under-representation and unfairness, but also a lingering hopefulness about different ways to engage politically. On the one hand, 'bitterness' is a key affective characteristic of resentment; it denotes the feeling that emerges after long-lasting struggles, frustrations and disillusions. On the other hand, the 'sweet' element denotes democratic ideals and the remaining trust some citizens still have vis-à-vis existing institutions and democracy at large, albeit sometimes with the impression that these ideals are out of reach, or being structurally ignored. After deciding on the title, we also realized that the first verses of 'Bitter-Sweet Symphony' (The Verve, 1997), from which our title takes inspiration, captures some of the spirit of the times in which the project was carried out and this book was put together.

Contents

List of Figures and Tables

Figures

Tables

*Online resources may be viewed at https://doi.org/10.11647/OBP.0401#resources

Acknowledgements

In this book we hope to provide helpful knowledge about the phenomenon of political resentment in Belgium and contribute to ongoing public debates on the state of democratic societies overall. We are hugely thankful for the contributions of the citizens who participated in our research. Over the course of the project on which this book is based, 7351 people took part in our panel survey and 150 people came and spent more than two hours with us in focus group discussions in Brussels, discussing matters related to politics. Our research would not have been possible without the time and responses of all of them.

We would like to thank all the colleagues in the RepResent project who participated in the numerous exchanges and meetings needed to prepare this book. It is therefore a testimony to the collective spirit that grew during the years of the project and helped us to put together this edited volume.

A special thanks goes to Heidi Mercenier for her crucial work at key moments of the RepResent project, and this book project in particular. In the same spirit, thank you to Kenza Amara-Hammou, Guillaume Petit, François Randour, Ramon van der Does and Soetkin Verhaegen for their valuable help in the focus group data collection effort and many research activities which made this book possible.

We would also like to thank the research institutions who supported us: the Fonds Wetenschappelijk Onderzoek (FWO) and the Fonds National de la Recherche Scientifique (FNRS), under the Excellence of Science (EoS) project FNRS-FWO n°G0F0218N, which provided the means to undertake fundamental research. The EoS financing scheme has provided a unique and rich opportunity for researchers across different universities and linguistic communities in Belgium to work together around common research themes and topics. The research presented in this volume would have not been possible without these inter-cultural and cross-linguistic exchanges. We would like to thank the universities that supported us in this project: the Vrije Universiteit Brussel, the Université Catholique de Louvain, the Université libre de Bruxelles, the University of Antwerp and the Katholieke Universiteit Leuven. Beyond the EoS project, our research also involved close collaborations and partnerships with other projects such as the FWO project G062917N (2017-2021), the MSCA project IF@ULB N°4012Y000001 and the F.R.S.-FNRS postdoctoral fellowship 1.B.421.19F. T.

Finally, we would like to warmly thank the editorial team of Open Book Publishers, and in particular Alessandra Tosi, Lucy Barnes and Cameron Craig, who have significantly helped us in every single editorial step leading to the publication of the book. Thank you as well to the two anonymous reviewers whose comments and feedback have greatly helped us to improve an earlier version of the manuscript.

Contributors

Kenza Amara-Hammou is a postdoctoral researcher at the Institut de Sciences Politiques Louvain-Europe, UCLouvain. She completed her dissertation on how people in socio-economically difficult situations think about political representation. Her main research interests are political theory, representation, activist research, participatory action and cross-disciplinary research. She is currently working on bottom-up normative theory building and co-creation.

Pierre Baudewyns is associate professor of political behaviour at the School of Political and Social Sciences, UCLouvain. His research focuses on electoral behaviour among citizens and elites, and survey methodology. He has published on these topics in journals such as *Electoral Studies*, *West European Politics* and *Comparative European Politics*.

Luca Bettarelli was a research fellow at the Centre d'Étude de la Vie Politique (CEVIPOL) in the framework of the Marie-Curie program at ULB. Since 2023 he has been a research fellow at the University of Palermo. His current research focuses on trends and drivers of political polarization, using a regional approach. He is Editorial Manager of the *Italian Journal of Regional Science*. His recent work has appeared in *Research Policy*.

Karen Celis is full professor affiliated to the Vrije Universiteit Brussel (VUB) Department of Political Sciences. She co-chairs the VUB Center for Democratic Futures (DFUTURE) and RHEA, the Centre of Expertise on Gender, Diversity and Intersectionality, and, until last year, the VUB Academic Advisor on Equality Policy. She conducts theoretical and empirical research on the democratic quality of political representation from an intersectional perspective. She leads political science and interdisciplinary research programmes and projects about gender, diversity and intersectionality; about resentment and polarization; and about democratic design and innovations.

Caroline Close is professor in the Department of Political Science at the Université libre de Bruxelles (ULB) and she is a researcher at the Centre d'Étude de la Vie Politique (CEVIPOL). Her research interests include party politics, political behaviour, representation, and democratic innovations. Her work has appeared in *Party Politics*, *Acta Politica*, *Parliamentary Affairs*, *Political Studies*, and *Representation*.

Kris Deschouwer is emeritus professor in the Department of Political Science of the Vrije Universiteit Brussel. His research and publications deal with political parties, elections, political representation, regionalism, federalism and consociational democracy and Belgian politics.

August De Mulder is a PhD student at the department of political science at the University of Antwerp, as part of the M²P research group. His main research interests are political communication, political representation and public opinion. In his doctoral dissertation, he examines the various representative claims that politicians make about citizens and how these claims may affect citizens' feeling of being represented.

Fernando Feitosa is a lecturer in politics at Griffith University, Australia, and a former FNRS postdoctoral researcher at the Université Libre de Bruxelles. His research focuses on political behaviour and public opinion. He has published on these topics in several peer-reviewed journals, such as the *European Journal of Political Research*, *Party Politics*, and the *International Journal of Public Opinion Research*.

Laura Jacobs obtained her PhD at the University KU Leuven in 2017. She is a postdoctoral researcher at the University of Antwerp and scientific collaborator at the Université Libre de Bruxelles. Her research interests include voting behaviour, political communication, populism, public opinion, and media effects. She has published numerous SSCI-ranked journal articles in high-quality journals in the field of political science and political communication.

Isaïa Jennart is a PhD researcher at the University of Antwerp and the Vrije Universiteit Brussel. His research focuses on political knowledge and, more precisely, citizens' knowledge of the issue positions of political parties. He is further interested in public opinion, voters, electoral campaigns and voting advice applications.

Louise Knops is assistant professor in environmental humanities at the Université libre de Bruxelles. During the writing and editing of this book, she was a post-doctoral researcher at the Université Catholique de Louvain and the Vrije Universiteit Brussel. Her research interests range from affect and emotions, to political theory, social movements studies and environmental politics.

Jonas Lefevere is assistant professor of political communication at the Vrije Universiteit Brussel. His research focuses on political communication, electoral behaviour and the strategic communication of political parties. He has published in these topics in, amongst others, *Political Communication*, *Public Opinion Quarterly* and *Party Politics*.

Heidi Mercenier was a postdoctoral researcher at Vrije Universiteit Brussels and the Université Catholique de Louvain. She was also a Visiting Professor at the Université Saint-Louis–Bruxelles. Heidi Mercenier's main research interest lies in citizens' relationships with politics, especially the EU, as well as how current digitalisation processes affect such relationships. She has published in leading political science journals such as the *Journal of European Public Policy* and *Politique européenne*, and she has co-edited two collective volumes. She completed her PhD at the Université Saint-Louis–Bruxelles and she worked as a lecturer at the Vrije Universiteit Amsterdam and as a visiting fellow at the Center for European Studies (ARENA) of the University of Oslo.

Jean-Benoit Pilet is a full professor of political science at Université libre de Bruxelles (ULB). He coordinates the project POLITICIZE on public attitudes towards non-elected politics (deliberative democracy, direct democracy, technocracy). Several findings of this project have been recently published in journals including the *British Journal of Political Science*, *European Journal of Political Research*, *Political Behaviour*, *Party Politics*, *Political Studies* and the *European Political Science Review*. He has also published books and articles on elections, electoral systems, political parties, members of parliament, and the personalization of politics. He was co-PI at ULB (with Emilie van Haute) for the Excellence of Science project RepResent.

François Randour is a guest lecturer at the department of political, social and communication sciences at the University of Namur. His research and teaching interests focus on EU decision-making processes, regional, national and European parliaments, multi-level governance, federalism, and political discourse analysis. He has been a visiting fellow at Sciences Po, Mannheim University and at the University of Antwerp and a guest lecturer at the Université Catholique de Louvain, the University of Antwerp, Sciences Po and the University of Namur.

Benoît Rihoux is full professor in political science at the School of Political and Social Sciences, UCLouvain. He is an international leader in the field of comparative methods and designs, focusing in particular on Configurational Comparative Methods (CCMs) and Qualitative Comparative Analysis (QCA). He also publishes on mixed- and multi-method designs and is involved in diverse disciplinary, interdisciplinary and transdisciplinary projects, also including management, evaluation, development, health systems research and medicine, involving QCA and multi-method designs.

Maria-Jimena Sanhueza was a doctoral researcher at Université Libre de Bruxelles, under the project RepResent (2018-2021). Her research interests cover political representation, and citizens' attitudes towards the institutions of representative democracy.

Eline Severs is associate professor at the Department of Political Science, Vrije Universiteit Brussel (VUB). Her research interests fall within the field of democratic theory. Her expertise lies in democratic representation, the relationships between civil society and democratic governance, citizens' conceptions of democracy, democratic norms, and what it means to include historically disadvantaged groups. She is the chair of the European Consortium for Political Research (ECPR) Standing Group on Political Representation and the VUB lead in the REDIRECT (Horizon Europe funded) project that identifies strategies for rectifying the representative disconnect.

David Talukder is a postdoctoral fellow at the University of Namur. His research focuses mainly on political representation, political attitudes, democratic reforms, and deliberative democracy. He has published on these topics in journal such as the *British Journal of Political Science, Acta Politica* and *The European Journal of Politics and Gender*.

Ramon van der Does is a writer and political scientist (PhD, Université catholique de Louvain, 2023). He writes about deliberation and the representation of non-human animals and natural ecosystems in political decision-making. His work has appeared in journals such as *Public Administration*, *Political Studies*, and *Political Science Research and Methods*.

Patrick F. A. van Erkel is an assistant professor at the University of Amsterdam. His research interests include electoral behaviour, public opinion, political communication and polarization. He has published in journals such as the *European Journal of Political Research*, *Party Politics*, *Electoral Studies* and *Political Communication*.

Emilie van Haute is professor of Political Science at the Université libre de Bruxelles (ULB) and researcher at the Centre d'Étude de la Vie Politique (CEVIPOL). Her research interests focus on party membership, intra-party dynamics, elections, and voting behaviour. Her research has appeared in the *European Journal of Political Research*, *West European Politics*, *Party Politics*, *Electoral Studies*, *Political Studies*, and *European Political Science*. She is co-editor of *Acta Politica*.

Virginie Van Ingelgom is a F.R.S.–FNRS Senior Research Associate and professor of Political Science at the Institut de Sciences Politiques Louvain-Europe, UCLouvain. Her research interests focus on the issue of democracy and legitimacy at the subnational, national, European and global levels, on citizens' attitudes towards European integration, on policy feedback, and in qualitative and mixed methods. Her previous work has been awarded the Jean Blondel Ph.D. Prize by the European Consortium for Political Research (2012) and an ERC Starting Grant (Qualidem, 2017-2023).

Soetkin Verhaegen is assistant professor of European Politics at the Faculty of Arts and Social Sciences, Department of Political Science, at Maastricht University. She is associate researcher at the Institute of Political Science Louvain-Europe (ISPOLE) at UCLouvain. Her research inquires into citizens' perceptions of the (il)legitimacy of governance at different levels, European identity, youth, socialization, political participation and elites. Her work has been published in, amongst others, *American Political Science Review*, Oxford University Press, *European Journal of International Relations*, *Comparative European Politics*, and *Journal of Common Market Studies*.

Stefaan Walgrave is professor of Political Science and Head of the Media, Movements and Politics research unit at the University of Antwerp. His work deals with social movements and protest, public opinion and elections, media and politics, and the information-processing of political elites. He has published widely on these topics in, amongst others, the *American Journal of Political Science*, *Political Communication*, *Political Behaviour*, and the *American Sociological Review*.

1. Political resentment: an empirical and conceptual introduction

Louise Knops, Karen Celis &

Virginie Van Ingelgom

Abstract: In this chapter, Knops, Celis, and Van Ingelgom lay out the context–both empirical and theoretical–in which the book is rooted. The authors, first, briefly situate the study of resentment in the literature and against the contemporary political context. They present a rationale for focusing on resentment as key concept of studies on the crisis of democracy. The chapter then provides a conceptual introduction on resentment along three dimensions–morality, complexity and temporality–before giving a short description of the project EoS-RepResent from which the contributions of the book emerged, the specificities of the Belgian context, the objectives of the book, its structure and a preview of the individual chapters.

Times of resentment

For a long time now, we have been hearing that democracy is in 'crisis' (Przeworski, 2019). This crisis is foremost a crisis of representative democracy, evidenced by widening 'gaps' between citizens and representatives and the declining levels of citizens' trust in representative institutions (Dalton, 2004; Norris, 2011). Some scholars argue however that what we are witnessing today is rather a 'post-crisis' age of *un*democratization where 'post-democratic' practices (Crouch, 2004) and anti-democratic ideals are on the rise (Mittiga, 2022). Others suggest that the crisis of democracy has taken a new shape by expressing itself through a deep-seated and lingering political 'malaise' and resentment

https://doi.org/10.11647/OBP.0401.01

(Fukuyama, 2018; Hochschild, 2016), illustrated, among other things, by outbursts of popular anger (Mishra, 2017) and hate against political elites, in the streets, on social media, or in the form protest voting.

At the heart of this context lies 'resentment'. Resentment is a complex moral emotion, rooted in anger, and it is believed to underlie different political phenomena that characterize our current political times: votes for populist parties, electoral abstention, or record-high protest votes. Resentment vis-à-vis the political establishment, but also radically different types of resentful feelings towards 'migrants' and differently situated 'others' are thought to have pushed voters towards 'Brexit' (Bachman and Sideway, 2016), or towards Donald Trump (Cramer, 2016; Hochschild, 2016), among others. Resentment has also been identified as a key driver of protest and collective action against governmental institutions, for example by Yellow Vests activists in the years 2018-2020 (Knops and Petit, 2022) and protesters against COVID-19 related measures (Vieten, 2020). Beyond specific political events, resentment is tied to the broader and more structural trends of declining levels of trust in representative institutions and democracy (e.g., Ure, 2015; Fleury, 2020) and increasing feelings of alienation towards 'others' and towards established institutions (e.g., Hochschild, 2016; Fukuyama, 2018; Foessel, 2018).

However, far from being merely a symptom of 'our times' tied to the specificities of the contemporary political context, resentment also has other roots–both 'objective' and 'subjective'. Resentment can be caused by structural, systemic imbalances of power found, in particular, in historical systems of discrimination and inequality (Hoggett et al., 2013; Van Hootegem et al., 2021; Cramer, 2016; Hochschild, 2016). In this regard, the conditions for resentment to (re-)emerge in society have become increasingly favourable, as socio-economic inequalities are deepening across modern capitalist societies (Picketty, 2013; 2019), as ultra-conservative movements are fighting back against the pursuit of equality for gender or ethnic minorities, and as welfare states in many Western democracies are being dismantled (McKay, 2019). Resentment is also caused by subjective experiences of inequality and unfairness, for instance a sense of loss (Hoggett et al., 2013) or a sense of unfairness and relative deprivation in comparison to other social groups (Pettigrew, 2016; Smith et al., 2012). Here, the concept of felt inequality developed by Cynthia Fleury (2020) is useful to grasp the difference between subjective and objective situations of inequality, injustice or deprivation which may cause resentment; and how this is also linked to the broader democratic expectation of 'equality'. As Fleury explains, resentment, and *ressentiment* in particular (we will return to this distinction later), emerges at the moment when individuals feel unequal compared to others, and therefore unfairly treated, precisely because of the democratic belief that they 'should' be treated equal. This means, she says, that resentment can sometimes swing together with the notion of entitlement; of feeling entitled to equality, equal rights and treatment.[1] Relatedly, this also means that there is an important link between resentment, democracy and equality; some democratic theories (which draw on Max Scheler's understanding of resentment and Tocqueville's democratic theory) even consider democracy, by essence, as a system that breeds resentment, precisely because of the central position occupied by equality and the feelings that emerge when the expectation of equality is unmet (Fleury, 2020, p. 28).

Resentment may thus be expected to arise in many existing democracies, and among a variety of socio-demographic groups for different socio-economic and experiential reasons. There is political resentment among groups which are sometimes stigmatized as the 'losers of globalization' (Kriesi et al., 2008), but also among groups that suffer from historical discrimination and oppression, most importantly racialized and ethnic minorities (Fassin, 2013).[2] Relatively 'new' groups of resentful citizens may also emerge or become visible, as the material possibilities for resentment to be expressed diversify and intensify; in particular on social media platforms, which are now recognized for channelling and breeding resentment, fear and indignation among specific radical-right online audiences (Ganesh, 2020).

---

1   In French, Cynthia Fleury says: 'La frustration se développe sur un terreau du *droit à*'.

2   Didier Fassin distinguishes in this regard resentment from 'ressentiment' but situates both emotions in the context of the emotions that were expressed in the post-Apartheid South-African context to denote the reality of the perpetuation of 'racial, gender and spatial disparities born of a very long period of colonial and apartheid white domination.' (Fassin, 2013). On resentment and ressentiment: the politics and ethics of moral emotions. *Current Anthropology*, 54(3), 249-267.

The RepResent project

It is in these 'times of resentment' that the collective project RepResent–a word contraction between Representation and Resentment[3]–emerged. During the years 2018-2022, a team of Belgian political scientists embarked on a collective project to study resentment and democracy in Belgium. The RepResent project pooled a wide variety of methods (see Chapter 2 in this volume), and multiple epistemological, theoretical and methodological frameworks to improve existing understandings and knowledge about political resentment, where to observe it, how to study it, and what types of political lessons should be drawn from it.

The empirical study of resentment and its further conceptualisation were at the heart of RepResent–albeit not always explicitly or centre-stage in the early days of the project. During the first years of RepResent, the team developed broad surveys across the Belgian population, mapping electoral behaviour, democratic preferences, issue-congruence between citizens and representatives and ideological polarization across society. Six surveys were carried out in total, among which four waves of a panel survey carried out before and after the general elections of May 2019 in Belgium: pre-2019 elections (N = 7351), post-2019 elections (N = 3909), one year after the elections (N = 1996), and two years after the elections (N = 1119) (see the general methodological appendix placed at the end of the book)[4]. Together, these panel surveys produced a unique dataset designed to analyse voters' political attitudes and behaviours, notably on different dimensions of democratic representation, and with a specific focus on democratic resentment (e.g., citizens' attitudes towards democracy, such as distrust and alienation, but also behaviours such as abstention, protest, or voting for anti-establishment parties).

---

3   RepResent is a research team of political scientists from the University of Antwerp, Université Catholique de Louvain, Vrije Universiteit Brussel, Université Libre de Bruxelles and KU Leuven. The consortium was funded jointly by FWO and FNRS under their Excellence of Science Program fostering fundamental research collaborations between universities of the Flemish and French-speaking communities. For an overview of the principal investigators and other researchers in the RepResent consortium see: https://represent-project.be/

4   Throughout the book, contributors draw to various extents on the survey data and include in their analyses different sections of the total survey data. In addition to the four waves of the panel survey data, two "cross-sectional" surveys were carried out (see the general methodological appendix).

The longitudinal structure of the surveys also allowed the project teams to explore the political dynamics at play in Belgium throughout the lengthy government formation process (Elie Michel, Fernando Feitosa, Jonas Lefevere, Jean-Benoît Pilet, Patrick van Erkel & Emilie van Haute, 2023). In addition to the surveys, the project teams organized a large number of focus groups (28 focus groups in total) with different sets of citizens, ranging from activists to citizens in marginalized socio-economic positions and citizens who were invited to discuss politics in the aftermath of the first COVID-19 lockdown in 2020.[5] Regarding the researchers and contributors to this book, although we cannot speak for individual positionalities, the consortium as a whole gathered early-career and more senior researchers; it was gender-balance and epistemologically mixed, in the sense of bringing together researchers from various sub-fields and traditions within political science, albeit all predominantly anchored in Western literature and scientific knowledge. These methodological aspects are important to mention here because they invariably influence our approaches to emotions, politics and resentment. They are also reflected in the varied approaches to resentment gathered in this book: different attempts to study resentment, taking different angles and perspectives, and drawing on different methods and research epistemologies.

The results of the surveys (Pilet et al., 2020) provided, among other things, an overview of electoral behaviour among the Belgian population.[6] Early contributions made by the project also showed the importance of taking emotions into account to understand contemporary politics. Close and Van Haute demonstrated, in particular, that the interplay of 'positive' and 'negative' emotions towards politics and political institutions are central to understand voters' choices and electoral behaviour (Close and Van Haute, 2020). Similarly, Van Erkel and Turkenburg (2020) highlighted the importance of affective polarization and the 'affective distance' that persists between different social groups with different

---

5   Amara-Hammou, Kenza, Knops, Louise, Petit, Guillaume, Randour, François, Mercenier, Heidi, van der Does, Ramon, Verhaegen, Soetkin, Celis, Karen, Deschouwer, Kris, Rihoux, Benoît, Van Ingelgom, Virginie (2020). RepResent Focus Group Dataset: Representation and Democratic Resentment in Belgium, Excellence of science project (EOS)-FNRS-FWO funding n°G0F0218N (2018-2022).

6   The books in French and Dutch, as well as other publications, are freely accessible: https://represent-project.be/results/

ideological beliefs. Celis, Knops, Van Ingelgom and Verhaegen (2021) discussed how citizens are caught between feelings of anger and betrayal and remaining hopes vis-à-vis democracy and democratic institutions, and Knops and Petit (2022) analysed specifically what happens when resentment turns into indignation in the specific context of protest and mobilization (here, notably, in the Belgian Yellow Vests movement).

Overall, these studies are rooted in an epistemological position that underlines the importance of taking emotions and their broader societal implications seriously. They start from the premise that, if emotions are not considered, political scientists are often unable to see the full picture of politics—whether in terms of electoral behaviour, political participation or mobilisation, for example. And that, without taking emotions into account, important pieces of the puzzle (Groenendyck, 2011) go missing, on different sides of political relationships: what moves people, what mobilizes them and divides them; and how representatives and political institutions (can and should) act in return. For instance, without taking emotions into account, we cannot fully make sense of why voters with a low income persistently vote for representatives who explicitly favour less redistributive politics (Cramer, 2016) (even though emotions are evidently not the only explanatory factor); or why, in the face of abundant scientific information and evidence about catastrophic climate change, there is still a lack of social and political action (Norgaard, 2011).[7]

This book is also rooted in this premise, and thus takes inspiration from the scholarship which is broadly understood as 'the affective turn' (Clough and Halley, 2007; Athanasiou et al., 2009; Slaby & von Scheve, 2019). Under the affective turn, emotions are seen as the 'fabric of politics' (Lordon, 2016) (2016); its 'blood-life' (Marcus, 2002); as the foundation of passionate democratic engagement and conflict (Mouffe, 2018); and a constitutive aspect of the emergence of political subjectivities and representation (Knops, 2022; Williams 2007). The affective turn appeared, in part, as a reaction to a chronic neglect of emotions in political analyses, where studies of the crisis of representative democracy remain largely rooted in the epistemology of rational-choice theory and interest-based evaluations. Throughout this book, contributors take stock of the

---

7   Cramer shows that resentment vis-à-vis other groups of citizens defines the ways in which citizens relate to political institutions. Norgaard explains how modern societies manage to carry on with their 'lives, practically unchanged' through different types of denial.

affective turn in their analyses of resentment, while also linking it to more classical concepts of political science, such as congruence, political behaviour and democratic attitudes.

The theoretical motivations to study emotions, coupled with an empirical reality that may be characterized as 'resentful times' encouraged the team of the RepResent project to hone in on political resentment, to understand what it is, and draw lessons from its broader political and democratic implications. To be sure, this does not mean that the book is an exhaustive or complete attempt to take emotions and resentment seriously in political analyses; it rather provides a tentative framework to do so and illustrates how resentment may be understood and studied by political scientists coming from a range of different epistemological and methodological backgrounds.

To carry out the project and study of resentment–both empirically and conceptually–the team adopted an approach that may be characterized as 'abductive'. Abduction entails a 'back-and-forth' between theory and empirical analysis; it combines features of deductive and inductive research methods (Timmermans and Tavory, 2012; Tavory and Timmermans, 2014; Pierce, 1994; Vila-Henninger, et al., 2022). Abduction starts with a set of theories and seeks to further develop them by looking out for theoretically surprising empirical cases. Once discovered and analysed, abductive researchers return to existing theories, often combining them, to formulate a theoretical account that might explain the unexpected case (Reichertz, 2007). Subsequently, they test these inductive, theoretically grounded explanations against existing and additional empirical data, which may result in another round of theory-building.

In line with abductive analysis principles, our conceptual work was rooted both in previous studies of resentment and in our own empirical analyses and discussions thereof.[8] We started our conceptual work with existing theories and knowledge of what resentment might be, where it

---

8   The conceptual discussions were primarily driven by Work Package 3 of the RepResent team, including Guillaume Petit (UCLouvain/VUB), Kenza Amara-Hammou (VUB), Heidi Mercenier (UCLouvain/VUB), François Randour (UNamur/UCLouvain), Virginie Van Ingelgom (UCLouvain), Soetkin Verhaegen (UCLouvain), Karen Celis (VUB), Louise Knops (UCLouvain/VUB), and Ramon van der Does (UCLouvain) and draws on an earlier working paper prepared by Heidi Mercenier and Louise Knops 'Unpacking the concept of resentment: A theoretical and methodological introduction', 15 June 2021.

might be expressed and in what form. For this we turned to literature on the crisis of representative democracy, the affective turn in social sciences, and existing work on resentment. Resentment, we soon found out, is both abundantly defined, yet rarely unpacked and conceptualized. It is often defined as a form of moral, bitter anger, mixed with feelings of unfairness and betrayal that breed over time, creating, amongst other things, the conditions for populism to thrive. But this conceptualization of resentment seemed too narrow to capture the multiple ways in which resentment materializes empirically, and the many different groups that express it. To delineate a common understanding of resentment and identify methodological pathways to study it empirically, we engaged in a collective conceptual and methodological discussion. This required, first, the development of a common language, across the different political traditions and epistemologies of the project. We then used our empirical analyses to further enhance our understanding of what resentment is, how it can be operationalized for empirical studies and what may be its normative implications. This book presents the outcome of this 'slow science' process: the evolutive and incremental trajectory of continuous exchanges amongst us, long discussions with citizens, and, in some cases, long periods of field work.

Other defining features of our project are its explicit normative ambitions and ethical positionality. As democratic scholars, we are driven by a strong commitment to democratic values and the work presented in this volume is born out of a deep concern about democratic backsliding, the emergence of illiberal democracies and new forms of legitimation for authoritarianism (Foa and Monk, 2016; Mittiga, 2022). Our book thus attempts to respond to the call for impactful political research which seeks to describe and provide tentative explanations, but also reflects on how to resist current anti-democratic trends and how to strengthen democracies (Merkel 2019; Saward, 2020).

Finally, in our study of resentment, we have placed citizens centre stage. The theoretical and empirical insights presented in the book are anchored in citizens' own understandings of and emotions towards politics, and some of the methodological approaches developed during the project are anchored in the principles of co-creation, participatory action research and collaborative research practices with high societal impact (Amara-Hammou, 2023). Over the course of our project, 7351 people took part in our panel survey and 150 people spent more than two hours with us in Brussels for focus groups discussions. We owe an enormous debt to all the citizens who agreed to participate in our study, and we seek to acknowledge this as often as possible by integrating their own words and political analyses into our findings.[9]

Resentment: our approach & contribution

Drawing on various literatures (among others political philosophy, political psychology, political representation, affect theory, and social movements studies), and on the abductive analyses of our empirical data, we conceptualize resentment first and foremost as an emotion.

Our understanding of emotion brings together classic definitions of emotions from political psychology and an understanding of emotion that takes inspiration from affect theory. Like Sara Ahmed (2004; 2014) we use emotion and affect interchangeably. We understand emotion as a broad conceptual category that brings together the simultaneous cognitive, psychological, and physiological reactions that individuals experience in response to the evaluation of a threat, or when faced with a source of pleasure, anger, or sadness (Scherer, 2005). To this, we add the explicit acknowledgment of the performative and relational dimensions of emotions that turn them into explicitly political objects, because they 'do' things. As Sara Ahmed explains, emotions are political because, among other functions, they bridge the individual and collective by binding bodies and subjects together; they play a crucial role in the deeply political process of collective identification and subjectivation (Ahmed, 2004; 2014).

Based on this understanding of emotion, we identify the following distinctive features and dimensions of resentment:

1. morality–an emotion that responds to situations of injustice or unfairness and casts a normative judgement;

2. complexity–characterized by more than one emotion;

3. temporality–a complex emotion that builds and grows over time.

---

9   They are necessarily anonymous; readers can get an idea of the range of individuals who helped us in this way from Appendices 2 and 3 of Chapter 2.

First, the emotional core of resentment is anger, but a specifically *moral* form of anger. Resentment is defined, for example, as 'bitterness and anger that someone feels about something' (Collins English Dictionary); a feeling of 'anger about a situation you think is unfair' (Cambridge English Dictionary). Resentment carries an explicitly moral and normative load because it implies a certain conception of what a 'fair' or 'just' situation should look like for a given social group. As Ure notes (2015, p. 600):

> We resent what we judge unjust. We judge unjust intentional, undeserved harmful acts or slights. [...] Resentment is an emotion through which we express the judgment that we have suffered a deliberate injustice, resentment explicitly or implicitly identifies norms of justice that we believe do or ought to regulate social and political interaction.

In the same vein, Engels (2015, p. 25) defines resentment as a moral emotion along the following lines:

> (1) the perception that one has suffered an unwarranted injury [...] and thus a judgment of moral wrong; (2) a feeling of hostility at the perpetrator of the injury; and (3) the manifestation of that hostility, in words or deeds.

Second, while most common definitions situate resentment as a moral form of 'anger', resentment may also include other emotions. Resentment is defined, for example, as 'a complex, multi-layered emotion; a mixture of *disappointment, anger* and *fear*' (Tenhouten, 2007). Solomon (1993) places resentment on the same trajectory as anger and contempt, and resentment is also sometimes associated with other complex feelings such as vengeance, rancour, and acrimony (Fassin, 2013) and the distinctive bitterness that comes with frustrations that have been chewed on for a long time (Fleury, 2020). Adding to the emotional complexity of resentment, scholars have recently described resentment as including fear and anxiety but also hope (Capelos and Demertzis, 2018)–more commonly understood as a positive emotion. In sum, resentment is not a single, firm, or well-defined emotional state, but a combination of emotions, which may vary from situation to situation and carry different implications depending on who expresses resentment in the first place.

Third, the emotions that compose resentment are also seen as 'growing' over time, which heightens the specific temporality of resentment compared to other forms of moral anger; it is an incremental feeling of frustration and anger which produces the characteristic 'bitterness' often ascribed to resentment. Resentment is also a reaction to situations that are judged to be unfair or discriminatory over time– here neighbouring with the classic notion of 'relative deprivation'. Relative deprivation is a political concept which describes 'the judgment that one is worse off compared to some standard'. Among other things, the concept draws on Marxist social class theory, whereby comparisons and the feelings that emerge within and between social groups are key to understanding social and political behaviour. In social psychology, relative deprivation is closely associated with resentment. As is well documented in their analytical review of the term, Smith et al. (2012) explain: 'Marx (1847/1935) captures the intuitive appeal of relative deprivation (RD) as an explanation for social behaviour. If comparisons to other people, groups, or even *themselves at different points in time* lead people to believe that they do not have what they deserve, they will be angry and resentful.' (Smith et al., 2012, p. 203, emphasis added).

Although emotions are the conceptual core of resentment, our understanding of resentment goes beyond the language of emotions only. On the one hand, this is consistent with our epistemological position, which does not consider emotions from a binary perspective as distinctive from other cognitive, behavioural dimensions; we prefer to see emotions, actions and cognition as interwoven in a more circular manner. On the other hand, and relatedly, studying resentment from a political science perspective requires us to include other related political 'neighbours' such as relative deprivation (see above) but also political distrust, democratic illegitimacy, protest. This understanding is also motivated by empirical reasons: to fully understand the political effects of resentment on society and democracy, it is important to expand the conceptual scope from *'what resentment is'* to *'what resentment does'* in terms of political behaviour, attitudes and broader implications. To this end, we found much inspiration in the work of Cramer (2016), who uses resentment as a heuristic tool to investigate the crises of representative politics, as well as in the innovative work of political psychologists Capelos and Demertzis (2018, 2021) who coined 'resentful affectivity' in order capture the emotions and political attitudes and behaviours that may derive from resentment (itself comprised of multiple emotions).

The concept of 'resentful affectivity' was foregrounded to make sense of the grievances, anti-establishment sentiment, anti-expert scepticism, anti-immigration demands, and support for populist parties–all different expressions of contemporary 'resentment'–in the Greek political context, which was marked by the drastic austerity measures taken in the aftermath of the economic and financial crisis (Capelos and Demertzis, 2018; 2021). Capelos and Demertzis found that resentful affectivity was composed of a distinctive yet ever changing set of emotions (shame, hope, anger, anxiety, fear, sadness, disappointment, pride, apathy) which characterizes citizens' relations to politics and political behaviour. Importantly, they determined whether and when resentful affectivity resulted in apathy or, in contrast, political engagement (Capelos and Demertzis, 2018, p. 3). By including apathy as part of resentful affectivity, Capelos and Demertzis resolve the distinction between 'resentment' and its French translation 'ressentiment' whereby the former is linked to a sense of political efficacy and the latter to a sense of powerlessness and impotence (Ure, 2015; Fassin, 2013).[10]

Siding with Capelos and Demertzis and earlier work carried out by members of the RepResent team (e.g., Celis et al., 2021), we apply resentful affectivity as a 'heuristic tool'. By this we mean that rather than investigating resentment based on a fixed and pre-defined set of emotions, processes, and actions, we ask questions about what kinds of emotions are at play in situations where we expect to observe resentment, which processes are they part of and in which actions do they result, or not. Applying resentful affectivity as a heuristic tool in our empirical studies has enabled us to study resentment along the three dimensions outlined above, and combine questions about what resentment is, where it exists and what it does. In particular:

---

10   As well explained by anthropologist Didier Fassin, this difference can be traced back to different philosophical traditions, and designates different types of affective reactions. While the former (resentment) seems to derive from Adam Smith's theory of moral sentiments, and is linked to frustration and acrimony, the latter (ressentiment) finds its roots in the work of Nietzsche and is related to historical situations of oppression and domination. Ure (2015) suggests a normative differentiation between what he calls 'moral and socio-political resentment', emphasizing the situation of resentment as part of the affective 'equipment' of social life (and hence overall a 'good' emotion), as distinct from a kind of pathologizing and ontological 'ressentiment' that results in hatred, passivity, and impotence (seen largely as a 'negative' emotion).

i. the complex, dynamic, and evolutive character of resentment in terms of emotions at play, and the various objects these emotions relate to (e.g., anger and fear as the constitutive components of a resentful affectivity can, for instance, have a different object than feelings of hope, which are constitutive of the same affectivity);

ii. the situations and contexts from which resentment emerges, the groups and communities which express resentment;

iii. how various affective constellations produce different, and at times even contradictory stances (attitudes, preferences, ...) vis-à-vis politics, thereby crucially nuancing simplistic and static 'positive' vs 'negative' evaluations;

iv. the kinds of political (in)actions it motivates (for instance, forms of protest and collective action, or alienation, abstention, or apathy), and importantly both the negative and the positive impact of resentment on society and democracy.

In sum, our conceptualization of resentment relies on, first, a performative and relational understanding of emotions. Second, it includes the identification of key dimensions and components of political resentment, as a complex cluster of emotions made of anger, fear and hope; a moral emotion that responds to subjective and objective situations of unfairness; and an emotion that has a distinctive temporality, in the sense of breeding over time. This may be found, for example, in citizens' long-lasting dissatisfaction towards politics, or in the continuous and repeated experiences of injustice and misrepresentations. Third, our conceptualization proposes that we should consider resentment as a 'resentful affectivity', which acknowledges that resentment is an 'open-boundary' and context- and time-specific constellation of emotions; that these emotions might well have shifting and multiple objects, and they may evolve over time, and across social groups; and that the attitudes and political behaviours it gives rise to are not pre-defined but rather remain open to empirical investigation. Concretely, and this is important to outline upfront, this means that, whilst resentment is first and foremost an emotion, the contributions gathered in this book do not focus only on the emotional components of resentment, but also include a multiplicity of related concepts and political attitudes.

The Case of Belgium

Although the RepResent project was carried out in Belgium, and concerns the political behaviour, attitudes and feelings of Belgian citizens, this book is not about a typically 'Belgian' resentment, compared to other national contexts. Yet, the findings presented in this book are closely tied to the Belgian context and we refrain from generalizing our empirical findings beyond Belgium. Hence a few remarks on the 'Belgian case' are necessary to situate resentment in the Belgian socio-economic and political context and identify why Belgium offers a relevant empirical field for resentment to be observed. To be sure, what we present below is by no means an exhaustive account of the historical roots of the many forms that resentment may take in Belgium; we merely signal a few important highlights that are useful to re-situate the findings and discussions we present in the book.

First, Belgium, like most Western democracies, has not been immune to the crisis of representative democracy and declining levels of trust towards political elites and institutions. Although Belgium's consociational model of democracy has enabled successive governments to overcome the deep divisions cutting across Belgian society, recent years have also been marked by repeated and deep political crises, causing major disruptions to Belgian political, social, and economic life (Xhardez et al., 2020).[11] The Belgian elections in May 2019, for instance, around which our research project was carried out, took place in a context of strong political instability (Pilet, Baudewyns, Deschouwer, Kern and Lefevre, 2020) and resulted in an important rise in protest voting. This was illustrated, among other things, by the sharp rise of the far-right nationalist party Vlaams Belang which became the second biggest party in Flanders with 11.9% of votes in 2019. At the same time, Belgium has also been a scene of what is sometimes called "democratic vitality", through the experimentation of democratic innovations, including mini-publics and citizens assemblies (Caluwaert and Reuchamps, 2018; Vrydagh et al., 2021) and a historically vibrant civil society (made of

---

11   Belgium has experienced a series of governmental crises, in particular over issues of federal and constitutional reform, sometimes leaving the country without a federal government for over a year. It took 494 days after the general election of May 2019 for Belgium to have a federal government.

trade unions, social movements, non-governmental organisations, among others). This is a situation that gives rise to a range of possible hypotheses on the different and competing democratic demands voiced by resentful citizens (we discuss this topic further in Chapter 10 of this volume).

Second, the specificities of Belgian federalism and its history are important to mention here to situate our study of resentment and the multiple causes and origins it may have in the Belgian context. Resentment is tied to the history of Belgium in and of itself. As well documented by Liesbeth Hooghe (2004), most of Belgian politics since its secession from the Netherlands in 1830 have been tied to territorial, cultural and linguistic conflicts between Walloons (in the south of the country) and Flemings (in the north of the country). These conflicts–and the inequalities and power differentials between the respective communities in both regions–have generated different types of resentment, which continue today. On the one hand, there is a historical feeling of resentment which is tied to the specific relation of domination exerted, historically, by the French-speaking bourgeoisie on the Dutch-speaking population in Belgium. Indeed, even though Dutch was a dominant language on Belgian territory, French became the sole official language throughout the entire central administration of Belgium, which created discrimination and feelings of injustice among the Dutch-speaking population. This, as explained by Fahrat, Rosoux and Poirier (2014), 'triggered the emergence of the so-called "Flemish movement" against the French-speaking elite and was intensified by the socio-economic disparities between the French-speaking provinces in early industrialized Wallonia and the Dutch-speaking areas plagued by large-scale poverty' (Fahrat et al., 2021, p. 394).

The situation of structural inequality between the two linguistic communities generated a long series of territorial conflicts and protests during the 1950s and 1960s and triggered a series of constitutional reforms, which started in the 1970s and culminated in the creation of a Belgian federal state in 1993. Subsequent constitutional reforms have also taken place to deepen and diversify the process of Belgian federalization. The move from a unitary state to a federal state led to a situation often described as the 'paradox of federalism' (Erk and Anderson, 2009) which both tempered existing feelings of resentment and created new ones: it created a situation where 'granting autonomy to the linguistic groups was initially considered a means of pacifying ethnolinguistic tensions, but at the same time it also legitimized and exacerbated the underlying identity conflicts' (Pascolo et al., 2021). Throughout the federalization of Belgium, resentment significantly evolved along with the evolution of the socio-economic disparities between the north and the south of the country; while the Walloon region had long been the economic powerhouse of Belgium, the situation began to reverse in the aftermath of World War II, with Flanders rising to become one of the wealthiest regions of Western Europe, and Wallonia becoming one of the poorest.

As a result, the resentment observed in Belgium today is multifaceted. It is expressed, among other ways, by a reaction to a federalization process which is perceived as going too far by some, but mostly as not going far enough by others, in particular in the north where citizens feel that they are contributing an unfair or disproportionate amount towards a federal state that they no longer believe in. These feelings have been particularly well channelled by the Flemish nationalist party N-VA and the far-right party Vlaams Belang, both claiming to protect the interests of the Flemish population as their number one priority, and who have been enjoying very high levels of popularity in recent years.

Across both communities, another type of resentment has also emerged in reaction to the loss of purchasing power, the rise of unemployment and the general decline of living conditions experienced by a section of the middle-class Belgian population. These feelings found a direct site of expression in the Yellow Vests movement in the years 2018—2019, which gave a voice to broader feelings of resentment among the Belgian population and combined a range of heterogeneous political identities.

Third, and relatedly, the socio-economic inequalities that characterize Belgium find a particular materialization in Brussels, which is important to highlight for the purpose of situating our study of resentment in the Belgian context (and in Brussels in particular, where some of our empirical field work was carried out). Although the average income in Brussels is higher than in other regions, Brussels remains the poorest region of Belgium, when one considers the amount of citizens at risk of—or experiencing—poverty: the proportion of individuals living below the poverty line amounts to 25% in Brussels, versus 9% in Flanders and 18% in Wallonia (Englert et al., 2021). Brussels is also marked by strong disparities of income and other types of discrimination linked to gender and race, inherited from Belgium's migration history and colonial past. Brussels is a highly multicultural and diverse city; the demographic figures of 2022 for Brussels show that 59% of its population holds a non-Belgian identity (a figure that is based on a person's nationality at birth) (IBSA & Statbel, 2022), a socio-demographic situation that is instrumentalized by radical-right and nationalist parties to fuel further resentment based on anti-immigration sentiments.

To be sure, the different dimensions of Belgium's federal structure and history, and the specificity of the socio-economic inequalities that cut across Belgian society are not the sole explanation for the resentment we observe, nor, we want to stress, the main focus of our book. However, these elements are crucial pointers to situate our findings in the Belgian socio-economic and political context.

Throughout the chapters of this volume, contributors to the project will illustrate, document and unpack different facets of citizens' resentment towards politics in the Belgian context (in the years 2018—2022). Collectively, these contributions fulfil an important empirical objective of documenting multiple facets of resentment in a context of deepening democratic crisis. They also contribute to ongoing conceptualizations of resentment and normative discussions about its implications for democracy and society. Lastly, the book has a strong methodological ambition in the sense that, by pooling together teams and researchers from different epistemological backgrounds, it provides a tentative roadmap for future political scientists eager to take our study of resentment further. The innovation of our work lies partly in the questions we have asked, the combination of approaches we have brought together, and the way we proceeded collectively to provide answers. As such, and because of the multiple objectives pursued by this edited volume, the chapters below inform ongoing work on resentment beyond Belgium and provide the grounds for comparative analyses with other political and socio-economic contexts.

About this book

Bitter-Sweet Democracy is a testimony to the complexity, contradictions, and ambivalences we observe in the relationship of citizens to politics in Belgium. Yes, there is resentment across society, but there is also a lot of hope. Yes, democracy is sometimes perceived as 'fake', an 'illusion'; a site of betrayal and exclusion; but democracy also remains an ideal to strive for, and a semantic signifier that remains associated in citizens' minds with the values of equality and freedom.

This edited volume presents a series of findings and results that attempt to bridge the gap between the language of political affect, emotions and affectivity, and core political science concepts such as congruence, democratic preferences, and legitimacy. It is also an attempt to strike a balance between providing a consistent approach and a thread that ties the chapters together, and offering a celebration of the differences and the diversity–in content and form–between them. In the following chapters, the contributors document political resentment through one or several of its emotional components; by investigating resentment's conceptual *entourage* (for instance, feelings of being represented, incongruence, democratic preferences, protest); or zooming in on morality and the temporal aspects or resentment; identifying who the resentful citizens are and how resentment leads to different democratic preferences and imaginaries.

In Chapter 2, Randour, Verhaegen and De Mulder show how the multifaceted concept of resentment has been approached and studied throughout the RepResent project, using different methods and gathering different types of data–mainly, surveys and focus groups. The chapter reviews the different methodological steps from different parts of the project that have followed an iterative logic based on the conceptual evolution of resentment, its understanding, and its mobilization. The chapter first discusses the use of quantitative and deductive methods for the study of resentment, and more precisely the application of different surveys, types of questions and their rationale. Second, the chapter discusses the use of qualitative and inductive methods in the study of resentment. Third, the chapter presents how qualitative and quantitative methods were combined, integrating insights from focus group research in the development of new survey questions. The chapter concludes with an assessment of the different approaches and the theoretical and methodological challenges associated with the study of political resentment. The general methodological appendix at the end of the book gathers some of the main methodological aspects related to the project and will serve as a methodological reference for the remainder of the chapters.

In Chapter 3, Feitosa, Baudewyns, Pilet and Talukder attempt to delineate who the resentful citizens are in Belgium by identifying and discussing where, i.e., across which socio-economic and demographic variables, resentment lies in society. Using data from the 2021 RepResent cross-sectional survey, the authors explore the distribution of resentment across five dimensions: gender, age, education, vote choice, and region of residence. The findings indicate significant variations in resentment levels among different age groups: resentment is highest among the middle-aged population rather than younger individuals. Additionally, there are remarkable differences across vote choices, with protest voters exhibiting higher levels of resentment compared to other voters. However, no substantial differences are observed when considering gender, educational levels, or regions of residence. These results also lead to a discussion of the specific situation of marginalized groups and reveal that protest voters experience a profound sense of exclusion from the political system.

After setting the scene, the book continues by including a series of chapters that empirically examine some of the emotional and behavioural dimensions of resentment. In Chapter 4, Bettarelli, Close, Jacobs and Van Haute investigate the affective complexity of resentment and how it relates to different types of political behaviour. Using the 2019 RepResent Voter Panel Survey, this chapter investigates the affective complexity of resentment and its impact on protest behaviour, understood as non-electoral protest participation and protest voting. It focuses on the combination of two core emotions towards politics and their intensity levels: anger and hope. Five groups that vary in their intensity of anger and hope are distinguished: neutral, high-intensity hopeful, high-intensity angry, high-intensity emotive, and apathetic. The results of these analyses show that different emotional clusters guide distinct types of protest actions. Apathy leads to 'exit' and decreases the probability of protest participation and protest voting. Citizens experiencing high-intensity anger turn away from mainstream parties and are more likely to vote for protest parties. The combination of high intensities of anger and hope motivates the expression of resentment through non-electoral protest actions. These findings reaffirm the significance of the affective dimension of political action, and support a conception of affective arrangements in which emotions combine to produce political outcomes. Finally, they interrogate the relevance of common binaries and distinctions that classify emotions as either positive or negative.

In Chapter 5, van der Does, Amara-Hammou and Talukder dive into the political dissatisfaction of people in socio-economic difficulties and marginalized situations, and discuss the objects of their political dissatisfaction, i.e., the political institutions and practices they are resentful about. People who face socio-economic disadvantages tend to be underrepresented in politics. Drawing on both survey data and focus group discussions conducted among socio-economically disadvantaged people in Brussels, the authors find that socio-economically disadvantaged people are generally more resentful, but this research also underlines the difficulty of reaching these groups, and the importance of deploying qualitative research methods and having a continuous presence in the field. The analyses of the focus groups specifically show that the targets of participants' resentment were mostly local actors and that expressions of resentment seemed tied to the experience of concrete problems. Second, even though resentment manifested itself in frustration, disappointment, and, at times, indifference towards politics, it also went hand in hand with at least some hope that politics could offer a solution to societal challenges. Most strikingly, and in contrast to some common assumptions about resentment and anti-establishment attitudes, participants wanted to be heard by existing representatives and sought to deepen their relationships with them rather than rejecting them entirely.

In Chapter 6, Lefevere, van Erkel, Walgrave, Jennart, Baudewyns and Rihoux take a different perspective and study resentment in relation to the political concept of 'incongruence'. In particular, the authors investigate the relation between voters' policy incongruence– the mismatch between their own preferences and parties' preferences– and resentment. Here, Lefevere et al. hypothesize that incongruence is positively related to resentment: the more incongruent voters are with either their own preferred party (egotropic incongruence) or the whole party system (sociotropic incongruence), the less likely it is that voters will expect policy that aligns with their preferences, and thus benefits them. Such incongruence likely fosters resentment. The authors further hypothesize that the relation between incongruence and resentment is moderated by voters' knowledge of parties' positions on different issues. Using some of the 2019 survey data from the RepResent project (the 2019 Panel Survey Data and the 2019 survey with party chairs), the authors find no support for the hypothesized relationship between incongruence and resentment. Rather, the authors find strong indications that citizens' knowledge of a party's position moderates the relation between incongruence and resentment. This indicates that it does not just matter that citizens *are* incongruent with their preferred party and/or the party system, but also that they *know* they are incongruent. More broadly, their findings have important implications for a deeper understanding of resentment and its distribution across society, in particular with regard to unequal access to information and inequalities of education, for example.

In the last part of the book, the authors zoom in on the relationship between resentment and crises of democracy, and explore how resentful citizens imagine democracy to be, and how they hope it could and should be. In Chapter 7, De Mulder engages with resentment and the 'crisis of representative democracy' by investigating what may be one of its key underlying causes: citizens' feelings of (un)representation. Using data from the 2021 Belgian election survey and drawing on an innovative measure of feeling represented, this chapter first examines how well citizens feel represented. The results show that, while the majority of citizens feel represented by at least some representatives, more than a third do not feel represented by anyone. Second, De Mulder shows that feeling unrepresented by any politician or party goes together political resentment resulting in disengagement: people who show low levels of trust, high levels of anger and hopelessness and are more likely to abstain from voting. By contrast, citizens who feel unrepresented by most politicians, yet who do feel represented by at least some of them, experience a more engaged kind of resentment as they are no longer likely to abstain nor likely to feel hopeless. Lastly, De Mulder highlights that feelings of being unrepresented by all politicians and parties are especially prevalent among historically disadvantaged groups, which carries important implications for our understanding of resentment in relation to inequalities and to the democratic ideal of equality.

Drawing on the affective turn in social sciences and increasing scholarly attention to political temporalities, in Chapter 8, Knops, Mercenier and Severs investigate the entanglement between feelings of injustice, resentment and time in citizens' discourses on politics. Based on a qualitative analysis of focus groups with activists (in the Yellow Vests and Youth for Climate movement) and with individuals interviewed during the COVID-19 pandemic (employees of the cultural sector and students), the findings highlight different temporal facets of citizens' resentment and situate their discontent as the result of clashing temporalities: between the temporalities of capitalism and human societies, and between different temporalities that structure politics within the boundaries of representative democracy. The chapter sheds light on the relevance of adopting an affective-temporal lens to understand citizens' resentment within a broader macro-political context in which the crisis of representative democracy is playing out.

In Chapter 9, Knops, Sanhueza, Severs and Deschouwer present a citizen-centred analysis of the meaning of democracy. While citizens' dissatisfaction with contemporary democracy has become somewhat commonplace, scholars routinely struggle to make sense of citizens' critiques and expectations of representative democracy. In this context, the authors attempt to account for the diverse and potentially contradictory beliefs that citizens may hold towards representative democracy, by advancing a citizen-led analysis of the concept of 'democracy'. Drawing on 4,366 responses to an open question 'what does democracy mean to you?' formulated in two Belgian national surveys (2009 and 2019), the chapter shows that citizens' accounts of democracy have changed over time. While representation was central to respondents' reflections in 2009, in 2019 they more frequently defined democracy in relation to elections and rules of decision-making. The findings also show that citizens' resentment correlates with these concerns and gives expression to unmet expectations. The authors identify three resentful tropes of democracy: democracy is unfair, democracy is fake, and democracy is cold-hearted.

In Chapter 10, Verhaegen, Van Ingelgom, Knops, Celis and Amara-Hammou further contribute to our understanding of resentment by asking two sets of questions. First, the chapter inquires what resentful citizens identify as problematic in the current functioning of democracy, and what they are resentful about. Second, the chapter asks what resentful citizens' (anti-)democratic preferences are, and what alternative democratic designs they prefer. These questions are answered using survey data of representative samples of Flemish and Walloon citizens, focus groups with resentful citizens, and democratic theory. The analyses show that respondents with higher levels of political resentment show lower satisfaction with the way in which democracy works, hold more populist attitudes, are more likely to vote blank or abstain, and are more supportive of referenda and citizen fora. Authors show that the latter democratic innovations may attract the support of resentful citizens because of their perceived novelty and because they mark a shift away from the 'distrusted representatives', but this also shows that resentful citizens have not lost all hope in representative institutions. The chapter wraps up by offering a speculative discussion on recursive and reflexive representative relationships as a pathway for democratic reform.

The book concludes with a final chapter, Chapter 11, which pursues a dual objective. On the one hand, it brings together the key empirical and conceptual findings on resentment presented throughout the book; on the other hand, it draws on these findings to define new conceptual boundaries around resentment and open paths for future research on resentment and democracy, and on emotions and politics more broadly.

References

Amara-Hammou, K. (2023). Theorizing representation from the perspective of the represented: How people in socio-economically difficult situations in Brussels understand representation. VUB: Unpublished PhD manuscript.

Ahmed, S. (2014). *The Cultural Politics of Emotion*. Edinburgh: Edinburgh University Press.

Athanasiou, H., Hantzaroula, P. and Yannakopoulos, K. (2009). 'Towards a new epistemology: The "affective turn". *Historein*, 8, 5–16, https://doi.org/10.12681/historein.33

Averill, J. R. (1975). 'A Semantic atlas of emotional concepts.' *JSAS Catalog of Selected Documents in Psychology*, 5, 330. (Ms. No. 421), https://doi.org/10.1037/e450182008-001

Bachman, V. and Sideway, J. (2016). 'Brexit geopolitics.' *Geoforum*, 77, 47–50, https://doi.org/10.1016/j.geoforum.2016.10.001

Bertsou, E. (2019). 'Rethinking political distrust.' *European Political Science Review*, 11(2), 213–230, https://doi.org/10.1017/s1755773919000080

Calhoun, C. (2001). 'Putting emotions in their place.' In J. Goodwin, J. M. Jasper, and F. Polletta (eds.). *Passionate Politics: Emotions and Social Movements* (pp. 45–57). Chicago: University of Chicago Press.

Caluwaerts, D., Reuchamps, M. (2018). *The Legitimacy of Citizen-led Deliberative Democracy: The G1000 in Belgium*. London, New York: Routledge.

Capelos, T., and Demertzis, N. (2018). 'Political action and resentful affectivity in critical times.' *Humanity and Society*, 42(4), 410–433, https://doi.org/10.1177/0160597618802517

Close, C., and van Haute, E. (2020). 'Emotions and vote choice.' *Politics of the Low Countries*, 2(3), 353–379, https://doi.org/10.5553/plc/258999292020002003006

Clough, P. and Halley, J. (2007). *The Affective Turn: Theorising the Social*. UK: Duke University Press.

Cordell, C. (2017). 'L'indignation entre pitié et dégoût: les ambiguïtés d'une émotion morale.' *Raisons politiques*, Cairn, 1(65), 67–90.

Cramer Walsh, K. (2016). *The Politics of Resentment: Rural consciousness in Wisconsin and the Rise of Scott Walker*. Chicago and London: The University of Chicago Press.

Dahl, V., Amnå, E., Banaji, S., Landberg, M., Šerek, J., Ribeiro, N., Zani, B. (2017). 'Apathy or alienation? Political passivity among youths across eight European Union countries.' *European Journal of Developmental Psychology*, 15(3), 284–301, https://doi.org/10.1080/17405629.2017.1404985

Dalton, R. J. (2004). *Democratic Challenges, Democratic Choices: The Erosion of Political Support in Advanced Industrial Democracies*. New York: Oxford University Press.

Easton, D. (1975). 'A re-assessment of the concept of political support.' *British Journal of Political Science*, 5(4), 435–457.

Engels, J. (2015). *The Politics of Resentment: A Genealogy*. Pennsylvania: The Pennsylvania State University Press.

Englert et al. (2021). *Baromètre Social: Rapport bruxellois sur l'état de la pauvreté*, https://www.ccc-ggc.brussels/sites/default/files/documents/graphics/rapport-pauvrete/barometre-welzijnsbarometer/baromere_social_2021.pdf

Erk, J., & Anderson, L. (2009). 'The paradox of federalism: Does self-rule accommodate or exacerbate ethnic divisions?' *Regional & Federal Studies*, 19(2), 191–202, https://doi.org/10.1080/13597560902753388

Farhat, N., Rosoux, V., & Poirier, P. (2014). 'The causal pattern of collective memory in a community conflict: "Constant causes" in the Belgium case.' *Nationalism and Ethnic Politics*, 20(4), 393–414, https://doi.org/10.1080/1353 7113.2014.969145

Fassin, D. (2013). 'On resentment and ressentiment.' *Current Anthropology*, 54(3), 249–267, https://doi.org/10.1086/670390

Fassin, D. (2018). 'Ressentiment d'extrême droite et indignation de gauche.' *Cause Commune*, revue d'action politique du PCF.

Fleury, C. (2020). *Ci-gît l'Amer: guérir du ressentiment*. Paris: Editions Gallimard.

Foessel, M. (2011). 'L'indignation, une passion morale à double sens.' *Liberation*, 2 August, https://www.liberation.fr/france/2011/08/02/l-indignation-une-passion-morale-a-double-sens_752696

Frijda, N.H., Markam, S., Sato, K. and Wiers, R. (1995). 'Emotions and Emotion Words.' In J. A. Russell, J.M. Fernandez-Dols, A. S. R. Manstead and J. C. Wellenkamp (eds.). *Everyday Conceptions of Emotion: An Introduction to the Psychology, Anthropology and Linguistics of Emotion*, vol. 81, pp. 121–43. Dordrecht: Kluwer Academic Publishers.

Fukuyama, F. (2018). *Identity: The Demand for Dignity and the Politics of Resentment*. New York: Farrar, Stras and Giroux.

Ganesh, B. (2020). 'Weaponizing white thymos: flows of rage in the online audiences of the alt-right.' *Cultural Studies*, https://doi.org/10.1080/095023 86.2020.1714687

Hay, C. (2007). *Why We Hate Politics*. Cambridge: Polity Press.

Hochschild, A. R. (2016). *Strangers in Their Own Land: Anger and Mourning on the American Right*. New York: The New Press.

Hoggett, P., Wilkinson, H. E. N., and Beedell, P. (2013). 'Fairness and the Politics of Resentment.' *Journal of Social Policy*, 42(3), 567–585, https://doi.org/10.1017/s0047279413000056

Hooghe, M., and Dassonneville, R. (2018). 'Explaining the Trump Vote: The Effect of Racist Resentment and Anti-Immigrant Sentiments.' *PS: Political Science and Politics*, 51(03), 528–534, https://doi.org/10.1017/s1049096518000367

Hooghe, L. (2004). 'Belgium: Hollowing the center.' *Federalism and Territorial Cleavages*, 55–92.

Inglehart, R., and Norris, P. (2016). 'Trump, Brexit, and the Rise of Populism: Economic Have-Nots and Cultural Backlash.' *Faculty Research Working Paper Series*, Havard Kennedy School.

Jasper, J. M. (2014). 'Constructing indignation: anger dynamics in protest movements.' *Emotion Review*, 6(3), 208–2013, https://doi.org/10.1177/1754073914522863

Knops, L. and Petit, G. (2022). 'Indignation as Affective Transformation: An Affect-Theoretical Approach to the Belgian Yellow Vests Movement.' *Mobilization: An International Quarterly*, 27(2), 170–192, https://doi.org/10.17813/1086-671x-27-2-169

Knops, L. (2022). 'Towards an Affective Turn in Theories of Representation: The Case of Indignation.' *Representation*, https://doi.org/10.1080/00344893.2022.2091011

Knops, L. (2021). *Political Indignation: a Conceptual and Empirical Investigation of Indignant Citizens* (2017-2021). Doctoral dissertation, Vrije Universiteit Brussel, defended on 18 June 2021.

Klingemann, H.-D. (1999). 'Mapping Political Support in the 1990s: A Global Analysis.' In P. Norris (ed.), *Critical Citizens: Global Support for Democratic Government* (pp. 31-56). Oxford: Oxford University Press.

Lamont, M. and White, P. (2009). *Workshop on Interdisciplinary Standards for Systematic Qualitative Research* (Final Report). Arlington, VA: National Science Foundation.

Lane, R. E. (1962). *Political Ideology: Why the American Common Man Believes What He Does*. New York, NY: Free Press.

Lordon, F. (2016). *Les affects de la politique*. Paris: Le Seuil.

Marcus, G. E. (2002). *The Sentimental Citizen: Emotion in Democratic Politics*. University Park, PA.: The Pennsylvania State University Press.

Michel, Elie, Feitosa, Fernando, Lefevere, Jonas, Pilet, Jean-Benoît, Van Erkel, Patrick, & Van Haute, Emilie. (2023). 'Studying dimensions of representation: introducing the Belgian RepResent panel (2019–2021).' *Eur Polit Sci*, https://doi.org/10.1057/s41304-023-00430-z

Mishra, P. (2017). *Age of Anger: A History of the Present*. New-York: Farrar, Straus and Giroux.

Mittiga, R. (2021). 'Political Legitimacy, Authoritarianism, and Climate Change.' *American Political Science Review*, 1–14.

Norris, P. (2011). *Democratic Deficit: Critical Citizens Revisited*. Cambridge: Cambridge University Press.

Pascolo, L., Vermassen, D., Reuchamps, M., & Caluwaerts, D. (2021). 'The Changing Dynamics of Belgian Federalism: Is there a reversal of the paradox of federalism?.' In *Belgian Exceptionalism* (pp. 138–152). Taylor & Francis, London: Routledge.

Pettigrew, T. F. (2016). 'In Pursuit of Three Theories: Authoritarianism, Relative Deprivation, and Intergroup Contact.' *Annu Rev Psychol*, 67, 1–21, https://doi.org/10.1146/annurev-psych-122414-033327

Peirce, C. 1934. *Collected Papers of Charles Sanders Peirce. Vol. 5, Pragmatism and Pragmaticism*, ed. by Charles Hartshorne and Paul Weiss. Cambridge, MA: Harvard University Press.

Przeworski A. 2019. *Crises of Democracy*. Cambridge: Cambridge University Press.

Reichertz, Jo. 2007 "Abduction: The Logic of Discovery of Grounded Theory." In *The SAGE Handbook of Grounded Theory*, edited by A. Bryant and K. C. Charmaz (pp. 214–28). London: Sage.

Scherer, K. R. (2005). 'What are emotions? And how can they be measured?' *Social Sciences Information*, 44(4), 695–729, https://doi.org/10.1177/0539018405058216

Slaby, J. Von Scheve, C. (2019). *Affective Societies: Key Concepts*. Routledge Studies in Affective Societies. London: Routledge.

Smith, H. J., Pettigrew, T. F., Pippin, G. M., and Bialosiewicz, S. (2012). 'Relative deprivation: a theoretical and meta-analytic review.' *Pers Soc Psychol Rev*, 16(3), 203–232, https://doi.org/10.1177/1088868311430825

Solomon, R. C. (1993). *The Passions: Emotions and the Meaning of Life*. Indianapolis: Hackett Publishing.

Tavory, I. and Timmermans, S. (2014). *Abductive Analysis: Theorizing Qualitative Research*. Chicago: University of Chicago Press.

Timmermans, S. and Tavory, I. (2012). 'Theory Construction in Qualitative Research from Grounded Theory to Abductive Analysis.' *Sociological Theory*, 30(3), 167–86, https://doi.org/10.1177/0735275112457914

Thompson, S., and Hoggett, P. (2012). *Politics and the Emotions*. London: Continuum.

Tenhouten, W. D. (2007). *General Theory of Emotions and Social Life*. London: Routledge.

Ure, M. (2015). 'Resentment/Ressentiment.' *Constellations*, 22(4), 599–613, https://doi.org/10.1111/1467-8675.12098

Valentino, N. A., Brader, T., Groenendyk, E. W., Gregorowicz, K., and Hutchings, V. L. (2011). 'Election Night's Alright for Fighting: The Role of Emotions in Political Participation.' *The Journal of Politics*, 73(1), 156–170, https://doi.org/10.1017/s0022381610000939

Valentino, N. A., Hutchings, V. L., Banks, A. J., and Davis, A. K. (2008). 'Is a Worried Citizen a Good Citizen? Emotions, Political Information Seeking, and Learning via the Internet.' *Political Psychology*, 29(2), 247–273, https://doi.org/10.1111/j.1467-9221.2008.00625.x

Van Hootegem, A., Abts, K., and Meuleman, B. (2021). 'The welfare state criticism of the losers of modernization: How social experiences of resentment shape populist welfare critique.' *Acta Sociologica*, https://doi.org/10.1177/0001699321994191

Vila-Henninger, L., Dupuy, C., Van Ingelgom, V., Caprioli, M., Teuber, F., Pennetreau, D., Bussi, M., & Le Gall, C. (2024). Abductive Coding: Theory Building and Qualitative (Re)Analysis. *Sociological Methods & Research*, 53(2), 968-1001. https://doi.org/10.1177/00491241211067508

Vrydagh, J. Devillers, S. Talukder, D. Jacquet, V. Bottin, J. (2021). 'Les mini-publics en Belgique (2001-2018): expériences de panels citoyens délibératifs.' *Le courrier hebdomadaire du CRISP*, 2477–2478.

Xhardez, C. Counet, M. Randour, F. Niessen, C. (dir) (2020). *50 ans de fédéralisation de l'Etat belge: institutions, acteurs, politiques publiques et particularités du fédéralisme belge*. Louvain-la-Neuve: Academia.

2. Studying political resentment: a methodological overview

Soetkin Verhaegen, August de Mulder &
François Randour

Abstract: Political resentment is a theoretically and methodologically challenging concept to study. It requires the observation of complex emotions, moral judgement and the over-time persistence of this sentiment, both in specific groups and in entire populations. To reach this goal, the RepResent project relied on large scale population-based surveys and focus groups. This chapter discusses the rationale, strengths and weaknesses of the different methodological choices and operationalisations which emerged from the research project. In doing so, the contribution helps the reader to make sense of the different approaches used in the book to study political resentment. More specifically, the chapter first examines the quantitative methods used to study resentment (i.e., waves of surveys, types of questions and rationale). Second, the chapter discusses the use of qualitative methods aimed at understanding resentment (i.e., waves of focus groups, types of questions and rationale). Third, the chapter presents how qualitative and quantitative methods have cross-fertilized to integrate insights from focus group research in the development of a new survey question. We conclude with an assessment of the different approaches in light of the theoretical and methodological challenges associated with the study of political resentment.

https://doi.org/10.11647/OBP.0401.02

Introduction

Political resentment is a complex and multi-dimensional concept, which makes it a theoretically and methodologically challenging concept to study. To take up this challenge and to unpack the complexity of resentment among Belgian citizens, this book is structured around four objectives. It aims to (1) define political resentment and identify the dominant traits of resentful citizens in Belgium; (2) empirically study the emotional and behavioural dimensions of resentment as well as (3) examine the feelings of injustice experienced by (disadvantaged) citizens and the feeling of being unrepresented. Finally, the book (4) explores the link between resentment and democracy, both in how resentful citizens feel towards democracy, and the hopes they have about democracy.

Different levels of empirical detail and scope are required to meet these objectives. For instance, mapping the characteristics of resentful citizens, and examining the relationship between resentment and political behaviour requires a standardized measure of political resentment that allows us to observe this sentiment among a representative sample of a population. To answer questions about how citizens think about political representation, or how the personal experiences of citizens are linked to resentment, more detailed accounts of the experiences, views and emotions of specific groups within the population are required. To provide both scope and detail, as well as observations of general and specific populations, and snapshots and observations undertaken over a duration, the RepResent project combined both large-scale population-based (panel) surveys and focus groups as methods of data collection.

The concept of political resentment itself raises some methodological challenges. It is defined in this book as a complex emotion, with anger as a core aspect that can commingle in a broader 'resentful affectivity' consisting of fear and disappointment and which involves a moral judgement resulting from the persistent and cumulative experiences of unfairness across time (Celis et al., this book; Capelos and Demertzis, 2018; Celis et al., 2021; Fleury, 2020). Hence, to observe the full sentiment, one needs to observe various aspects at the same time. One must explore the co-relation of various emotions and of resentful affectivities, moral judgment, and how resentment is related to time and experiences, which are very personal. Qualitative and quantitative methods can contribute to this in different ways.

Finally, our goal to study a concept that has not been widely researched requires us to distinguish it from, and relate it to, neighbouring concepts. While Chapter 1 accomplishes this on a theoretical level, the research methods we have used allow us to do so empirically as well. They make it possible, to a certain extent, to compare our findings with previous research.

In sum, studying political resentment triggers important methodological questions, which are reflected in the diversity of data sources and methods of analysis used in this book. Following an abductive approach, as explained in Chapter 1, the project started off with the collection of quantitative and qualitative data in parallel (see Figure 2.1).

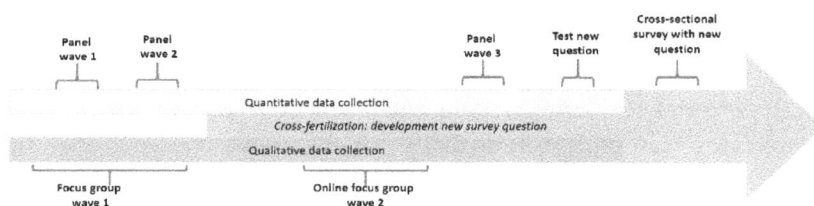

Fig. 2.1 Data collection stages of the RepResent research project.

Note: The data collection started in January 2019 and ended in November 2021.

Quantitively, the project started with a set of 'waves' of online surveys (a three-wave panel)[1] that aimed to capture political resentment and perceptions of democratic representation among the Belgian population (discussed in Section 1 below). Qualitatively, focus groups were organized among samples of the population in which political resentment is most likely to be observed, and that are typically underrepresented in large-scale survey research (Section 2). After this initial phase, the analysis of the focus group data and the consideration of the strengths and limitations of the survey data collected thus far led to the development of a new measurement instrument for political

---

[1] In this chapter we base our discussion on the three first waves of the EoS Panel survey; for the full overview of the surveys, see the Appendix.

resentment in survey research, which was included in a cross-sectional survey, which was the final survey of the project (Section 3).

The chapter then goes on to discuss the different methodological choices and operationalisations used in the research project.[2] The chapter concludes with an assessment of the different approaches taken in relation to the challenges identified in the study of political resentment (Section 4).

Section 1: Studying resentment with surveys

In order to capture political resentment (and its relationship to other attitudes and behaviour) in society at large, the RepResent project conducted a three-wave, online panel survey among Belgian citizens. The data collection was structured around the elections of 26 May 2019 in Belgium.[3] In a pre-electoral wave, respondents were surveyed between 5 April and 21 May 2019 (see Figure 2.1). The post-electoral wave surveyed the same respondents immediately after the elections between 28 May and 18 June 2019. Finally, about one year after the elections, these respondents were surveyed a third time between 7–27 April 2020. The panel design makes it possible to examine the evolution of resentment over time.

The target population of these surveys were the inhabitants of the Flemish, Walloon, and Brussels regions who were eligible to vote in the 2019 elections. The sample was targeted to match the gender, age, and education distribution for the voting-age population in the respective regions. Anticipating panel attrition due to the longevity of the panel, we began with a very large sample of 7351 respondents in Wave 1 (Flanders N= 3298; Wallonia N= 3025; Brussels N= 1028). The sample shrank to 3917 respondents in Wave 2 (Flanders N= 1971; Wallonia N= 1429; Brussels N= 509). For the third wave, only the Flemish and Walloon respondents who participated in the two previous waves were

---

2   The methodological choices and the data collection are the outcome of a collective process involving all researchers of the RepResent research project.

3   Belgium is an interesting case, since rising support for parties with extreme ideological positions and the mobilization of social movements suggests that political resentment may be present in substantial parts of the population, which raises questions about the role of political resentment in the development of political attitudes and behaviour.

contacted, resulting in 1996 completed responses, with a response rate of 58.6% compared to the second wave (Flanders N= 1266; Wallonia N= 730). Respondents from Brussels were not contacted for this wave, because the sample had become too small.

The representativeness of the sample was checked by comparing the sample to the population of reference in terms of age, gender and education. Although we aimed to have a representative sample at Wave 1, a sample is never a perfect reflection of the population from which the sample is drawn. Indeed, Chi-square statistics showed that there are statistically significant differences between the sample of Wave 1 and the population ($p<0.001$) (more information can be found in the technical report of the survey, see the general methodological appendix in this book). Further, due to panel attrition, Waves 2 and 3 also showed significant differences on most variables. To account for the differences between the samples and the population, weights were calculated for each sample based on the known distribution of the population in terms of age, gender and education, and computed through the iterative proportional fitting procedure (ipfraking module–Stata). This ensures that the weights correct the marginal distributions of the sample to match the population distribution.

Survey questions on resentment

The complex nature of political resentment provides various methodological challenges, including the development of survey questions that can capture the full concept. As explained in Chapter 1, our project defined political resentment in terms of three key components: (1) its nature as a complex emotion, (2) that is rooted in a moral judgement and experienced unfairness and (3) which is long-lasting, due to accumulated experiences over time. The temporality aspect is incorporated into the design of the panel survey.[4] To capture

---

4   The panel design allows us to examine the evolution of resentment over time. Most emotions remain stable between wave 1 and wave 2 of the panel. Results of the paired t-test (same respondents, two time points) show significant statistical mean differences for anger (Mean Diff: 0.138, $p< 0.010$), bitterness (Mean Diff: 0.135, $p<0.010$), fear (Mean Diff: 0.191, $p< 0.001$) and contentment (Mean Diff: -0.096, $p< 0.010$). Most of the panel respondents moved up one to two points on the 0-10 scale between the waves, except for the emotion of contentment, which went down.

the other two aspects, the project (initially) chose to draw on a number of well-established survey questions for concepts that are related to political resentment, which, taken together, would cover all its key aspects. This allows us to situate the findings of the RepResent project within the long tradition of empirical research on citizens' attitudes vis-à-vis politics. Yet, there are also some limitations to this approach, in terms of its conceptual match with the definition of political resentment. In the last phase of the project, the insights from these surveys and from focus groups were therefore used to develop a novel survey measure of political resentment (see Section 3), which can be directly compared with more established indicators such as political trust, cynicism and efficacy (see for example, Chapter 10 in this volume).

The surveys had to capture political resentment as a complex cluster of emotions. While resentment is most commonly associated with anger, many scholars point to its being a complex mixture of multiple emotions besides anger, perhaps including, for example, disappointment or fear (Tenhouten, 2007). This ongoing conceptual discussion raises the question: which emotions should be included in a measure of political resentment? For example, Capelos and Demertzis (2018) approach political resentment by measuring a multitude of 'resentful affectivities', including emotions of anger, fear, anxiety and hope. The advantage of their approach is that it avoids setting strict boundaries in advance to determine what political resentment is and is not. Similarly, we built on the question on emotions developed by Valentino (2008) and extended it to an 8-item battery that tapped into various emotions related to politics (Box 2.1).

Box 2.1 Measure of emotions towards politics.

When you think of Belgian politics in general, to what extent do you feel each of the following emotions?" [0-10 scale: 0 = Not at all; 10 = To a great extent]
1. Anger
2. Bitterness
3. Anxiety
4. Fear
5. Hope
6. Relief
7. Happiness
8. Contentment

Note: This question is included in wave 1 and 2.

Political resentment is also characterized as a moral judgement that emerges in the face of experiences of unfairness or injustice. This implies certain norms about how one should be represented, and a judgment that these norms are not complied with. This aspect of political resentment connects to a long tradition of survey research that tries to capture citizens' attitudes towards politics using concepts that are closely related to political resentment. Most notable in this regard are the American National Election Surveys (ANES), which introduced empirical measures of various sub-dimensions of political alienation. Among other things, they introduced indicators of concepts such as trust in government, political cynicism and political efficacy. Although these concepts do not deal with resentment per se, they do capture the experiences of unfairness and the moral judgement that are key aspects of political resentment. The included measures are presented in Box 2.2.

One of the most frequently used indicators dealing with citizens' relation vis-à-vis politics is political trust. Although there is no consensus about the exact definition of political trust (Seyd, 2016), it is most frequently referred to as a relational concept, in which a person expects another person or an organization to behave in a certain (beneficial) way in the face of uncertainty and dependency on the outcome of those actions (e.g., Hardin, 2000; Van der Meer and Hakhverdian, 2017; Van der Meer, 2017; Seyd, 2016). When this trusting relationship is broken, and one or more characteristic components of a trusting relationship—commitment, care, predictability and competence (Kasperson et al., 1992; Van Der Meer, 2010)—are perceived to be absent, resentful attitudes may arise. Specifically, a lack of trust implies that one believes that the elites (or the system) cannot be expected to treat one fairly (hence, perceived unfairness). To measure political trust, we followed the example of the European Social Survey (ESS) and limited political trust to a specific set of political objects. In this research, these are: political parties, the Federal Parliament, politicians and the European Union.

In contrast, in much empirical research—especially in American studies—conceptions of political trust or 'trust in government' are often characterized by a stronger focus on norms and morals. This research looks at whether political actors are complying with certain normative expectations, or instead are corrupt, and whether they waste tax money, or only look out for special interests or themselves (Hetherington, 1998). Political actors that are perceived as scoring badly on those indicators are regarded as not to be trusted. In this tradition, trust is sometimes posited as the inverse of political cynicism (e.g., Easton, 1975; Mason, House, and Martin, 1985), which involves an attitude 'that the political process and its actors are inherently corrupt, incompetent and self-serving' (Van der Meer and Zmerli, 2017, p. 5). Political cynicism is most clearly connected to the notion of resentment and has even been defined as being a 'bitter or resentful attitude' about the morality of political actors (Cappella and Jamieson, 1997, p. 142). Based on the ANES trust scale, which has often been used to measure political cynicism (e.g., Dardis et al., 2008 and Pinkleton and Austin, 2002), the three panel waves include a 7-item scale of political cynicism, specifically selected to tap into key elements of political resentment: experiences of unfairness and moral judgement.

Furthermore, the surveys included questions to measure an individual's perceived political efficacy. Political efficacy refers to 'the feeling that individual political action does have, or can have, an impact upon the political process' (Campbell et al., 1954, p. 187, via Craig et al., 1990, p. 290). One can distinguish internal and external components of political efficacy (e.g., Lane, 1959). Internal efficacy refers to an individual's beliefs about one's own competence to understand and participate effectively in politics. External efficacy is an individual's beliefs about the responsiveness of government authorities and institutions to citizens' preferences (Chamberlain, 2012). External efficacy is relevant to the study of political resentment as it deals with citizens' perception about whether or not political parties (or the system as a whole) allow regular citizens to have an input, thereby again tapping into perceptions about (un)fairness. The three survey waves included elaborate efficacy batteries.

Box 2.2 Measures of moral judgements towards politics.

---

1. Political trust

Can you indicate the extent to which you agree with the statements below?
[0-10 scale: 0 = No trust at all, 10 = Full trust]
  1. Political Parties
  2. The Federal Parliament
  3. Politicians
  4. The European Union

2. Political cynicism

Can you indicate the extent to which you agree with the statements below?
[1-5 scale: 1 = Totally disagree; 2 = Somewhat disagree; 3 = Neither agree
nor disagree; 4 = Somewhat agree; 5 = Totally agree]
  1. Politicians are corrupt.
  2. Most politicians are competent.
  3. Politicians are trying to keep their promises.
  4. Politicians do not understand what is going on in society.
  5. Many politicians have been around for too long.
  6. The way we organize elections in this country is fair.
  7. Political parties take sufficient account of independent experts
     when making decisions.

3. Political efficacy

Please indicate to what extent you disagree or agree with the following
statements. [1 = Totally disagree; 2 = Somewhat disagree; 3 = Neither
agree nor disagree; 4 = Somewhat agree; 5 = Totally agree]
  1. Most citizens do not have clear political preferences.
  2. Political parties do not offer real political alternatives to the people.
  3. Political parties give too much freedom to campaign advisers to
     determine important political issues. The influence of interest
     groups and lobbyists on policies is too big.
  4. Voting is pointless because parties do what they want anyway.
  5. In general, our political system functions fairly.
  6. Our political decision-making processes are sufficiently
     transparent.
  7. In general, our political system functions in an efficient way.
  8. I feel that I have a fairly good understanding of important political
     values in Belgium.

Note: The question on trust was included in wave 1 and 3, the question on cynicism
and efficacy were included all three waves. Efficacy item 9, however, was only
included in wave 2 and 3.

Limits of using survey data for the study of political resentment

There are, however, some limitations to this approach when studying political resentment. First, the chosen measurement is not ideal. Although using well-established indicators has the advantage of comparability with earlier public opinion research, and these indicators together capture the key theoretical aspects of political resentment, the fragmentated manner in which political resentment is captured in the panel surveys (spread across the surveys) also has a number of disadvantages. Most importantly, by using scales of related concepts instead of one scale focused specifically on political resentment, it is impossible to make inferences about 'how resentful' citizens are towards politics. Rather, the included measures give indications of how resentful citizens are in terms of certain key elements. Therefore, these measures may be useful to examine the relationship between aspects of political resentment and other variables such as political participation (Chapter 4 in this volume), substantive representation (Chapter 6 in this volume) or feeling represented (Chapter 7 in this volume). However, a more detailed analysis mapping how resentful citizens are and who the resentful citizens are requires a standardized measure of political resentment (Chapter 3 in this volume). Also, while the temporal aspect of political resentment was incorporated into the survey design with its panel setup, this key aspect of resentment was neglected in the actual survey items. A standardized measure of political resentment also needs to take the long-lasting character of political resentment into account more substantively.

Furthermore, using large-scale online surveys also creates some limitations for the study of political resentment. Asking respondents to answer closed questions pre-emptively narrows the scope of their answers to fit the researchers' theoretical assumptions. A more bottom-up approach, in contrast, can bring forward new insights from the perspectives of the citizens themselves. Relatedly, as people are largely unable to elaborate on their answers in online surveys, the insights one gets from survey data often lacks nuance in comparison to more in-depth interviewing methods.

The final limitation of using survey data to measure resentment is that it is challenging to reach marginalized groups as these citizens are simply unlikely to participate in survey research (Dillman et al., 2002).

Section 2: Studying resentment with focus groups

Since political resentment is a relatively new field of empirical study, and given the limitations of the survey approach elaborated above, the RepResent project complements the deductive quantitative approach for which large-scale surveys were used with a more inductive qualitative approach relying on focus groups. The focus groups aim to develop a deeper understanding of what political resentment is, how individuals experience it, and how they express it. Focus groups are conversations between research subjects—participants—that are organized by a researcher, about a specific topic. This method is useful to shed light on a topic that does not typically spontaneously become visible in an interviewing context, while, at the same time, the method limits the intervention of the researcher so that plenty of room is left for the free expression of views and experiences by the participants (Hennink, 2014; Kapiszewski, Maclean, Read, 2015). This setting permits participants to collectively define and highlight issues that are important to them, thereby giving prominence to research participants' perspectives, perceptions and understanding of a political issue (Hennink, 2014: Van Ingelgom, 2020). A key characteristic of focus groups is the interaction among participants (see Hennink, 2014; Kitzinger, 1994; Morgan, 1996; Van Ingelgom, 2020; Wilkinson, 1998). This interactive setting encourages participants to react to other participants' experiences, thereby allowing for the collection of more complex and 'fully articulated' accounts. This makes focus groups a method of observation that is particularly well-suited for studying political resentment. Overall, this method allows to capture unanticipated issues and enables more nuance than a fixed list of items proposed by a researcher would permit, thereby rendering data that would not otherwise be available for study.

Focus groups are also appropriate when a researcher wants to gain insight into the views of 'hard-to-reach' or marginalized groups in society (Barbour, 2007). On the one hand, a targeted recruitment strategy makes it possible to contact people who 'may slip through the net of surveys' (Barbour, 2007, p. 20). The organization of focus groups close to the spaces where participants spend much of their time contributes to their willingness to participate in research and to share their views. On the other hand, standardized (survey) approaches may not be a sufficiently close fit with the life-worlds of certain parts of society. Focus groups allow participants to talk about what they know and experience, using the words that are familiar to them, thus allowing the researcher to observe which words and references people spontaneously use when discussing certain issues (Wilkinson, 1998). These aspects that relate to access and inclusion are another key reason why the RepResent project uses focus groups.

In sum, using focus groups, the researcher can unpack both what citizens think, and how they think about political issues (Van Ingelgom, 2020). These advantages are of major importance when studying a multi-dimensional concept such as political resentment. The more flexible approach used by focus groups and their interactive nature are key to letting participants reflect on politics in a way that is relevant to them and that is close to their life and their own experiences (i.e., life-world in context). Focus group data thus allow us to explore the diversity and complexity of feelings of resentment towards politics in detail.

A focus on (potentially) resentful citizens

Participants for the focus groups were recruited following a logic of purposive sampling and the selection of participants was theoretically driven (Van Ingelgom, 2020). In the RepResent project, the objective of the focus groups was to capture a diverse sample of citizens among whom we expected to observe political resentment, while ensuring a certain homogeneity within each focus group (Wilkinson, 1998; Hennink, 2014; Van Ingelgom, 2020).

Focus groups were organized in two 'waves' of data collection. The first wave (January 2019–February 2020) aimed to explore resentment among two main categories of participants: (1) politicized citizens (Chapter 8) and (2) disadvantaged citizens (Chapter 5). Politicized citizens are understood as citizens involved in a protest or social movement, or an activist association. Due to their (protest) activities, these citizens were expected to express resentful attitudes and feelings towards current political institutions and politicians. In particular, two focus groups consisted of citizens belonging to the Youth for Climate movement, three focus groups consisted of members of the Yellow Vests and three focus groups were conducted with members of non-profit associations active in the social sector ('Expert du Vécu' and 'Syndicat des Immenses').

The second category aimed to document (potential) feelings of resentment among (dis)advantaged citizens who are confronted with very visible (economic) disparities and who do not engage in explicit expressions of resentment through protest activities. We focused on two geographically proximate—yet very distinct—areas of the 'Canal Zone' in Brussels: the Molenbeek and Dansaert areas. While Molenbeek is mainly residential, commercial (hosting mostly local shops) and is a socio-economically disadvantaged area, the Dansaert area across the Canal of Molenbeek is more touristic, commercial (hosting mostly high-end shops) and very popular with young middle-class adults (Van Criekingen, Fleury, 2006).

We also conducted two focus groups with 'blue-collar workers' employed at the European Parliament in Brussels. We expected that these workers (i.e., contractual employees working in maintenance, logistics and the IT sectors) might hold resentful feelings as they were working in an organization where people with very different economic backgrounds and access to political decision-making are employed (i.e., members of the European parliament and EU civil servants). In total, seven focus groups were conducted along this spatial dimension (four in Molenbeek, one in Dansaert and two with blue-collar workers). The focus groups were organized in person, in the areas where people were recruited.

The second wave of focus groups (December 2020–March 2021) was conducted online and aimed to document how citizens expressed resentment in a time of crisis (Chapter 8). With the COVID-19 pandemic as the common context of this wave, four categories of participants were sampled: (1) far-right voters; (2) COVID-19 vaccine sceptics; (3) participants (heavily) affected by COVID-19 restrictions and finally, (4) non-politicized 'middle-class' citizens dissatisfied with politics. A recruitment survey and an external survey company were used to identify and recruit participants. We conducted two focus groups with Belgian citizens who had far-right or right-wing Flemish nationalist political preferences (VB and N-VA). We also conducted two focus groups with citizens who were suspicious of, or opposed to the COVID-19 vaccine. We expected these participants to depict relatively high levels of resentment towards 'mainstream' political representatives. The third category focused on citizens who have been presented in the public debate as being particularly affected by the COVID-19 pandemic:[5] professionals from the cultural sector (two focus groups) and university students (three groups). In addition to these very specific groups, three focus groups were organized with non-politicized 'middle-class' citizens who are generally dissatisfied with politics. They serve as a point of comparison for the other specific groups.

Documenting resentment through the prism of societal issues

The focus groups used an experience-based and context-sensitive approach to study political resentment. The organizers started from the personal experiences of the participants and let them identify what (societal) issues or problems were most important to them. We thus used a problem-based approach, which begins with the identification of problems before exploring the means available to tackle them (Chapter 9) (Goodin, 1996; Saward, 2020; Warren, 2017; White, 2010).

Embedded in this approach and inspired by previous studies on citizens and politics (Mercenier, 2019; White, 2010), the focus groups were organized around three central questions (see Appendix 1 for a generic version of the topic guide). The first question dealt with *what* participants considered to be the most important societal challenges that Belgium is facing today. This allowed respondents to reflect on politics in a way that is concrete and relevant to them, enabling substantive discussions where views on representation and resentment could be expressed. The second guiding question focused on *who* should take care of resolving these societal challenges. With this question,

---

5   It can be argued that many other groups have been strongly affected by the COVID-19 crisis. Yet, in the Belgian public debate and in the media when the focus groups took place—a period of a couple of weeks—the effects for students (social isolation) and the cultural sector (economic consequences) were very salient.

participants could collectively debate the role of various types of actors—not solely political representatives—whom they think should be in charge of resolving problems. This question permitted participants to discuss the role of actors beyond the usual suspects (i.e., 'politicians') and to understand if participants were making specific connections and comparisons between groups of actors within society. Finally, the third guiding question introduced a discussion about *how* these issues could be resolved. As a follow-up to the open discussion of this question, participants were offered six images representing ways in which societal issues can be addressed. The pictures could be described as: people voting; citizens coming together to discuss societal issues; a non-violent street demonstration; a violent protest; experts getting together to discuss societal challenges; citizens directly helping others. Finally, the facilitator could ask a concluding question about what it means for the participants to be represented, and ways in which people of their group could be represented.

Overall, by using focus groups, it was possible to unpack two important dimensions of resentment. The first major finding outlines the necessity to embrace the complexity of emotions. The varying affective associations that resentful citizens express towards politics confront them with a 'democratic dilemma' (Celis et al., 2021; Chapter 1). While resentful citizens express a combination of feelings of anger, frustration, fear, disappointment and unfairness towards the institutions and actors of the Belgian representative democratic system, they also show some form of trust and hope in that same representative democratic system. The second major finding is that resentment is an incremental emotion that builds up over time. For instance, it can be the accumulation of emotions, such as fears and grievances, that lay the foundations for 'tipping points' of indignation (Knops and Petit, 2022). Beside this incremental—linear—perspective, Knops et al. (Chapter 8) explore the cyclical nature of resentment, which could also emerge from a perceived clash of temporalities and a synchronicity between citizens' life and politics. In sum, the use of focus groups contributes to our understanding of the various affective aspects of political resentment, and of the role of temporality.

Limits of using focus group data for the study of political resentment

Regardless of the important advantages of using focus groups, there are also some limitations to studying resentment with focus group data, which lead to a number of remaining questions. The first limitation relates to the sampling of participants. The purposive sampling of participants among whom we are likely to observe political resentment leaves us with a sample that is not representative of any defined population. However, this method does allow us to reach relevant participants, and individuals that less easily show up in surveys. Yet, at the same time, there is also bias in those who decide to participate in the study. Participating in a focus group requires a substantial amount of time (two to three hours), and one needs to feel comfortable enough to engage in a discussion with strangers. The qualitative nature of the data and the context-specific approach of focus groups thus does not aim to produce findings that can be generalized to the broader population. Rather, it provides a rich exploration of the complex nature of resentment.

Second, as outlined by Celis et al. (2021), the focus group data we collected constitute a (static) snapshot of emotions at a certain moment in time. Emotions—and combinations of them—evolve through time and should be apprehended as dynamic so as to fully understand them. Indeed, previous findings highlighted the incremental and evolving nature of resentment. While various accounts in the focus groups that reflect (aspects of) political resentment include reflections on the past, and on a perceived evolution of the state of politics and society and how they relate to this, more should be done to identify the different temporalities of resentment and to reflect on the broader role of time on (political) representation.

Third, while the focus group discussions provide context for the observed expressions of political resentment, the focus groups do not allow for a systematic analysis of what characteristics, attitudes, experiences and beliefs are related to political resentment. For instance, it is a pressing question how resentment is associated with views and preferences towards democratic arrangements and alternatives, and to undemocratic alternatives. It is therefore important to question how the politically resentful challenge the current government system, and whether resentment undermines or strengthens democracy overall. More systematic research should be pursued to understand the relationship between resentment, democracy, and attitudes about the governing system more broadly.

Section 3: Cross-fertilization across methods: from focus groups to new survey questions

In the previous sections, we explained how the project approached the study of political resentment with both quantitative and qualitative methods. Drawing on the insights of both the panel surveys and the focus groups, a new survey instrument for measuring political resentment was developed. The measure combines insights from the conceptual literature on what political resentment entails, and insights from the focus groups organized as part of the project. The result is a survey question with seven statements tapping into disappointment, anger, feeling infantilized, unfairness, and the perception that the bad situation has persisted.

This standardized measure of political resentment allows us to make inferences about how resentful citizens relate to politics, and which characteristics are systematically related to higher levels of resentment. It also allows us to inquire into the relationship between resentment, democracy, and attitudes about the governing system more broadly. As such, through the cross-fertilization between qualitative and quantitative methods, we are able to offer an alternative to studying political resentment in all its dimensions in an ungeneralisable qualitative way, or studying it in large samples solely through basic questions about emotions that people associate with politics and through indicators that are only partially related to resentment (trust, cynicism and efficacy).

The process of integrating qualitative and quantitative research proceeded in five steps: (1) conceptualizing the various dimensions of political resentment; (2) identifying quotes from focus group data capturing these dimensions; (3) formulating a new survey question; (4) testing the new question and finally (5) including the new measurement instrument in a cross-sectional survey, which was the final survey of the research project. This question is used in the analyses in Chapters 3 and 11 of this book. In this part of the chapter, we lay out each of these steps, and present the resulting survey instrument.

To start with, we conceptualized political resentment as a complex emotion with anger as a core emotion that can commingle to form a broader 'resentful affectivity' consisting of fear and disappointment, which involves a moral judgement resulting from the persistent and cumulative experiences of unfairness across time (Chapter 1 in this volume; Capelos and Demertzis, 2018; Celis et al., 2021; Fleury, 2020). It requires observing the co-relation of various emotions, moral judgment, as well as how resentment is related to time and experiences. Specifically, we derived five key elements from this definition: disappointment, anger, fear, feelings of unfairness, and a lasting sentiment. While anger, fear, and feelings of unfairness are indeed captured by parts of the survey questions presented in the first part of this chapter, we noticed that feelings of unfairness are included in a very limited way (only about elections), and that disappointment and the lasting aspect of the sentiment are entirely missing from the measurement. Moreover, elements of political resentment are dispersed across measures of other concepts.

To fill these gaps, we[6] analysed the first wave of focus group data (i.e., the conversations with Yellow Vests, Youth for Climate, and individuals who occupy a socially disadvantaged position—see section 2 of this chapter; January 2019–February 2020) and searched for quotes and expressions matching the different aspects of political resentment that we identified in the literature. At various instances, we noticed anger in the tone of voice, facial expressions, gestures, and choice of words. For instance, when participants say that they feel infantilized because politicians treat them like children, they express anger and frustration about this situation. At times, it is literally mentioned, e.g., 'I'm so tired, right, I'm angry' (Syndicat des Immenses). As concluded in the study of Celis et al. (2021) that also draws on these data, both disappointment and its opposite—hope—also appear in the conversations. For instance, in a group with participants from the Syndicat des Immenses, it is mentioned that 'They [politicians] talk about transparency, make promises, but when they are in power, they don't apply it.' Feelings

6   Kenza Amara-Hammou, Louise Knops, François Randour, Ramon van der Does, Soetkin Verhaegen.

of unfairness are also expressed at various points in the focus groups: unfairness in terms of who gets access to public spaces, the distribution of the costs and benefits of public policy, and more generally about who is (not) taken into account by the governing system. Participants are very clear in explaining that their evaluations of the political system are persistent, hence the time element is also very clear in the data in quotes such as 'There is always a mismatch between the intentions they have and the results that come out. And this interaction will always persist and continue to be there.' (Dansaert area), 'It's always the same thing, the same problems, they get repeated.' (blue-collar workers at the European Parliament), and 'I don't see any progress' (blue-collar workers at the European Parliament).

We used the quotes from the first wave of focus group data to develop a measure for political resentment. Since political resentment is a multidimensional concept and as we want to use formulations that speak to respondents' life-worlds, we opted for a battery question with statements that reflect as closely as possible the words that participants in the focus groups used. Yet, considering guidelines on the formulation of effective survey questions and translations (the focus groups were either in Dutch or French and the survey was in both languages), adaptations to the formulations were required. Box 2.3 presents the formulated survey question. This survey question was then pre-tested in a (non-representative) sample of respondents in Flanders between 23 August and 14 September 2021. Using these results, we checked the distribution and variation of answers to the items, how they correlate, and whether they load on a single factor. We also inquired whether the items correlate in expected ways with concepts that are theoretically expected to be positively associated with political resentment and for which validated measures already existed, i.e., emotions related to politics, populism, cynicism, efficacy, and feeling represented. These tests showed that the answers to the new items are well distributed, generally load on a single factor, that correlations with other concepts are as expected, but not to such a degree as to suggest that we were measuring exactly the same attitudes and feelings as captured by other items in the survey.[7]

---

7   This chapter focusses on the items that made it to the final survey that is used in
     Chapters 3 and 10 in the book. However, one additional item was included in the
     pre-test: 'One cannot say that politics systematically favours certain groups'. This

Box 2.3 Developed survey question.

How strongly do the following statements correspond to your opinion about politics? [0= Doesn't correspond to my opinion at all; 10= Corresponds to my opinion very well]

1. What the government decides is often less good than what I hoped for.*
2. I'm generally disappointed in politics in Belgium.*
3. I get angry when I think about politics.*
4. Most politicians don't take citizens seriously, they rather treat us as children.*
5. Policy is usually better for others than for people like me.*
6. I'm afraid that the government will use it against me if I negatively express myself about politics.
7. Elections don't matter, everything has been decided on beforehand anyway.*
8. Politics treats all groups in society fairly.
9. Political decisions often have a positive impact on the majority of the people.
10. The political system in Belgium has been malfunctioning for a long time.*
11. I believe that politics is capable of solving people's problems.

* These items are kept in the final measurement for political resentment.

Note: The 11 items were asked in the test survey in August—September 2021 (but see footnote 6 on item 8), and in the final survey in November 2021. The items marked with * are part of the final measurement for political resentment.

We finally included the new survey questions in a representative survey of the Flemish and Walloon population of Belgium, fielded in November 2021. Theoretically, we have good reasons to expect that this survey battery as a whole provides a rich and encompassing measurement of respondents' political resentment. Yet, we also explore whether, statistically, the different items of the battery load on a single factor in a principal component factor analysis (Mooi et al., 2018). As a first step in the factor analysis, all 11 items included in the survey are included in the analysis using Stata SE 16.1. Here, we observe that the positively formulated items do not load on the same factor as the negatively

---

item does not load on the factor. We concluded that this is probably due to the formulation. The item includes a negation, and it can be interpreted both literally and metaphorically. It was therefore reformulated to 'Politics treats all groups in society fairly'.

formulated items. We formulated some items so as to tap into fairness, as the counterpart of items that tapped into unfairness, and we included an item that expresses the believe that politics is capable of solving people's problems as an expression of hope. Yet, as noted in previous research on survey question formulation, we do not find that these formulations tap into the same concept as the negatively formulated items in a positive way (Roszkowski and Margot, 2010). Rather, we find a second factor of positively formulated attitudes towards politics. For this reason, we exclude these items from the measurement for the concept of political resentment, which is an affect that reflects negative rather than positive evaluations of politics. Additionally, we observe that item 6, tapping into fear, does not load well on what we label the 'political resentment factor', so this item is excluded from the analysis too. The result is a measurement for political resentment consisting of seven survey items in total, tapping into disappointment, anger, feeling infantilized (which in the focus groups was used as an expression of anger), unfairness, and the perception that the bad situation has been lasting. The factor analysis is presented in Table 2.1.

Table 2.1 Principal factor analysis: political resentment battery.

Survey item	Factor scores
1. What the government decides is often less good than what I hoped for.	0.781
2. I'm generally disappointed in politics in Belgium.	0.833
3. I get angry when I think about politics.	0.755
4. Most politicians don't take citizens seriously, they rather treat us as children.	0.821
5. Policy is usually better for others than for people like me.	0.568
6. Elections don't matter, everything has been decided on beforehand anyway.	0.771
7. The political system in Belgium has been malfunctioning for a long time.	0.831

Source: 4th EOS RepResent Cross-Sectional survey, 2021.

Note: Cronbach's Alpha is 0.883

Conclusion

As outlined throughout this contribution, studying political resentment is a theoretically and methodologically challenging task for which there is no 'one size fits all' research method. The diverse chapters in this book illustrate how different research questions and objectives require diverse methodological approaches. This chapter laid out the main quantitative and qualitative approaches that are used in this book to observe political resentment. It presented the rationale, strengths, and weaknesses of population-based surveys and focus groups to study political resentment. It also demonstrated how both methods fruitfully cross-fertilized, by using the rich insights from the focus groups to develop a new—standardized—survey measurement of political resentment, allowing us to move beyond the fragmented manner in which political resentment was captured by previous surveys. Moreover, the coordinated collection of focus group and survey data using the new measurement makes it possible to answer research questions using a mixed-methods design, as done in Chapter 10.

However, with the selected methods, there are still some facets of resentment and important questions that we cannot tackle in the present book. One of the major limitations relates to the analysis of the different temporalities of resentment and, more generally, on the incremental and long-lasting character of political resentment. Indeed, despite the panel setup of the surveys, the temporality of resentment could not be captured consistently in the (fragmented) selected survey items. Moreover, focus groups only constitute a snapshot of citizens' resentful feelings at a certain moment in time. While some participants evoked their past (experiences) to explain their current feelings, more needs to be done in forthcoming research to understand the role of time and its impact on political representation. Second, despite the efforts of the research team to adopt an experience-based and context-sensitive approach to political resentment, the chosen methods and the data we collected also imply that we focused on expressions of political resentment collected in a research setting. Therefore, we still know little about how citizens express political resentment in 'real-world' configurations, for instance during protests or on social media. Some of these limitations could be addressed by refining the research design of the (panel) surveys and of the focus groups so as to draw in contextual information about participants' experiences. Yet other purposes require the collection of different kinds of data or the use of other types of data-collection methods that allow for more direct observation of both context and feelings.

One way forward is to collect different kinds of data. Previous studies have shown that the communication context in which discourses are produced have an impact on the linguistic register used by the participants (Perez et al., 2019). Therefore, it could be interesting to compare expressions of political resentment in focus groups with expressions of political resentment in other contexts, such as the interventions of citizens during (political) television debates, in the written press, on social media or during protests ((non)participant observation). This would allow us to analyse 'real-world' expressions of resentment rather than expressions of resentment is a research setting. Moreover, these types of data would allow for a comparison of expressions of political resentment across different types of actors and communication contexts. This would contribute to our understanding of the conditions under which political resentment discourse is produced, how it circulates among actors in society and how it might impact the democratic functioning of society.

In terms of methods of analysis, new methods of text analysis could aid the detection of emotions, and specifically political resentment, in this type of observational data. In recent years, computational sciences have made important steps forward in the study of emotions of large corpora (Soroka et al., 2015). Sentiment analysis makes it possible to grade sentiment (i.e., from very positive to very negative), detect emotions (i.e., frustration, anger, sadness etc.), and to conduct 'aspect-based' sentiment analysis (i.e., linking emotions with particular objects). These can be useful strategies to analyse large amounts of data where citizens express themselves spontaneously, and thus where the researcher is unable to ask about, or probe, some (aspects of) political resentment in particular.

In sum, this book draws on different types of qualitative and quantitative data that shed light on feelings of political resentment in Belgium. The purpose of this chapter was to lay out the reasons for the choices made, the strengths and weaknesses of each method, and to help the reader understand how a dialogue between types of data collection and methods of analysis has led to an innovation in the measurement of political resentment in large-scale survey research.

References

Barbour, R. (2007). *Doing Focus Groups*. London: Sage, https://dx.doi.org/10.4135/9781849208956

Campbell, A., Gurin, G., and Miller, W. E. (1954). *The Voter Decides*. Evanston, IL: Row, Peterson.

Capelos, T., and Demertzis, N. (2018). 'Political Action and Resentful Affectivity in Critical Times.' *Humanity and Society*, 42(4), 410–433, https://doi.org/10.1177/0160597618802517

Cappella, J. N., and Jamieson, K. H. (1997). *Spiral of Cynicism: The Press and the Public Good*. New York: Oxford University Press.

Celis, K., Knops, L., Van Ingelgom, V., Verhaegen, S. (2021). 'Resentment and Coping with the Democratic Dilemma', *Politics and Governance*, 9(3), 237–247, https://doi.org/10.17645/pag.v9i3.4026

Chamberlain, A. (2012). 'A time-series analysis of external efficacy.' *Public Opinion Quarterly*, 76(1), 117–130, https://doi.org/10.1093/poq/nfr064

Close, C., van Haute, E. (2020). 'Emotions and vote choice.' *Politics of the Low Countries*, 2(3), 353–379, https://doi.org/10.5553/PLC/258999292020002003006

Craig, S., Niemi, R. and Silver, G. (1990). 'Political efficacy and trust: A Report on the NES Pilot Study Items.' *Political Behavior*, 12(3), 289-314, https://doi.org/10.1007/bf00992337

Dardis, F. E., Shen, F., and Edwards, H. H. (2008). 'Effects of negative political advertising on individuals' cynicism and self-efficacy: The impact of ad type and message exposures.' *Mass Communication and Society*, 11(1), 24–42, https://doi.org/10.1080/15205430701582512

Dillman, D. A., Eltinge, J. L., Groves, R. M., and Little, R. J. (2002). 'Survey nonresponse in design, data collection, and analysis.' In R. M. Groves, D. A. Dillman, J. L. Eltinge, and R. J. Little (eds.), pp. 3–26. *Survey Nonresponse*. New York: Wiley.

Easton, D. (1975). 'A re-assessment of the concept of political support.' *British Journal of Political Science*, 5, 435–457, https://doi.org/10.1017/s0007123400008309

Fleury, C. (2020). *Ci-gît l'amer: Guérir du ressentiment* [Here lies the bitter: To heal resentment]. Louise: Editions Gallimard.

Hardin, R. (2000). 'Do We Want Trust in Government?' In Warren, M. E. (ed.), *Democracy and Trust* (pp. 22–41). Cambridge: Cambridge University Press, https://doi.org/10.1017/CBO9780511659959

Hennink, M. M. (2014). *Focus Group Discussions*. Oxford: Oxford University Press, https://doi.org/10.1093/acprof:osobl/9780199856169.001.0001

Kasperson, R. E., Golding, D., and Tuler, S. (1992). 'Social distrust as a factor in siting hazardous facilities and communicating risks.' *Journal of Social Issues*, 48(4), 161–187, https://doi.org/10.1111/j.1540-4560.1992.tb01950.x

Kapiszewski, D., MacLean, L. M., and Read, B. L. (2015). *Field Research in Political Science: Practices and Principles*. Cambridge: Cambridge University Press, https://doi.org/10.1017/CBO9780511794551

Kitzinger, J. (1994). 'The methodology of focus groups: The importance of interaction between research participants.' *Sociology of Health and Illness*, 16, 103–121, https://doi.org/10.1111/1467-9566.ep11347023

Lane, R. E. (1959). *Political Life: Why People Get Involved in Politics*. Glencoe, IL: Free Press.

Mason, W. M., House, J. S., and Martin, S. S. (1985). 'On the Dimensions of Political Alienation in America.' *Sociological Methodology*, 15, 111–151, https://doi.org/10.2307/270848

Mercenier, H, 2019. 'L'Union européenne vue par des jeunes Bruxellois. Contribution à l'étude des rapports des citoyens à la politique.' In *Thèse de sciences politiques*. Singapore: Université Saint-Louis Bruxelles.

Mooi, E., Sarstedt, M., Mooi-Reci, I. (2018). 'Principal Component and Factor Analysis.' In Mooi, E., Sarstedt, M., Mooi-Reci, I. (eds.). *Market Research, Springer Texts in Business and Economics* (pp. 265–311). Springer, https://doi.org/10.1007/978-981-10-5218-7_8

Morgan, D. L. (1996). 'Focus group.' *Annual Review of Sociology*, 22, 129–152, https://doi.org/10.1146/annurev.soc.22.1.129

Pinkleton, B. E., and Austin, E. W. (2002). 'Exploring relationships among media use frequency, perceived media importance, and media satisfaction in political disaffection and efficacy.' *Mass Communication and Society*, 5(2), 141–163, https://doi.org/10.1207/S15327825MCS0502_3

Perrez, J., Randour, F., Reuchamps, M. (2019). 'De l'uniformité du discours politique: analyse bibliométrique et linguistique de la catégorisation des discours politiques.' *Cognitextes*, 19, https://doi.org/10.4000/cognitextes.1337

Roszkowski, M. J., and Soven, M.(2010). 'Shifting gears: consequences of including two negatively worded items in the middle of a positively worded questionnaire.' *Assessment and Evaluation in Higher Education*, 35(1), 113–130, https://doi.org/10.1080/02602930802618344

Seyd, B. (2016). 'Exploring Political Disappointment.' *Parliamentary Affairs*, 69(2), 327–347, https://doi.org/10.1093/pa/gsv018

Soroka, S., Young, L., Balmas, M. (2015). 'Bad news or mad news? Sentiment scoring of negativity, fear, and anger in news content.' *Ann. Am. Acad. Polit. Soc. Sci.* 659(1), 108–121, https://doi.org/10.1177/0002716215569217

Tenhouten, W. D. (2007). *A General Theory of Emotions and Social Life*. London: Routledge, https://doi.org/10.4324/9780203013441

Valentino, N. A., Hutchings, V. L., Banks, A. J. and Davis, A. K. (2008). 'Is a worried citizen a good citizen? Emotions, political information seeking, and learning via the internet.' *Political Psychology*, 29, 247–273, https://doi.org/10.1111/j.1467-9221.2008.00625.x

Van Criekingen, M., Fleury, A. (2006). 'La ville branchée: gentrification et dynamiques commerciales à Bruxelles et à Paris.' *Revue Belge de Géographie*, 1–2, 113–134, https://doi.org/10.4000/belgeo.10950

Van der Meer, T. (2010). 'In what we trust? A multi-level study into trust in parliament as an evaluation of state characteristics.' *International Review of Administrative Sciences*, 76(3), 517–536, https://doi.org/10.1177/0020852310372450

Van der Meer, T., Hakhverdian, A. (2017). 'Political Trust as the Evaluation of Process and Performance: A Cross-National Study of 42 European Countries.' *Political Studies*, 65(1), 81–102, https://doi.org/10.1177/0032321715607514

Van der Meer, T., Zmerli, S. (2017). 'The deeply rooted concern with political trust.' In S. Zmerli, and T. W. G. van der Meer (eds.). *Handbook on Political Trust* (pp. 1–18). Cheltenham: Edward Elgar, https://doi.org/10.4337/9781782545118

van der Meer, T. (2017). 'Political Trust and the 'Crisis of Democracy'. In R. Dalton (Ed.), *Oxford Research Encyclopedia of Politics* (pp. 1–25). Oxford: Oxford University Press, https://doi.org/10.1093/acrefore/9780190228637.013.77

Van Ingelgom, V. (2020). 'Focus Groups: From Qualitative Data Generation to Analysis.' In Curini, L., Franzese, R. (eds.). *The SAGE Handbook of Research Methods in Political Science and International Relations* (pp. 1190–1210). London: Sage Publication, https://dx.doi.org/10.4135/9781526486387.n65

Verhoeven, I., Tonkens, E. (2018). 'Joining the Citizens: Forging new collaborations between government and citizens in deprived neighbourhoods.' In *From Austerity to Abundance? Critical Perspectives on International Public Sector Management* (pp. 161–179). Bingley: Emerald Publishing Limited, https://doi.org/10.1108/s2045-794420180000006007

Warren, M. E. (2017). 'A Problem-Based Approach to Democratic Theory.' *American Political Science Review*, 111(1), 39–53, https://doi.org/10.1017/S0003055416000605

Wilkinson, S. (1998). 'Focus groups in health research: Exploring the meaning of health and illness.' *Journal of Health Psychology*, 3(3), 329–348, https://doi.org/ 10.1177/135910539800300304

White, J. (2010). 'Europe in the political imagination.' *Journal of Common Market Studies*, 48(4), 1015–1038, https://doi.org/10.1111/j.1468-5965.2010.02084.x

Appendix 1: Simplified generic version–Topic guide Focus group (2020-2022)

Welcome and introduction

Presentation of the research project: *who we are, what we do, what we are interested in, what we will do together.*

Discussion rules: *consent form, anonymity and recording, duration.*

Get to know each other: *can you briefly introduce yourself to the rest of the group?*

Societal issues

Main question: *What are the most important societal issues today?*
   (1) *Inner deliberation*: Each participant writes their answers on a post-it; (2) *Tour de table:* Each participant shares their answers; (3) *Collective discussion*: Reactions and collective discussion

Follow-up questions:
   We would like to ask you to discuss together which of these issues are for you–as a group–the most (second and third) important issues and challenges.
   Have there been any moments, or important changes, or evolutions that stood out to you?
   Who is to blame?
   When a participant expresses an emotion about politics (e.g., 'depressed', 'angry', 'sad'), ask if the other participants feel the same. If no one mentions an emotion, ask *how do you feel about politics today?*

Societal problems and political solutions

Main question: *What are the solutions to these societal problems?*

Main question: *Who is responsible? Who should take care of that?*

Stimuli (pictures): *Here are some examples of ways in which people try to address these problems. What comes to mind when you see these pictures? What do you think about these? How do they relate to our discussion so far?*

Description of the pictures [follow-ups with suggestions]

(1) **Voting** [e.g., elections; referendum]; (2) **Citizens** coming together to talk about an issue [e.g., citizens coming together to talk about the problems and potential solutions; citizen summit that gives *advice* to the government; citizen summit that can *make decisions* for the community]; (3) **Demonstrate**; (4) **Helping people that are having a hard time**; (5) **Experts** getting together to make decisions [experts = scientists; professionals in their field]; (6) **Violent protest**

Follow-up question:

In the discussions, you mentioned the mayor/Belgian government/ EU, Brussels/Flanders/Wallonia a few times, but there are also other places where decisions and laws are being made, like local/federal/Belgium/ EU/Brussels/Flanders/ Wallonia. What do you think about these levels? What are the problems or good things about this?

Conclusive question

Main question: In all of this, what about the [label of the group]? How are you represented?

Follow-up: *What does it mean for you to feel represented? Who should take care of that (i.e., representing you)?*

Appendix 2: RepResent Focus Group Dataset–Wave 1 (2019-2020)

The focus group data were collected between January 2019 and February 2020 in the framework of the EOS RepResent project (FNRS-FWO n°G0F0218N). This project examines the relationship between democratic resentment and political representation in Belgium. In particular, the RepResent Focus Group Dataset originates from work package 3 and focuses on symbolic representation. Symbolic representation mostly concerns the linkage between citizens and representatives and deals with questions such as: do people feel represented by their representatives? Do they believe that representatives are representing their concerns in the political arena?

To inquire citizens' experiences with, views about, and feelings (such as democratic resentment) towards political representation in an open manner, focus groups were organized around three guiding questions: What are the most important societal issues that Belgium is facing today?; Who should take care of those issues?; How should they be resolved (i.e., political solutions)?[1] These three questions were asked in 16[2] focus groups carried out in the Brussels region. On average, six people participated in each focus group (92 participants in total). The average length of the focus groups was 2.5 hours. All focus groups were audio recorded —and, when participants agreed (written informed consent was required for participation), filmed (14 out of 16). Based on these recordings, anonymized verbatim transcripts were produced.

While all focus groups followed the same structure, the selection criteria and recruitment strategies aimed to achieve diversity in terms of participants and groups. Participants were selected along two main dimensions: a socio-political proxy and a socio-spatial proxy. The goal of these selection criteria was to capture a diverse sample of citizens from whom resentful feelings might be expected and to examine how these feelings are linked to matters of political participation. A first set of focus groups examined the expression of democratic resentment and views on political representation in political spaces (i.e., socio-political proxy) with politicized and/or pre-identified groups (i.e., Yellow Vests, Youth for Climate, social workers, Experts du vécu, Syndicat des Immenses and blue-collar workers in the European Parliament —59 out of 92 participants). A second set of focus groups included people based on the social spaces they are part of (i.e., socio-spatial proxy), focusing on both mixed or less advantaged areas (i.e., 'Marolles' and Molenbeek — 30 out of 92 participants) and, to a lesser extent, on more advantaged areas of Brussels (i.e., 'Dansaert' — three out of 92 participants). To guarantee the distinction between the socio-political and the socio-spatial proxy,

---

1   The two focus groups conducted in French among the *Gilets Jaunes* [Yellow Vests] followed a slightly different structure. Indeed, these groups served as pilot groups. The main questions were addressed in the same order (What are the most important societal issues that Belgium is facing today?; Who should take care of those issues?; How should they be resolved (i.e., political solutions)?; but some more specific questions relative to this particular context of mobilization were also asked. Our experience with these first groups helped us to fine-tune the topic guide that served for the remainder of the focus groups. For example, a new vignette exercise among participants (discussing different solutions) was introduced after the two pilot groups with the Yellow Vests activists.

2   Fourteen in French and two in Dutch.

researchers made sure that prospective participants for the latter groups were not part of a politicized collective/activist movement.

Two types of recruitment strategies were used: (1) direct recruitment by the researcher on the field of study and (2) a mixed strategy, composed of direct and indirect recruitment via existing networks (i.e., pre-existing organization such as NGOs, foundations, etc.). The technical report of the study specifies which groups were recruited in what manner. Using these socio-political or socio-spatial proxies and recruitment strategies led to the inclusion of participants with varying socio-demographic characteristics: (1) 64% of participants are male (36% female); (2) apart from 65+, respondents of all ages are relatively evenly represented; (3) about half of the participants obtained either no diploma or a diploma from secondary school, 14.3% were still in secondary school at the time of the focus group, 14.1% had a university degree, and 20.7% completed professional secondary education.

Appendix 3: RepResent Focus Group Dataset–Wave 2 (2020-2021)

The focus group data were collected between December 2020 and March 2021 in the framework of the EOS RepResent project (FNRS-FWO n°G0F0218N). This project examines the relationship between political resentment and representation in Belgium. In particular, the RepResent Focus Group Dataset originates from work package 3 of the RepResent project and focuses on symbolic representation. Symbolic representation mostly concerns the linkage between citizens and representatives and deals with questions such as: do people feel represented by their representatives? Do they believe that representatives are representing their concerns in the political arena?

To inquire citizens' experiences with, views about, and feelings (such as political resentment) towards political representation in an open manner, the focus groups relied on an 'experienced-based' and a 'context-sensitive' approach, starting from the personal experiences of the participants. To do so, the focus groups were organized around the same three guiding questions used for the first wave of FG: What are the most important societal issues that Belgium is facing today?; Who should take care of those issues?; How should they be resolved (i.e., political solutions)? These three questions were asked in 12[3] focus groups conducted online, using Zoom. On average, five people participated in each focus group (58 participants in total). The average length of the focus groups was 2 hours and 25 minutes. All focus groups were audio and video recorded (written informed consent was required for participation). Based on these recordings, anonymized verbatim transcripts were produced.

Participants were recruited following a logic of purposive sampling and the selection of participants was theoretically driven. Overall, the objective of the focus groups was to capture a diverse sample of citizens where political resentment is expected to be observed, while ensuring a certain homogeneity within each focus group. In particular, the second wave of focus groups aimed to document how citizens expressed political resentment in a time of crisis (i.e., the COVID-19 pandemic). With the COVID-19 pandemic as the common context of this wave, four categories of participants were sampled: (1) far-right voters; (2) COVID-19 vaccine sceptics; (3) participants (heavily) affected by COVID-19 restrictions and finally, (4) non-politicized 'middle-class' citizens dissatisfied with politics.

More precisely, we conducted two focus groups with Belgian citizens who had far-right or right-wing Flemish nationalist political preferences (VB and N-VA). We also conducted two focus groups with citizens who were suspicious of or opposed to the COVID-19 vaccines. We expected these participants to demonstrate relatively high levels of resentment towards 'mainstream' political representatives. The third category focuses on citizens who have been presented in the public debate as being particularly affected by the COVID-19 pandemic: (1) professionals from the cultural sector (two groups) and university students (three groups). In addition to these very specific groups, three focus groups were organized with non-politicized 'middle-class' citizens who are generally dissatisfied with politics. They served as a point of comparison for the other specific groups.

A recruitment survey (for five groups) and an external survey company (for seven groups) were used to identify and recruit participants. Using these recruitment strategies led to the inclusion of

---

3   Seven in French and five in Dutch.

participants with varying socio-demographic characteristics: (1) 50% of participants are male (50% female); (2) in terms of age, respondents below 25 (n=15); 25–34 (N=11); 35–44 (N=12); 45–54 (N=6); 55–64 (N=6); 65–74 (N=7); 75+ (N=1); (3) in terms of education, six participants obtained either no diploma or a diploma from secondary school and two participants completed professional secondary education; 15 participants had a professional bachelor's degree (i.e., higher education, short type); 15 participants were currently studying at a university (i.e., bachelor's degree) and two obtained a bachelor's degree; and 17 participants had a university degree (master's degree or higher).

3. Who feels resentful?

Fernando Feitosa, Pierre Baudewyns,
Jean-Benoit Pilet & David Talukder

Abstract: This chapter investigates the groups of the population that harbor feelings of resentment. Utilizing data from the 2021 RepResent cross-sectional survey, we explore the distribution of resentment across five dimensions: gender, age, education, vote choice, and region of residence. The findings indicate significant variations in resentment levels among different age groups, but in an unexpected direction. Specifically, resentment is highest among the middle-aged population rather than younger individuals. Additionally, there are remarkable differences across vote choices, with protest voters exhibiting higher levels of resentment compared to other voters. However, no substantial differences are observed when considering gender, educational levels, or regions of residence. These results contribute to a better understanding of the relationship between marginalized individuals and protest voters and a sense of exclusion from the political system.

Introduction

As elaborated earlier in this book, political resentment is a major issue in contemporary democracies. However, political resentment is unlikely to be equally distributed within societies. First, one might suppose that a sense of exclusion should be particularly felt by the traditionally and historically marginalized. Second, given the prevalence of resentment-related attitudes among supporters of protest parties, these individuals should exhibit higher levels of political resentment compared to supporters of other parties. Third, the greater electoral support for protest

©2024 F. Feitosa, et al., CC BY-NC 4.0   https://doi.org/10.11647/OBP.0401.03

parties in Flanders compared to Wallonia suggests that resentment may be more pervasive in the former region.

This chapter explores these inequalities in the distribution of political resentment. By carefully examining the distribution of resentment along five dimensions (gender, education, age, vote choice, region of residence), we aim to contribute to our understanding of the nature and origins of political resentment. Additionally, our findings can help to inform initiatives aimed at addressing and reducing individuals' sense of exclusion from the political system. Note that our examination of the relationship between these five factors and resentment relies on the established terminology utilized in previous research (e.g., see Celis & Childs, 2012; Mayne & Peters, 2023). Our use of the terms does not entail adopting a normative position regarding the various social groups they represent, nor does it seek to further stigmatize or essentialize groups who may already be in structurally disadvantaged positions. We are mindful of the power differentials between the different sociological groups we speak about in this chapter. Our objective in this chapter is first and foremost to describe the distribution of resentment across the Belgian population, along a limited set of socio-demographic variables.

The investigation of data from the 2021 RepResent cross-sectional survey reveals that individuals who tend to experience underrepresentation do not necessarily harbour a sense of resentment, in the way we define it in this book. Specifically, no significant differences in levels of resentment are observed between genders. Additionally, the disparity in resentment levels between individuals with lower and higher levels of education is relatively modest. Age emerges as a significant factor, but younger individuals, who tend to be less politically represented, display lower rather than higher levels of resentment compared to middle-aged citizens. Voters who support protest parties — the Parti du travail de Belgique (PTB), the Partij van de Arbeid van België (PVDA), the Nieuw-Vlaamse Alliantie (N-VA), and the Vlaams Belang (VB) — exhibit higher levels of resentment compared to voters of other parties. Yet, resentment is not higher in Flanders compared to Wallonia.

This chapter is structured as follows: first, we provide a theoretical framework that explains the potential connections between resentment and the various factors examined in this chapter. Next, we discuss the data and the methodology employed to test these relationships. Following the presentation of the main findings, we delve into additional analyses that examine the relationships with an emotion-based resentment measure. We conclude the chapter with a discussion of the scholarly implications of our findings.

Gender, age, and educational differences in political resentment

While there is a paucity of studies focusing on inequalities in political resentment, existing literature on citizens' attitudes towards politics, democratic dissatisfaction, and political underrepresentation offers valuable insights. Specifically, empirical evidence demonstrates that women comprise, on average, only 32.8% of Members of Parliament (MPs) in the Americas and 31.2% of MPs in Europe (Inter-Parliamentary Union, 2022). Furthermore, individuals aged 30 or below constitute less than 2.8% of MPs, despite representing a relatively large proportion of the overall population. Note that while elections inherently involve the selection of a political elite from among the citizenry, these inequalities in political representation are concerning as inclusion remains an important democratic goal (Broockman, 2013; Mansbridge, 1999; Sobolewska, et al., 2018).

Individuals with lower levels of education are also underrepresented among elected politicians. While comprehensive global data on the educational background of MPs are not available, several studies have demonstrated that MPs in various European countries, such as Belgium, the Netherlands, Germany, the UK, France, and Italy, tend to hold university or higher education degrees (Talukder, 2022; Hakhverdian, 2015). This observation has led many to perceive political elites as a distinct social class that may be disconnected from the experiences and challenges faced by those who did not have the opportunity to go into higher education (Noordzij, et al., 2021).

Women, individuals with lower educational levels, and younger citizens are therefore descriptively less represented in politics than their counterparts. In other words, the proportion of politicians among those groups is lower than among men, individuals with higher educational levels, and older citizens. But in addition to a poor descriptive representation, women, individuals with lower educational levels, and younger citizens encounter difficulties in having their ideas and interests represented in parliament. Numerous studies have demonstrated, for instance, that representatives tend to prioritize the interests of socio-economically advantaged citizens over those who are socio-economically disadvantaged (Giger, et al., 2012; Lupu & Warner, 2022; Rosset, et al., 2013; Rosset & Stecker, 2019), pointing to a systemic substantive underrepresentation of the latter group.

One of the consequences of political underrepresentation is a sense of resentment. Individuals who are objectively excluded from politics, or not as well represented as their counterparts, may feel left out by the political elite, and develop resentful feelings. The existence of a relationship between political underrepresentation and political resentment seems plausible as well, when considering that lower levels of representation often lead to lower levels of attitudes such as support for democracy (Ezrow & Xezonakis, 2011; Mayne & Hakhverdian, 2017) and trust in parliament (Marié & Talukder, 2021) —a combination that is closely linked to political resentment. Moreover, researchers have shown that marginalized individuals often express lower levels of satisfaction with democracy compared to their socio-economically-advantaged counterparts (Bègue, 2007; Braconnier & Mayer, 2015; Ceka & Magalhaes, 2020; Talukder, 2022), and that they tend to harbour more negative evaluations of the political elite, explaining their support for reforms aimed at promoting participatory tools (Bowler, et al., 2007; Coffé & Michels, 2014; Talukder & Pilet, 2021; Webb, 2013) or those associated with stealth democracy (Hibbing & Theiss-Morse, 2002).

The link between political underrepresentation and political resentment has been more directly discussed by Stoker (2019, p. 145). Stoker has argued that factors like disconnection from a global and knowledge-based economy, recent changes in social structures, and political alienation can all create conditions that foster the emergence of resentment. Interpreted together, the literature therefore seems to support the idea that women, individuals with lower levels of education, and younger citizens are more susceptible to experiencing resentment than their counterparts.

Our first hypothesis is, consequently, that:

H1: Women, those with lower educational levels, and younger citizens display higher levels of political resentment than their counterparts.

While it seems reasonable to anticipate a relationship between gender, in particular, and political resentment, the strength of this relationship seems to vary depending on an individual's perception of political underrepresentation. Individuals who are unaware of their underrepresentation or who feel adequately represented should exhibit a weaker connection between their gender and political resentment. By being oblivious to or rejecting the disparities in representation, these individuals may not perceive a direct correlation between their gender and their feeling of resentment. On the other hand, individuals who recognize the underrepresentation of their gender may be more likely to experience stronger feelings of resentment. Their awareness and recognition of the disparities in representation expose them to the realities of gender-based discrimination or systemic biases, leading to a heightened sense of exclusion.

Our second hypothesis is therefore that:

H2: Perceived underrepresentation moderates the relationship between gender and political resentment.

The relationship between gender and resentment seems to be further nuanced by education. In social-psychological theory, it is widely recognized that individuals have multiple identities that shape their self-perception. Specifically, individuals possess a diversity of personal identities that reflect unique traits and self-characterizations, relational identities that pertain to their social roles and relationships with others, and collective identities that arise from shared characteristics or ascribed attributes within a group (Andersen & Chen, 2002; Ashmore, et al., 2004; Brewer & Gardiner, 1996; Sedikides & Brewer, 2001).

The combination of multiple personal, social, or collective identities gives rise to diverse perspectives and outcomes among individuals. For example, individuals who identify with both sexual and racial/ethnic minority groups often experience a unique set of challenges and adaptations related to the simultaneous development and expression of these identities (Crawford, et al., 2002). When it comes to gender and education specifically, a higher educational attainment may contribute to a greater sense of integration within the political system for women who obtained it compared to those with low levels of education. Similar dynamics should apply to men; however, due to their privileged position, education should have a lesser impact on their sense of exclusion. As a result, education should contribute to varying levels of the gender gap in representation.

Our third hypothesis therefore posits that:

> H3: Education moderates the relationship between gender and political resentment.

Vote choices and regional variances in political resentment

In addition to disparities in resentment across gender, age, and education, vote choice and regional residence may also contribute to varying levels of this political attitude. The literature suggests that individuals who harbour dissatisfaction with the political system, a correlate of political resentment, tend to align their vote choices with protest parties. For instance, Goovaerts and colleagues (2020) have found that supporters of the PTB-PVDA, two far-left parties, and the VB, a far-right party, generally express higher levels of discontentment with the political system compared to voters of other parties. A similar trend can be observed with the N-VA and the Green parties. Although not considered radical parties, they have still managed to attract protest voters (Hooghe, et al., 2011; Rihoux, 2003; Hino, 2012; van Haute, 2016).

The emergence of these parties as viable options for protest voters can be partially explained by their reliance on a discourse that taps into their feelings of dissatisfaction with the political system. In Figures 1 and 2, we present examples of the rhetoric employed by these parties, which serves this purpose. Figure 1 showcases a tweet from the PTB, highlighting the notion that the government prioritizes the interests of the economic elite when it comes to wealth redistribution, thereby neglecting those who face economic hardships. Meanwhile, Figure 2 displays a tweet from the VB, suggesting that the government is advocating for increased labour immigration despite the prevailing economic challenges in the country. Both messages have the potential to strike a chord with individuals who hold grievances against the system, feeling excluded from it.

PTB
5 mai, 20:33 · 🌐   ···

Electrabel vide nos poches pour gonfler celles de ses actionnaires. Et que fait le gouvernement ? Rien... Il est temps d'oser s'en prendre à ces surprofits pour protéger le pouvoir d'achat des ménages. Notre proposition de loi est prête à être votée. On ne peut plus attendre.

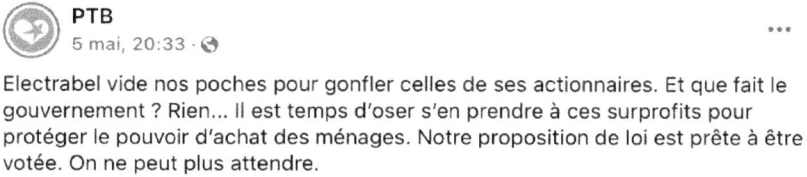

Fig. 3.1 Resentment-inducing discourse by the PTB-PVDA.

Note: The English translation reads as follows: 'Electrabel [a company that sells electricity] empties our pockets to inflate those of its shareholders. And what does the government do? Nothing... It is time to dare to attack these excess profits to protect the purchasing power of households. Our bill is ready to be voted on. We can't wait any longer.'

Vlaams Belang ✓
6 mai, 13:22 · 🌐   ···

Ondanks de stijgende energiearmoede, de sterk dalende koopkracht en de vervreemding van steden en dorpen, wil deze paars-groene regering nog méér arbeidsmigratie op gang trekken. Stop hiermee en denk eerst aan onze mensen!

- Tussenkomst van federaal parlementslid Dries Van Langenhove -

Fig. 3.2 Resentment-inducing discourse by the VB.

Note: The English translation reads as follows: 'Despite rising energy poverty, sharply declining purchasing power and the alienation of cities and villages, this purple-green government wants to initiate even more labour immigration. Stop this and think of our people first!'

Following this logic, our fourth hypothesis therefore proposes that:

H4: Voters of protest parties (i.e., PTB-PVDA, N-VA, VB, Green) exhibit higher levels of political resentment compared to voters of other parties.

If resentment is higher among supporters of protest parties, this political attitude should be more prevalent in Flanders than in Wallonia. Belgium is commonly regarded as a deeply divided society with two distinct party systems (Sinardet, 2012; Van Haute & Wauters, 2019). Notably, protest parties like the VB and the N-VA have a significant presence in Flanders, while their representation in Wallonia is limited. This disparity in the electoral support of protest parties between Flanders and Wallonia is indicative that levels of resentment may vary between the two regions. Specifically, individuals residing in Flanders may experience higher levels of resentment compared to their counterparts in Wallonia (although Walgrave, et al., 2020, present an alternative perspective).

Our fifth and final hypothesis is then that:

H5: Political resentment is higher in Flanders than Wallonia.

Data

To investigate the differences in levels of political resentment among individuals, we utilize data from the 2021 RepResent cross-sectional survey. This survey includes a unique set of questions designed to assess individuals' resentment towards politics. Specifically, respondents in this survey were asked to indicate their level of agreement or disagreement with the following statements: 'What the government decides is often worse than what I hoped for'; 'I am generally disappointed with Belgian politics'; 'I get angry when I think about politics'; 'Most politicians do not take citizens seriously; they rather treat us as children'; 'Politics is usually better for others than for people like me'; 'Elections do not matter; everything is decided beforehand'; 'The Belgian political system has been malfunctioning for a long time'. Two points should be made about these questions. First, they address the same underlying concept of political resentment. Indeed, not only is the Cronbach's alpha coefficient relatively high (.88), but a principal component analysis conducted on these items yields a single index. Second, the inclusion of an item asking respondents to evaluate whether politics is usually more beneficial for others than for people like themselves allows for the creation of a resentment index that captures a sense of group exclusion from politics.

To construct the index that will be used in the analysis, we initially transform the original responses to a -5 to +5 scale, assigning a value of 5 to the most extreme expression of resentment. Next, we compute an additive index of resentment by summing individuals' scores on the transformed -5 to +5 scale. The scores on this scale range from -35, representing the lowest level of resentment, to +35, indicating the highest level of resentment. As Figure 3 shows, citizens in our sample harbour a relatively moderate degree of resentment, with a mean value of 8.97 and a standard deviation of 15.02. However, it is notable that there is a greater number of individuals with high levels of resentment compared to those with low levels of resentment, which is consistent with the widespread democratic dissatisfaction discussed in the literature.

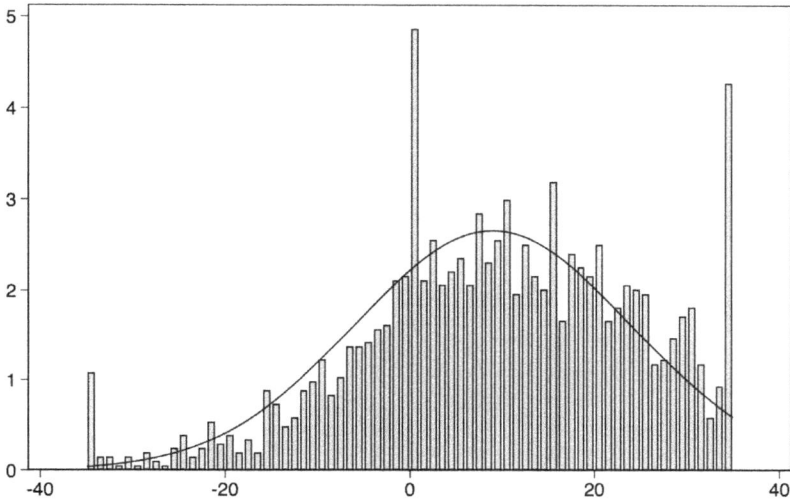

Fig. 3.3 Distribution of resentment index in the data.

Note: The index is created by summing individuals' responses to the seven resentment questions. In this index, a score of 35 represents the highest level of resentment, and -35 the lowest level.

When it comes to the five individual-level characteristics examined in this study, they are coded as follows: First, individuals identifying as men are coded as '0', while those identifying as women are coded as '1' (refer to Appendix 1 for descriptive statistics). Individuals with no schooling or only primary education are coded as '1'; those with incomplete secondary education are coded as '2'; those with complete secondary education are coded as '3'; those with tertiary education (not university) are coded as '4'; and those with university experience are coded as '5'. Residents of Flanders are coded as '0', while residents of Wallonia are coded as '1'. Age represents a continuous variable, while vote choice consists of a categorical variable with six different response options for respondents in Wallonia (cdH/Les Engagés, Ecolo, DéFI, MR, PS, and PTB), and seven options for respondents in Flanders (CD&V, Groen, N-VA, Open VLD, PVDA, Vooruit/SP.A, and VB).

To assess the moderating role of perceived underrepresentation, we utilize a unique battery of questions that gauges perceptions of women's and men's representation in politics. Our measure of perceived representation ranges from -10 to +10 (refer to Table 3.1). Individuals who believe that women are significantly *over*represented while men are significantly *under*represented are coded as +10. Conversely, those who perceive women as significantly *under*represented while men as significantly *over*represented are coded as -10. Individuals who perceive an equal level of representation of women and men are coded as 0.

Table 3.1 Possible values on the perceived representation index.

		Women				
		Very under	Under	Neither, nor	Over	Very over
	Very under	0	+1	+3	+6	+10
	Under	-7	0	+2	+5	+9
Men	Neither, nor	-8	-4	0	+4	+8
	Over	-9	-5	-2	0	+7
	Very over	-10	-6	-3	-1	0

Note: The index ranges from -10 to +10, with +10 representing the belief that women are *over*represented and men are *under*represented, and -10 representing the belief that women are *under*represented and men are *over*represented.

Method

We conduct multivariate linear regressions to examine the correlation between the five individual-level characteristics and political resentment. We chose this analytical approach because it allows us to isolate the impact of each independent variable (gender, education, age, vote choice, and region) on our dependent variable (resentment). To mitigate the potential underestimation of the impact of gender, age, education, and region on resentment, we employ two separate models. In Model 1, a subset of the independent variables is included (gender, age, education, and region), while in Model 2, all five independent variables are included (gender, age, education, region, and vote choice). In both models, age is included as a squared term to allow for curvilinear relationships. Model 2 is conducted separately for Flanders and Wallonia, as vote choice differs between these regions.

To examine the potential moderating effects of perceived representation and education on political resentment, we conduct additional tests using Model 1. For perceived representation, we include an interaction term between gender and the relative representation scale. For education, we include an interaction term between gender and education levels. To aid in the interpretation of the findings, we concentrate on estimated resentment levels in this chapter. The coefficients related to this are presented in tabular form in the Supporting Information.

Results

Figure 3.4 presents the estimated levels of resentment based on the multivariate linear regressions including gender, education, age, and region (Model 1). The figure reveals that both men and women exhibit a relatively mild degree of political resentment, with no significant difference between them. Although it cannot be demonstrated in this research, the absence of significant differences between men and women in terms of political resentment could be associated with the presence (though in low levels) of women elected politicians within all the parties of the political spectrum. Moreover, even if women's levels of resentment are equal to those of men, they could still be sufficient to drive change in the political system, facilitating meaningful progress towards more women's representation in parliament. Our results should also be read against the fact that not all emotions are legitimized in the same way across all gender groups or expressed in the same ways; resentful expressions may vary across society which may nuance the interpretations and findings we provide here (see for example Dittmar, 2020).

Figure 3.4 also reveals a minimal disparity in resentment levels between the least and most educated individuals, with only a 3.83-point difference on the resentment index (the least educated scoring 11.14 and the most educated scoring 7.30). In contrast, there is a notable variation in resentment across different age groups. While individuals aged 18 demonstrate a very low level of resentment (2.46), those aged 58 exhibit a moderate level (10.81). Furthermore, resentment undergoes significant changes as we move towards older age groups, with individuals aged 88 showing similar levels of resentment as the youth. These results challenge our initial expectations regarding age differences in resentment, as they reveal that younger individuals are actually less resentful than some of their older counterparts.

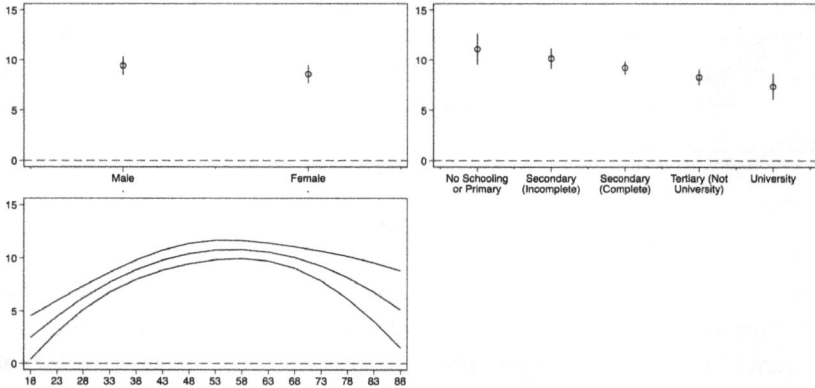

Fig. 3.4 Estimated resentment across gender, education, or age groups.

Note: Estimates based on Model 1 (excluding vote choice). 95% confidence intervals are reported. See the results in tabular format in Appendix 2.

As anticipated, women tend to experience greater resentment when they perceive a negative bias against women in politics compared to when they perceive no bias or even a positive bias. This can be observed in the left panel of Figure 3.5, where a shift from -10 (underrepresentation of women, overrepresentation of men) on the relative representative scale to 0 (equal representation of women and men) is associated with a decrease of 4.30 points on the resentment index (from 11.94 to 7.64) among female respondents. Likewise, a shift from 0 to +10 (overrepresentation of women, underrepresentation of men) is associated with a further decrease of 4.31 points (from 7.64 to 3.33). Despite these variations, the difference between men and women is statistically significant only when there is an overrepresentation of women and underrepresentation of men. In this case, women exhibit significantly lower levels of resentment compared to men.

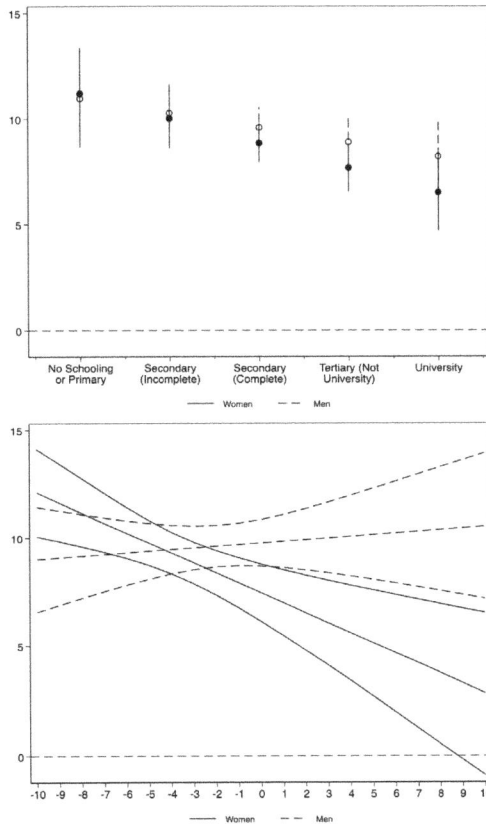

Fig. 3.5 Estimated resentment of women and men by representation perceptions (top) and education levels (bottom).

Note: Estimates based on Model 1 (excluding vote choice). 95% confidence intervals are reported. In the left panel, -10 indicates the underrepresentation of women and overrepresentation of men, while 10 signifies the overrepresentation of women and underrepresentation of men. See the results in tabular format in Appendix 3.

The top panel of Figure 3.5 highlights, in turn, that women with higher educational levels display lower levels of resentment in comparison to women with lower levels of education. Specifically, there is a notable (though statistically insignificant) decrease in resentment from 11.13 to 6.69 among female respondents. However, the anticipated gender gap is not more pronounced among individuals with low levels of education. This indicates that education does not lead to varying levels of a gender gap in resentment.

Turning to vote choices, Figure 3.6 reveals significant variations in resentment among supporters of parties. Specifically, in Flanders, supporters of Open VLD (2.18), CD&V (3.25), Groen (3.30), and Vooruit/ SP.A (5.38) exhibit relatively low levels of resentment. In contrast, N-VA (11.72), PVDA (12.78), and VB (16.36) voters demonstrate higher levels of resentment. These findings confirm our expectations regarding the relationship between vote choice and resentment. More specifically, resentment tends to be higher among supporters of parties that attract protest voters. However, our expectation regarding Groen voters is not confirmed. Despite the party's appeal to protest voters, Groen supporters do not differ significantly in terms of political resentment from supporters of liberal, socialist, and Christian-democratic parties (refer to Chapter 6 for tests on the link between policy congruence and resentment).

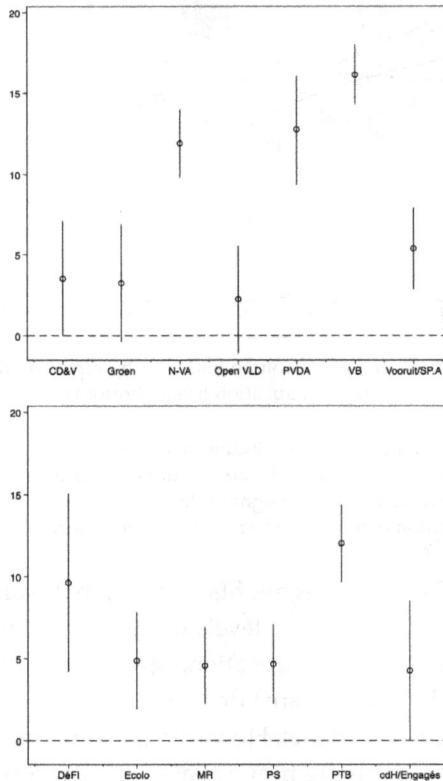

Fig. 3.6 Estimated resentment across vote choices.

Note: Estimates based on Model 2 (including vote choice). 95% confidence intervals are reported. See the results in tabular format in Appendix 2.

Similar patterns are observed in Wallonia. Political resentment is higher among PTB and DéFI voters compared to voters of the three most established parties in the Walloon party system (MR, PS, and cdH/ Les Engagés), as well as among Ecolo voters. These findings validate the PTB's ability to attract voters who harbour resentment. More importantly, they confirm that voters of protest parties in Wallonia exhibit higher levels of resentment, though Ecolo voters show similar levels of resentment as voters of other parties. In this sense, it appears that protest voters not only have higher levels of distrust in politicians and democratic discontent, but they seem to experience a profound sense of exclusion from the political system. Substantively, this finding suggests that the message associated with protest voting may be related to this sense of exclusion in addition to a distrust of politicians or general democratic dissatisfaction. Note that the limited number of DéFI voters in the sample cautions against drawing conclusions about the observed resentment levels among these voters.

While protest voters are more resentful than their counterparts, Figure 3.7 demonstrates that resentment levels are remarkably similar between residents of Flanders (9.56) and Wallonia (8.39). In other words, despite the prevalence of protest parties in Flanders, Flemish citizens are overall no more resentful than Walloon citizens. Our expectation regarding a regional difference in political resentment is therefore disconfirmed.

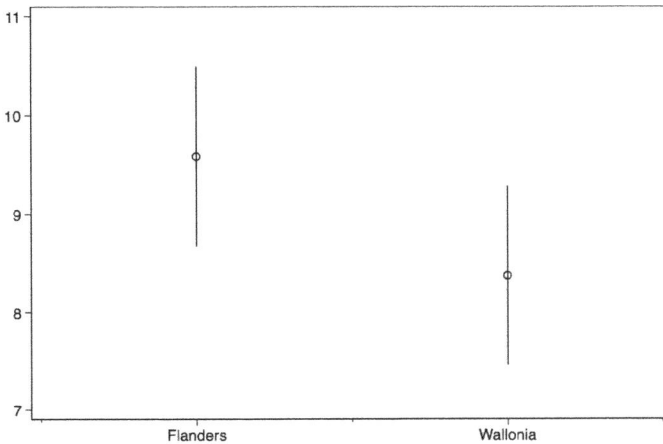

Fig. 3.7 Estimated resentment across regions.

Note: Estimates based on Model 1 (excluding vote choice). 95% confidence intervals are reported.

Robustness check using individuals' feelings about politics

Although our focus in this chapter has been on a measure of resentment that combines cognitive and affective dimensions, we also investigate disparities in resentment using an alternative measure based on an emotion index. This index draws on individuals' responses to the question, 'When you think of Belgian politics in general, to what extent do you feel each of the following emotions: Anger, Bitterness, Anxiety, Fear.' Similar to the resentment index, we recode the responses on a scale ranging from -10 to +10. For instance, individuals who experience a high level of anger are coded as +5, while those who do not feel any anger are coded as -5. By recoding the responses, our emotion index captures values between -20 (indicating the lowest levels of emotions) and +20 (indicating the highest levels of emotions).

We find a striking similarity between the analyses conducted using our resentment index and our emotion index. Specifically, women are not more emotional than men, and the middle-aged exhibit higher levels of emotion compared to both the youth and the elderly (see Appendix 4). This is important to highlight given gender-based stereotypes on who expresses emotions in society and the broader fact that gender roles define which emotions are suitable to express, and which are not, and crucially by whom. The only notable difference is that education is now found to be insignificantly associated with emotion, whereas in our main findings, it showed a significant but marginal association with resentment.

The findings pertaining to vote choice follow a similar pattern. Supporters of N-VA, PVDA, and VB in Flanders, as well as DéFI and PTB supporters in Wallonia, tend to score higher on the emotion index compared to supporters of other parties (see Appendix 5). Furthermore, residents of Flanders and Wallonia do not significantly differ in terms of their emotions (see Appendix 6). These results provide reassurance that the lack of substantial findings for gender and region, the weak findings for education, and the strong findings for age and vote choice are not driven by our use of the resentment index. They persist even when we utilize an alternative measure of political resentment.

Discussion and conclusion

This chapter examined whether resentment is unequally distributed among the Belgian population. Our investigation revealed significant variations in resentment levels based on age and vote choices. Specifically, we identified a curvilinear relationship between political resentment and age, with resentment peaking around the age of 50. Furthermore, our findings indicate that supporters of N-VA, PTB-PVDA, and VB tend to display higher levels of resentment compared to supporters of other parties. Surprisingly, women and residents of Flanders do not display higher levels of resentment than their counterparts, and the differences in these levels across education groups are relatively limited. Moreover, moderation tests reveal that the effect of gender on resentment is significant when women are perceived as overrepresented and men as underrepresented in politics, but not when the opposite scenario is observed. In contrast, education does not influence the association between gender and resentment.

By identifying who feels resentful along a set of socio-demographic variables, this chapter hopes to inform collective efforts to understand and respond to the resentment expressed across the population. It seems particularly important to address the middle aged and individuals who vote for protest parties as they harbour more resentment than their counterparts. One of these efforts may be direct democracy initiatives. By allowing citizens to have a more active role in decision-making and policy formulation, these initiatives have the potential to contribute to a greater sense of ownership and inclusion within the political system (refer to Chapters 5 and 8 of this book for a related discussion).

In contrast, the absence of a (strong) connection particularly between gender and resentment opens up important questions about who is allowed to express resentment, and suggests that different social groups may choose different affective repertoires to express their dissatisfaction with politics. While this finding may cast doubt on the efficacy of diversity policies aimed at augmenting the number of women MPs to reduce resentment, from a normative standpoint, diversity should be valued for its intrinsic worth. Consequently, even when women do not perceive themselves as more excluded than men, it is still relevant to undertake initiatives that address and mitigate inequalities in political representation.

Since our study focuses on Belgium, it is important to emphasize that our findings may not necessarily generalize to other political contexts, nor to other socio-demographic variables which were not included in our analysis. Therefore, future research could explore the extent to which the individual-level factors examined in this study correlate with resentment in different political contexts. By conducting cross-contextual investigations and studying resentment across more diverse social groups of citizens, we would gain a more comprehensive understanding of the distribution of resentment, including whether the observed levels of resentment among marginalized groups and protest voters are exclusive to Belgium or not. Such research endeavours will increase our understanding of inequalities in political resentment and how we can reduce it in the population.

References

Andersen, S. M., & Chen, S. (2002). 'The relational self: An interpersonal social-cognitive theory.' *Psychological Review*, 109, 619–645. https://doi.org/10.1037/0033-295X.109.4.619

Ashmore, R. D., Deaux, K., & McLaughlin-Volpe, T. (2004). 'An organizing framework for collective identity: Articulation and significance of multidimensionality.' *Psychological Bulletin*, 130, 80–114. https://doi.org/10.1037/0033-2909.130.1.80

Bègue, M. (2007). *Le rapport au politique des personnes en situation défavorisée: Une comparaison européenne: France, Grande-Bretagne, Espagne*. PhD Thesis, Institut d'Etudes Politiques de Paris. ParisTech Research Repository, http://www.theses.fr/2007IEPP0047/document

Best, H. (2007). 'New challenges, new elites? Changes in the recruitment and career patterns of European representative elites.' *Comparative Sociology*, 6(1–2), 85–113. https://doi.org/10.1163/156913307X187414

Bowler, S., Donovan, T., & Karp, J. A. (2007). 'Enraged or Engaged? Preferences for Direct Citizen Participation in Affluent Democracies.' *Political Research Quarterly*, 60(3), 351–362. https://doi.org/10.1177/1065912907304108

Braconnier, C., & Mayer, N. (2015). *Les inaudibles: Sociologie politique des précaires*. Paris: Presses de Sciences Po. https://doi.org/10.3917/scpo.braco.2015.01

Brewer, M. B., & Gardiner, W. (1996). 'Who is this "we?" Levels of collective identity and self representations.' *Journal of Personality and Social Psychology*, 71, 83–93. https://doi.org/10.1037/0022-3514.71.1.83

Broockman, D. E. (2013). 'Black Politicians Are More Intrinsically Motivated to Advance Blacks' Interests: A Field Experiment Manipulating Political Incentives.' *American Journal of Political Science*, 57(3), 521–536. https://doi.org/10.1111/ajps.12018

Ceka, B., & Magalhaes, P. C. (2020). 'Do the Rich and the Poor Have Different Conceptions of Democracy? Socioeconomic Status, Inequality, and the Political Status Quo.' *Comparative Politics*, 52(3), 383–412. https://doi.org/10.5129/001041520X15670823829196

Celis, K., & Childs, S. (2012). 'The substantive representation of women: What to do with conservative claims?' *Political Studies*, 60(1), 213–225. https://doi.org/10.1111/j.1467-9248.2011.00904.x

Coffé, H., & Michels, A. (2014). 'Education and support for representative, direct and stealth democracy.' *Electoral Studies*, 35, 1–11. https://doi.org/10.1016/j.electstud.2014.03.006

Cramer, K. J. (2016). *The Politics of Resentment: Rural Consciousness in Wisconsin and the Rise of Scott Walker*. Chicago: University of Chicago Press.

Crawford, I., Allison, K. W., Zamboni, B. D., & Soto, T. (2002). 'The influence of dual-identity development on the psychosocial functioning of African American gay and bisexual men.' *Journal of Sex Research*, 39(3), 179–189. https://doi.org/10.1080/00224490209552140

Dalton, R. J. (2004). *Democratic Challenges, Democratic Choices: The Erosion of Political Support in Advanced Industrial Democracies*. Oxford: Oxford University Press. https://doi.org/10.1093/acprof:oso/9780199268436.001.0001

Dittmar, K. (2020). 'Urgency and ambition: the influence of political environment and emotion in spurring US women's candidacies in 2018.' *European Journal of Politics and Gender*, 3(1), 143–160.

Ezrow, L., & Xezonakis, G. (2011). 'Citizen satisfaction with democracy and parties' policy offerings.' *Comparative Political Studies*, 44(9), 1152–1178. https://doi.org/10.1177/0010414011405461

Giger, N., Rosset, J., & Bernauer, J. (2012). 'The poor political representation of the poor in a comparative perspective.' *Representation*, 48(1), 47–61. https://doi.org/10.1080/00344893.2012.653238

Goovaerts, I., Kern, A., Van Haute, E., & Marien, S. (2020). 'Drivers of Support for the Populist Radical Left and Populist Radical Right in Belgium: An Analysis of the VB and the PVDA-PTB Vote at the 2019 Elections.' *Politics of the Low Countries*, 2(3), 228–264. https://doi.org/10.5553/PLC/258999292020002003002

Hakhverdian, A. (2015). 'Does it matter that most representatives are higher educated?' *Swiss Political Science Review*, 21(2), 237–245. https://doi.org/10.1111/spsr.12166

Han, K. J. (2016). 'Income inequality and voting for radical right-wing parties.' *Electoral Studies*, 42, 54–64. https://doi.org/10.1016/j.electstud.2016.02.001

Hibbing, J. R., & Theiss-Morse, E. (2002). *Stealth Democracy: Americans' Beliefs About How Government Should Work*. Cambridge: Cambridge University Press. https://doi.org/10.1017/CBO9780511613722

Hino, A. (2012). *New Challenger Parties in Western Europe: A Comparative Analysis*. London: Routledge. https://doi.org/10.4324/9780203130698

Hooghe, M., Marien, S., & Pauwels, T. (2011). 'Where do distrusting voters turn if there is no viable exit or voice option? The impact of political trust on electoral behaviour in the Belgian regional elections of June 2009.' *Government and Opposition*, 46(2), 245–273. https://doi.org/10.1111/j.1477-7053.2010.01338.x

Lefevere, J., Van Dijk, L., Walgrave, S., Celis, K., DeschouwerK., Marien, S., Pilet, J.B., Rihoux, B., Van Haute, E., Van Ingelgom, V., Baudewyns, P., Verhaegen, S., De Mulder, A. (2021). RepResent Cross Sectional Survey Fall 2021. DANS, https://doi.org/10.17026/dans-zkg-rftw

Lupu, N., & Warner, Z. (2022). 'Affluence and congruence: Unequal representation around the world.' *Journal of Politics*, 84(1), 276–290. https://doi.org/10.1086/714930

Mansbridge, J. (1999). 'Should Blacks Represent Blacks and Women Represent Women? A Contingent "Yes".' *Journal of Politics*, 61(3), 628–657. https://doi.org/10.2307/2647821

Marié, A., & Talukder, D. (2021). 'Think like me and I will trust you. The effects of policy opinion congruence on trust in the parliament.' *Politics of the Low Countries*, 3, 58–287. https://doi.org/10.5553/PLC/.000026

Mayne, Q., & Hakhverdian, A. (2017). 'Ideological congruence and citizen satisfaction: Evidence from 25 advanced democracies.' *Comparative Political Studies*, 50(6), 822–849. https://doi.org/10.1177/0010414016639708

Mayne, Q., & Peters, Y. (2023). 'Where you sit is where you stand: education-based descriptive representation and perceptions of democratic quality.' *West European Politics*, 46(3), 526–549. https://doi.org/10.1080/01402382.2022.2071044

Noordzij, K., de Koster, W., & van der Waal, J. (2021). '"They don't know what it's like to be at the bottom": Exploring the role of perceived cultural distance in less-educated citizens' discontent with politicians.' *British Journal of Sociology*, 72(3), 566–579. https://doi.org/10.1111/1468-4446.12800

Norris, P. (2011). *Democratic Deficit: Critical Citizens Revisited*. Cambridge: Cambridge University Press. https://doi.org/10.1017/CBO9780511973383

Pitkin, H. F. (1967). *The Concept of Representation*. Berkeley: University of California Press.

Rihoux, B., (2003). 'La percée d'Ecolo au 13 juin 1999 : un effet dioxine et des électeurs moins «verts» ?' In Frognier, A.-P. & Aish, A.-M. (eds.). *Elections: la rupture?* (pp. 44–53). De Boeck.

Rosset, J., Giger, N., & Bernauer, J. (2013). 'More money, fewer problems? Cross-level effects of economic deprivation on political representation.' *West European Politics*, 36(4), 817–835. https://doi.org/10.1080/01402382.2013.783353

Rosset, J., & Stecker, C. (2019). 'How well are citizens represented by their governments? Issue congruence and inequality in Europe.' *European Political Science Review*, 11(2), 145–160. https://doi.org/10.1017/S1755773919000043

Sedikides, C., & Brewer, M. B. (2001). *Individual Self, Relational Self, Collective Self*. New York: Psychology Press.

Sinardet, D. (2012). 'Is There a Belgian Public Sphere? What the Case of a Federal Multilingual Country Can Contribute to the Debate on Transnational Public Spheres, and Vice Versa.' In Seymour, M. & Gagnon, A.-G. (eds.). *Multinational Federalism* (pp. 172–202). Springer. https://doi.org/10.1057/9781137016744_9

Sobolewska, M., McKee, R., & Campbell, R. (2018). 'Explaining motivation to represent: How does descriptive representation lead to substantive representation of racial and ethnic minorities?' *West European Politics*, 41(6), 1237–1261. https://doi.org/10.1080/01402382.2018.1455408

Stoker, G. (2019). 'Relating and Responding to the Politics of Resentment.' *Political Quarterly*, 90, 138–151. https://doi.org/10.1111/1467-923X.12576

Talukder, D. (2022). *Légitimité politique et sous-représentation :comment les citoyens évaluent-ils le système politique*. PhD thesis, Universite Libre de Bruxelles. ULB Research Repository.

Talukder, D., & Pilet, J.-B. (2021). 'Public support for deliberative democracy. A specific look at the attitudes of citizens from disadvantaged groups.' *Innovation: The European Journal of Social Science Research*, 1–21. https://doi.org/10.1080/13511610.2021.1978284

Van Haute, E. (2016). *Green Parties in Europe*. London: Routledge. https://doi.org/10.4324/9781315585932

Van Haute, E., & Wauters, B. (2019). 'Do Characteristics of Consociational Democracies Still Apply to Belgian Parties?' *Politics of the Low Countries*, 1(1), 6–26. https://doi.org/10.5553/PLC/258999292019001001002

Vidal, G. (2018). 'Challenging business as usual? The rise of new parties in Spain in times of crisis.' *West European Politics*, 41(2), 261–286. https://doi.org/10.1080/01402382.2017.1376272

Walgrave, S., van Erkel, P., Jennart, I., Lefevere, J., & Baudewyns, P. (2020). 'How issue salience pushes voters to the left or to the right.' *Politics of the Low Countries*, 2(3), 320–353. https://doi.org/10.5553/PLC/258999292020002003005

Webb, P. (2013). 'Who is willing to participate? Dissatisfied democrats, stealth democrats and populists in the United Kingdom: Who is willing to participate?' *European Journal of Political Research*, 52(6), 747–772. https://doi.org/10.1111/1475-6765.12021

Supporting Information

Appendix 1. Descriptive statistics of variables in the analysis

	Mean	Standard Deviation	Minimum	Maximum	N
Political Resentment	8.97	15.02	-35	35	2,035
Gender	0.52	0.50	0	1	2,031
Education	3.25	1.01	1	5	2,035
Age	49.70	16.76	18	90	2,035
Vote Choice (Flanders)	4.49	1.90	1	7	760
Vote Choice (Wallonia)	3.70	1.31	1	6	609
Region	0.50	0.50	0	1	2,035
Perceived Representation	-2.64	3.65	-10	10	1,823
Emotions	3.40	8.87	-20	20	2,035

Note: Data comes from the 2021 RepResent cross-sectional survey.

Appendix 2. Association between political resentment and the five variables (gender, education, age, vote choice, and region)

	DV: Political Resentment		
	Model 1	Model 2 (Flanders)	Model 2 (Wallonia)
Gender	-0.851	-0.930	-1.099
	(0.672)	(1.057)	(1.184)
Education	-0.936**	-1.188*	0.163
	(0.327)	(0.496)	(0.615)
Age	0.641***	0.418*	0.698**
	(0.124)	(0.196)	(0.215)
Age squared	-0.006***	-0.004	-0.006**
	(0.001)	(0.002)	(0.002)
Region	-1.212		
	(0.659)		
Groen (ref: CD&V)		-0.283	
		(2.586)	
N-VA (ref: CD&V)		8.355***	
		(2.068)	
Open VLD (ref: CD&V)		-1.293	
		(2.451)	
PVDA (ref: CD&V)		9.199***	
		(2.515)	
VB (ref: CD&V)		12.639***	
		(2.076)	

Vooruit/SP.A		1.846	
(ref: CD&V)		(2.216)	
Ecolo			-4.770
(ref: DéFI)			(3.174)
MR			-5.076
(ref: DéFI)			(3.004)
PS			-4.979
(ref: DéFI)			(3.025)
PTB			2.393
(ref: DéFI)			(3.028)
cdH/Les Engagés			-5.376
(ref: DéFI)			(3.511)
Constant	-3.147	-2.553	-7.995
	(3.080)	(5.212)	(6.181)
N	2031	760	608
R^2	0.029	0.157	0.073

Note: The estimates presented in this table are based on linear regressions, with standard errors indicated in parentheses. * $p < 0.05$, ** $p < 0.01$, *** $p < 0.001$. Political resentment is measured by means of an index derived from the summation of individual responses to seven resentment items. Scores range from -35, representing the lowest level of resentment, to +35, representing the highest level of resentment. Gender is coded as '1' for female and '0' for male. Education is categorized into five levels, with '1' indicating no schooling or only primary education, and '5' corresponding to university education. Region is coded as '0' for Flanders and '1' for Wallonia. The reported effects of the socio-demographic variables in columns three and four may be underestimated due to the inclusion of vote choice in the models.

Appendix 3. Association between gender and political resentment moderated by perceived representation or education

	DV: Political Resentment	
	(1)	(2)
Gender	-2.318**	0.725
	(0.877)	(2.215)
Perceived representation	0.077	
	(0.139)	
Gender* Perceived representation	-0.540**	
	(0.194)	
Education	-1.446***	-0.686
	(0.351)	(0.468)
Gender* Education		-0.487
		(0.652)
Age	0.657***	0.645***
	(0.129)	(0.124)
Age squared	-0.006***	-0.006***
	(0.001)	(0.001)
Region	-1.360*	-1.205
	(0.693)	(0.659)
Constant	-1.103	-4.037
	(3.257)	(3.303)
N	1819	2031
R^2	0.038	0.030

Note: The estimates presented in this table are based on linear regressions, with standard errors indicated in parentheses. * p < 0.05, ** p < 0.01, *** p < 0.001. Political resentment is measured by means of an index derived from the summation of individual responses to seven resentment items. Scores range from -35, representing the lowest level of resentment, to +35, representing the highest level of resentment. Gender is coded as '1' for female and '0' for male. Perceived representation ranges from -10 to +10, with +10 representing the belief of women being overrepresented and men being underrepresented, and -10 representing the belief of women being underrepresented and men being overrepresented. Education is categorized into five levels, with '1' indicating no schooling or only primary education, and '5' corresponding to university education. Region is coded as '0' for Flanders and '1' for Wallonia.

Appendix 4. Estimated emotion across gender, education, or age groups

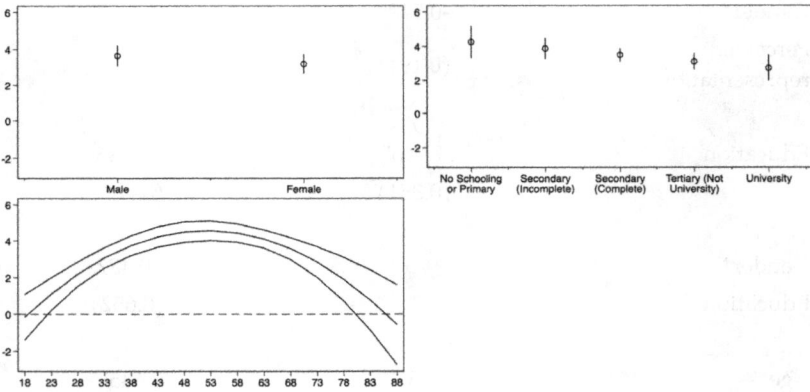

Note: Estimates based on Model 1 (excluding vote choice). 95% confidence intervals are reported. See the results in tabular format in Appendix 7.

Appendix 5. Estimated emotion across vote choices

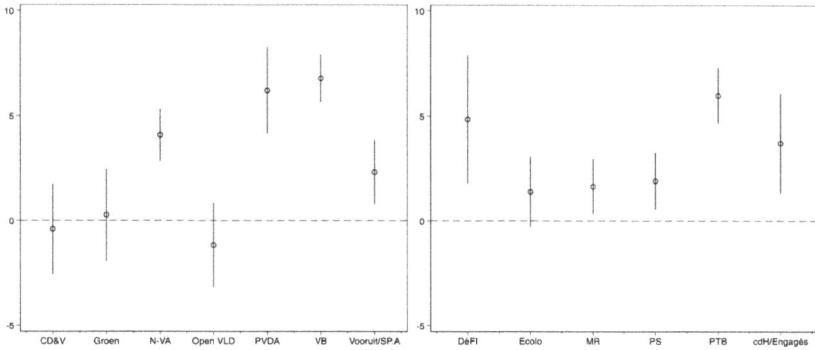

Note: Estimates based on Model 2 (including vote choice). 95% confidence intervals are reported. See the results in tabular format in Appendix 7.

Appendix 6. Estimated emotion across regions

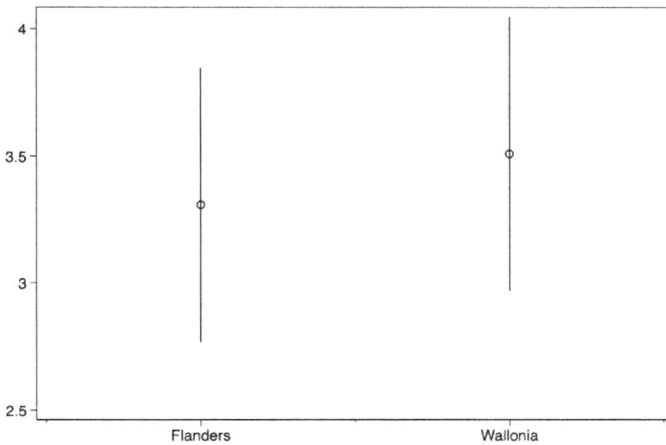

Note: Estimates based on Model 1 (including vote choice). 95% confidence intervals are reported. See the results in tabular format in Appendix 7.

Appendix 7. Association between political resentment, measured by individuals' emotions and the five factors (gender, education, age, vote choice, and region)

	DV: Political Resentment (Emotions)		
	Model 1	Model 2 (Flanders)	Model 2 (Wallonia)
Gender	-0.449	-1.285*	1.016
	(0.398)	(0.642)	(0.668)
Education	-0.377	-0.336	-0.067
	(0.194)	(0.301)	(0.347)
Age	0.419***	0.267*	0.270*
	(0.073)	(0.119)	(0.121)
Age squared	-0.004***	-0.003*	-0.002
	(0.001)	(0.001)	(0.001)
Region	0.201		
	(0.391)		
Groen (ref: CD&V)		0.671	
		(1.570)	
N-VA (ref: CD&V)		4.480***	
		(1.256)	
Open VLD (ref: CD&V)		-0.766	
		(1.488)	
PVDA (ref: CD&V)		6.618***	
		(1.527)	
VB (ref: CD&V)		7.202***	
		(1.260)	

Vooruit/SP.A		2.711*	
(ref: CD&V)		(1.346)	
Ecolo			-3.470
(ref: DéFI)			(1.790)
MR			-3.213
(ref: DéFI)			(1.695)
PS			-2.949
(ref: DéFI)			(1.706)
PTB			1.141
(ref: DéFI)			(1.708)
cdH/Les Engagés			-1.148
(ref: DéFI)			(1.981)
Constant	-5.045**	-4.102	-2.811
	(1.828)	(3.165)	(3.487)
N	2031	760	608
R^2	0.021	0.125	0.074

Note: The estimates presented in this table are based on linear regressions, with standard errors indicated in parentheses. * $p < 0.05$, ** $p < 0.01$, *** $p < 0.001$. Political resentment is measured by means of an index derived from the summation of individual responses to four emotion items. Scores range from -20, indicating the lowest levels of emotions, to +20, indicating the highest levels of emotions. Gender is coded as '1' for female and '0' for male. Education is categorized into five levels, with '1' indicating no schooling or only primary education, and '5' corresponding to university education. Region is coded as '0' for Flanders and '1' for Wallonia. The reported effects of the socio-demographic variables in columns three and four may be underestimated due to the inclusion of vote choice in the models.

4. Emotive participants? Emotions, apathy, and protest participation

Luca Bettarelli, Caroline Close, Laura Jacobs & Emilie van Haute

Abstract: Using the RepResent Voter Panel Survey conducted around the 2019 elections in Belgium, this chapter investigates the affective complexity of resentment and its impact on protest participation, understood as non-electoral protest participation and protest voting. We focus on the combination of two core emotions towards politics and their intensities: anger and hope. We highlight five groups that vary in their intensity of anger and hope: neutral, high-intensity hopeful, high-intensity angry, high-intensity emotive, and apathetic. We then connect these five groups to protest behaviours. Our results indicate that different emotional clusters guide distinct types of protest actions. Apathy leads to electoral exit and decreases the probability of non-electoral protest participation and protest voting. High intensities of anger turns citizens away from mainstream parties and increases their propensity to vote for protest parties. The combination of high intensities of anger and hope motivates the expression of resentment through non-electoral protest actions. Our findings reaffirm the significance of the affective dimension of political action. They support a conception of affective arrangements in which emotions combine to produce political outcomes. Finally, they nuance the idea that there would be absolute positive vs. negative emotions.

 https://doi.org/10.11647/OBP.0401.04

Introduction

This chapter investigates the affective complexity of resentment and its impact on protest participation, using the RepResent Voter Panel Survey conducted around the 2019 elections in Belgium. More specifically, we analyse whether specific combinations and intensities of anger and hope drive different choices in terms of protest participation, understood as non-electoral protest participation in between elections and protest voting on election day.

Our contributions are twofold. First, rather than looking at emotions as discrete concepts (Ekman, 2016), we unpack how emotions combine into clusters, with a specific focus on anger and hope. We identify five distinct classes of respondents depending on their combination of various intensities of anger and hope. In doing so, we emphasize that citizens are characterised by different 'clusters' of emotions (Cowen, et el., 2019) beyond a simplistic binary distinction between 'positive' and 'negative' affects (Watson et al., 1988). Second, we connect these five classes to protest participation. We demonstrate that each class develops distinct protest behaviours paralleling 'exit', 'voice', opposed to 'loyalty' conceived as the defense of the status quo (Hirschman, 1970). Citizens who display a combination of high intensities of anger and hope are more prone to take part in protest actions ('voice'); while low intensities of anger and hope decrease the propensity to participate in non-electoral protest and increase the likelihood that a person 'exits' the electoral process (i.e., abstains from voting). High intensities of anger increase the likelihood that a person voices their discontent and votes for a protest party. With these findings, we connect the affective/emotional dimension of resentment and the behavioural expression of resentment.

Overall, our findings give credit to the idea that politics is not only rational and evaluative, but also involves a significant affective dimension that should be taken into account (Theiss-Morse et al., 1993). We show that protest behaviours can result from the combination of both anger and hope, as well as from the absence of an affective relationship to politics.

Emotions, resentment and protest

The affective dimension of politics has received increasing attention in recent years. The role of emotions in social movement and collective action is nowadays well established (Flam & King, 2007; Jasper, 1998, 2011; Woods et al., 2012). The affective turn has also reached electoral studies, where various symptoms of the crisis of representative democracy, such as the success of protest parties, the growing voting abstention, etc., have increasingly been explained by citizens' affect towards politics (Close & van Haute, 2020; Vasilopoulos et al., 2019; Vasilopoulou & Wagner, 2017).

Our conceptualization of affect and emotions relies on two assumptions that are linked to our focus on resentment. First, we distance ourselves from most studies in political psychology that look at citizens' emotions towards specific events. Rather, we are interested in citizens' emotions towards politics in general, which is connected to the concept of political resentment vis-à-vis the political elites and institutions (Capelos & Demertzis, 2018). Second, we are interested in the effect of different combinations of emotions and their intensities, rather than in the effect of discrete emotions. We focus on anger and hope, as they are central in the existing studies and as they stand out in our empirical analysis as the most prominent emotional clusters (see below). This goes against what has been the dominant view in social psychology, which considers emotions as discrete concepts comprised of various categories (Ekman, 2016; Brader et al., 2019), some labeled as positive, others as negative (Watson et al., 1988). We side with a growing line of research that is interested in the complexity of emotions (Cowen et al., 2019). This is because we conceptualize resentment as characterised by affective complexity, involving a moral judgment of enduring and cumulative perceptions of unfairness across time (Celis et al., 2021; Capelos & Demertzis, 2018; Fleury, 2020). This conceptualization means that, in order to grasp resentment, various emotions or affects should be combined, leading to the notion of 'affective arrangment' (Knops & Petit, 2022). Affective arrangements offer a framework for understanding how emotions impact experiences of agency and the power to act, either via conventional (voting) or unconventional forms of political participation (protest) (Knops & Petit, 2022). We thereby acknowledge that these emotional clusters can drive distinct types of behavior, namely 'exit', 'voice', or 'loyalty'.

Emotions and non-electoral protest participation

Political psychology has so far mainly accepted the dominant discrete conceptualization of emotions. Studies have examined the interplay between single discrete emotions, especially anger or hope, and individual protest behaviours such as signing a petition, demonstrating, or boycotting (Landmann & Rohmann, 2020; Marcus, 2000; Roseman, 1991; van Stekelenburg & Klandermans, 2013). Anger has been pinpointed as a crucial driver of protest actions (Gaffney et al., 2018; Salmela & von Scheve, 2017; Vasilopoulos et al., 2019; Woods et al., 2012), as it closely relates to feelings of frustration, indignation (Jasper, 2014) or *ressentiment* (Capelos & Demertzis, 2018; Celis et al., 2021). By contrast, studies have emphasized that fear and anxiety deter individuals from engaging in protests, particularly in autocratic contexts where the risk of repression is high (Dornschneider, 2020; Nikolayenko, 2022). In democratic contexts, Capelos and Demertzis (2018) show that, during times of crisis in Greece, anxious people reported low levels of political activity while angry people reported a high degree of participation, especially in violent actions. Individual protest behaviour is also associated with positive emotions. Capelos and Demertzis (2018) again show that during times of crisis in Greece, hopeful people reported a high level of engagement in legal and illegal actions alike. Yet few of these studies look at the combination of emotions (for exceptions, see Dornschneider, 2020; Landmann & Rohmann, 2020; Nikolayenko, 2022). Conversely, social movement studies analysed the role of sets of emotions in the process of collective identity building and in creating, nurturing, and potentially breaking collective action (Jasper, 1998; Melucci, 1995, p. 45; Polletta & Jasper, 2001). Jasper refers to protest as being the result of 'pairs of positive and negative emotions' (Jasper, 2014, p. 211), such as outrage and hope (Castells, 2012), or the result of sequences of emotions, such as shame turning into pride through anger in groups sharing a stigmatized identity (Britt & Heise, 2000).

Given our conceptualisation of emotions, we side with social movement studies in arguing that it is the combination of anger and hope that prompts protest participation. In other words, being angry is not enough; hope—the belief that things may change—is also necessary. Consequently, we expect that:

> H1: A combination of hope and anger has a positive relationship with protest participation.

Emotions and protest voting

Emotions are also expected to affect electoral protest and voting behaviour (Close & Van Haute, 2020; Ladd & Lenz, 2008; Rico et al., 2017). Political psychology studies have examined the effect of single discrete emotions, especially anger or hope, on voting for protest parties (Altomonte et al., 2019; Marcus et al., 2019; Salmela & von Scheve, 2017; Vasilopoulos et al., 2019). Looking at voting behaviour during the Brexit referendum, Vasilopoulou and Wagner (2017) show that, while anger was positively associated with support for the Leave option, fear prompted more moderation. This is because fear enhanced individuals' reliance on evaluations of the situation and triggered risk-avoidance behaviours (Dornschneider, 2020; Valentino et al., 2008).

In this chapter, we explore the relationship between the combination of various intensities of anger and hope and three types of voting behaviour, based on the 'Exit, Loyalty and Voice' framework (ELV Model). This model, introduced by Hirschman (1970) posits that citizens within a society have two responses at their disposal if they perceive an institution as failing to deliver on its objectives: they can exit (withdraw) or voice (i.e., aim to improve the relationship with the institution by making their grievances explicit). Hence, citizens in an electoral context can choose to support the status quo or the mainstream parties that are in power ('loyalty'), express their dissatisfaction by supporting parties that promise to bring change ('voice'), or they could withdraw by not casting a vote ('exit'). We argue that in a situation of resentment, anger and hope will contribute to predict citizens' choice of voting behaviour (Close & Van Haute, 2020). We add to the prior literature by arguing that the absence of anger and hope, or apathy, drives protest behaviour too, but in a distinct way.

First, we expect hope to feed loyalty. Hope has been defined as 'the perceived capability to derive pathways to desired goals, and motivate oneself via agency thinking to use those pathways' (Snyder, 2002, p. 249). It is a prospective emotion that reflects a positive outlook for the future and is expressed whenever individuals believe that better outcomes are within reach (Chadwick, 2015; Just et al., 2007; Lazarus, 2001). Given that it is an emotion that entails a positive evaluation of a given situation, higher intensities of hope are expected to be positively linked to a desire to maintain the status quo ('loyalty'), while we expect them to be negatively related to voting for protest parties. Protest parties have been found to often make use of negative rhetoric, emphasizing what is going wrong in society and blaming the (political) elite or other groups (Nai, 2021; Widmann, 2021). They are less attractive to citizens who are not disillusioned with politics and mainstream political actors (Aron & Superti, 2001; Rooduijn, 2018). We therefore expect that:

> H2a: High intensities of hope have (a) a positive relationship with voting for mainstream parties, but (b) have a negative relationship with voting for protest parties.

Second, we expect anger to fuel 'voice'. Following cognitive appraisal theory (Roseman, 1991), anger is generally elicited whenever citizens feel their personal privileges or entitelments are jeopardized by an external actor who is considered to be to blame. In this case, citizens feel they should signal this grievance in order to change the situation. Therefore, high intensities of anger are theorized to result in 'voice', directed at repairing a situation. At elections, citizens can voice their anger via supporting political actors that claim to represent the ordinary people and act against the elite, and who promise to change the status quo (Aron & Superti, 2021; Cohen, 2019). This antagonism between the citizens and the elite is a core characteristic of protest parties that often also have a populist component (Mudde, 2004; Rooduijn, 2013). According to this view, populist actors advocate for corrections to the system, which resonates well with the anger component of resentment and voice. The reverse relationship is expected to arise for mainstream parties, as they are seen as defenders of the status quo. Hence, we expect that:

> H2b: High intensities of anger have (a) a positive relationship with voting for protest parties, but (b) have a negative relationship with voting for mainstream parties.

Third, we expect apathy, or low intensities of emotions towards politics (Ryan, 2017; Davis 2015), to be related to exit. Citizens who display low intensities of anger and hope towards politics have given up any effort to engage with it. What sets these citizens apart from other angry and dissatisfied voters is that they also have low levels of hope and they do not believe that another political actor (e.g., a protest party) will be able to deliver change and represent them, making them turn away from politics as a whole. Such apathy regarding politics is expected to drive 'exit' behaviours, such as abstention or casting a blank or invalid vote. Exit behaviours signal that citizens perceive themselves to be unable to exert any influence or gain control over a situation, so that their best option is to withdraw. A reverse relationship with voting is expected among supporters of mainstream and protest parties, as both are options that reflect a belief that a vote is still useful:

> H2c: Apathy, or low intensities of anger and hope, has (a) a positive relationship with exit behaviour, but (b) a negative relationship with voting for mainstream and protest parties.

Data and method

This chapter focuses on Belgium, using the RepResent Panel Voter Survey 2019 as our main data source (see Chapter 1). We are interested in the first two waves of the panel survey. Wave 1 was pre-electoral and conducted from 5 April to 21 May (3,298 respondents in Flanders; 3,025 in Wallonia; 1,056 in Brussels). Wave 2 was post-electoral and conducted from 28 May to 18 June (1,978 respondents in Flanders; 1,429 in Wallonia; 510 in Brussels). When we compute variables making use of the RepResent dataset, we weight for age, gender and education.

Dependent variables

To grasp respondents' reported participation in protest actions, we made use of the following question: 'There are different ways to improve things in Belgium or to be more politically active. How often did you do any of the following actions in the past 12 months?' (1 = never; 2 = seldom; 3 = sometimes; 4 = often). Nine types of political action were offered, of which we focus on four: a) signing petitions, b) participating in protest or demonstration, c) boycotting products and d) breaking rules for political reasons. Tables 4.1 and 4.2 report descriptive statistics for the above items and the correlation matrix, respectively.

Table 4.1 Descriptive statistics of types of protest participation.

Variable	Obs	Mean	Std. Dev.	Min	Max
a) petitions	3,904	1.94	.98	1	4
b) protest	3,904	1.44	.76	1	4
c) boycotting	3,904	1.92	1.07	1	4
d) breaking rules	3,904	1.39	.72	1	4

Table 4.2 Correlations matrix among types of protest participation.

Variables	(a)	(b)	(c)	(d)
(a) petitions	1.000			
(b) protest	.52	1.000		
(c) boycotting	.55	.46	1.000	
(d) breaking rules	.41	.50	.42	1.000

Operationally, we assembled an additive index that sums up the four items (Cronbach's alpha is equal to 0.8) to collapse the four items into a unique indicator of protest. The resulting variable ranges from 4 to 16: the higher the index, the more often respondents engage in protest actions.

Our second dependent variable is protest voting. We consider exit behaviour (i.e., blank and null votes, abstention), voice behaviour (voting for protest parties) and loyalty behaviour (voting for mainstream parties). The dependent variable is the party that respondents say they voted for in the 2019 federal elections in Belgium, as measured in Wave 2. Mainstream parties include the green (Ecolo, Groen), socialist (PS, Vooruit), liberal (MR, Open VLD), Christian-democrat (cdH, CD&V) and regionalist party families (DéFi, N-VA), while for protest parties we include the radical left party PTB-PVDA and the radical right VB. Some smaller parties (e.g., PP) were excluded from the analysis. We consider voters who did not vote, voted null, or invalidated their ballot as exhibiting exit behaviour. Table 4.3 below reports the decsriptive statistics of the three voting strategies.

Table 4.3 Descriptive statistics of voting strategies.

Variable	Obs	Mean	Std. Dev.	Min	Max
Mainstream vote	3,917	.66	.47	0	1
Exit vote	3,917	.08	.26	0	1
Protest vote	3,917	.22	.41	0	1

Independent variables

Our measure of respondents' emotions towards politics is captured by the following question: 'When you think of Belgian politics in general, to what extent do you feel each of the following emotions?'. Respondents were offered eight emotions (anger, bitterness, anxiety, fear, hope, relief, happiness, and satisfaction), and a scale ranging from 0 (not at all) to 10 (to a great extent). Previous research discussed in the literature review presented above pointed to the crucial role of two emotions: anger and hope. We made use of the Latent Class Analysis (LCA) to place respondents into emotional groups based on their levels of anger and hope. In this model, a categorical latent (unobserved) variable is used to identify the probability that each individual will belong to a specific category, by means of a Generalized Structural Equation Model. We obtain the best fit when our sample is split into five groups (see Figure 4.1). In light of these results, we define group (1) as neutral (Gasper et al., 2019), when respondents register average scores for both anger and hope; group (2) as apathetic, indicating individuals with low scores for both anger and hope; groups (3) and (4) as high-intensity hopeful and high-intensity angry, respectively, where the former includes people with high rates of hope and low rates of anger, while the latter is the other way around; group (5) as high-intensity emotive, which includes individuals showing high rates of both anger and hope. In the empirical analysis, neutral will represent the baseline category. Note that fear or anxiety have also appeared as factors constraining mobilization. In previous analyses, we considered fear in the latent class analysis, but we did not observe one class that was specifically related to fear.

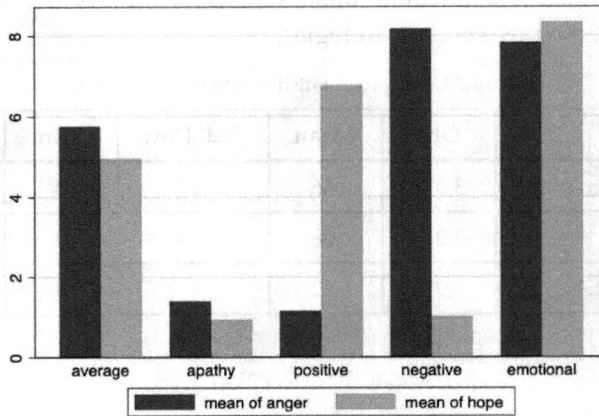

Fig. 4.1 Distribution of anger and hope across groups (Latent Class Analysis).

In terms of size (Table 4.4), two groups (neutral and high-intensity angry) account for over the 70% of the respondents. Nevertheless, no group contains fewer than 200 individuals. Note that the overall standard deviation of each emotion is consistently larger than that within each group, thus further supporting our modelling choice.

Table 4.4 Descriptive statistics of anger and hope across groups.

	N	Mean	SD	Min	Max
Overall					
Anger	3,909	5.99	2.65	0	10
Hope	3,909	3.85	2.55	0	10
Neutral					
Anger	1,985	5.55	1.65	3	9
Hope	1,985	4.95	1.13	3	7
Apathetic					
Anger	244	1.41	1.40	0	4
Hope	244	0.94	1.05	0	3
High-intensity hopeful					

Anger	251	1.15	1.10	0	4
Hope	251	6.77	1.42	4	10
High-intensity angry					
Anger	1,159	8,17	1.61	5	10
Hope	1,159	1.02	1,02	0	3
High-intensity emotive					
Anger	219	7.84	1.51	4	10
Hope	219	8.33	0.98	7	10

Table 4.5 reports the distribution of protest participation by group. It indicates that protest participation is significantly lower in the apathetic group, and larger in the high-intensity angry and (mostly) the high-intensity emotive groups, when compared to neutral. By contrast, no significant differences emerge among the neutral and high-intensity hopeful groups.

Table 4.5 Descriptive statistics of protest participation split by groups.

Categories	N	Mean	SD	Min	Max	p(x, y)
Neutral	1,981	6.63	2.67	4	16	
Apathetic	244	5.77	2.38	4	14	0.00
High-intensity hopeful	250	6.52	2.65	4	16	0.55
High-intensity angry	1,158	6.68	2.79	4	16	0.09
High-intensity emotive	218	8.28	3.42	4	16	0.00

Note: p (x,y) in last column is the t-test of equality of means across the baseline category neutral (x) and other categories (y), under the assumption of equal variances.

Controls

We included standard individual-level socio-demographic variables (gender, age, education) that contribute to determining political engagement (Brady et al., 1995; Marien et al., 2010). Gender is a dummy equal to one for female. Age ('What is your age?') is a continuous variable measured in years, while education is a five-category variable, ranging from 'none or elementary' to 'university degree'.

We also controlled for political attitudes that were identified as important for protest participation and protest voting (Hooghe & Marien, 2013). We included three PCA-based indices measuring respondents' degree of populism, trust in political institutions, and external efficacy, respectively. We measured populism with an index consisting of three items from the RepResent dataset, asking to respondents the extent to which they agree with the following (on a 1–5 scale): 'Politicians must follow the people's opinion', 'Political opposition is more present between citizens and the elite than between citizens themselves', 'I prefer being represented by an ordinary citizen rather than by a professional politician'. Trust in political institutions was assessed by considering the opinion of each respondent towards political parties, federal parliament, politicians, and the European Union, on a 0–10 scale. External efficacy relates to the extent to which political institutions are perceived as responsive to citizens' demands, thus capturing citizens' perception of whether they feel able to influence the political process (Balch, 1974; Niemi et al., 1991). As a result, we measured this by the extent to which respondents agree with the following statements, on a 1–5 scale: 'In general, our political system works honestly', 'Our political decision-making processes are sufficiently transparent', 'In general, our political system works effectively'. Then, we controlled for respondents' left–right self-placement, on a scale 0–10, with 0 meaning left, 5 the centre, and 10 the right. Finally, we controlled for the NUTS1 region of residence of each respondent, i.e., Brussels, Flanders and Wallonia. Tables 4.6 and 4.7 below report the descriptive statistics and correlation matrix of the set of controls.

Table 4.6 Descriptive statistics of control variables.

Variable	N	Mean	Std. Dev.	Min	Max
Age	3,909	49.68	15.59	18	91
Gender	3,909	1.46	.50	1	3
Education	3,909	3.54	.96	1	5
Populism index	3,899	0	1.35	-4.71	2.51
Efficacy index	3,904	0	1.54	-2.74	4.20
Trust index	3,908	0	1.84	-3.00	5.03
Left Right	3,904	5.36	2.33	0	10
Region	3,909	2.24	.66	1	3

Table 4.7 Matrix of correlations of control variables.

Variables	(1)	(2)	(3)	(4)	(5)	(6)	(7)	(8)
(1) Age	1.00							
(2) Gender	-0.20	1.00						
(3) Education	-0.10	0.03	1.00					
(4) Populism index	0.13	-0.01	-0.12	1.00				
(5) Efficacy index	-0.04	-0.06	0.09	-0.31	1.00			
(6) Trust index	-0.05	-0.05	0.11	-0.31	0.67	1.00		
(7) Left–Right	0.06	-0.11	-0.01	-0.01	0.05	0.10	1.00	
(8) Region	-0.10	0.06	-0.06	0.01	-0.09	-0.09	-0.08	1.00

Modelling strategy

Empirically, we estimated the following equation:

$$Y_i = \beta_0 + \beta_1 X_i + \beta_2 Emo\_Cluster_i + \gamma_r + \varepsilon_i \; (1)$$

where subscript *i* indicates survey respondent, *X* is the vector of controls, and are NUTS1 region dummies. *Emo_Cluster* includes our emotional groups, i.e., neutral, apathetic, high-intensity hopeful, high-intensity angry, and high-intensity emotive. Standard errors are clustered at NUTS1 region level.

We used two different econometric techniques to estimate eq. (1), according to the characteristics of the dependent variables. When we investigated the drivers of protest participation, as it is a continuous variable, we employed a standard OLS model. As voting strategies are dummies equal to one if voters cast a mainstream vote, a protest vote, and opts for an exit strategy, we used Logit models.

Analysis and findings

Table 4.8 presents the results of our regression analyses. For each model, we introduced our independent variable, the groups of respondents by type of emotion. Coefficients associated with these groups must be interpreted as differences with respect to the baseline group (neutral emotions). We also introduced our control variables.

Column 1 presents the results of our standard OLS regression for our first dependent variable, protest participation. Results provide very interesting insights. Non-electoral protest participation, as expected, is significantly lower in the apathetic group if compared to neutral category. The same holds but to a lower extent for the high-intensity hopeful group. This denotes that not having strong emotions (or at least the ones we measured) or being high-intensity hopeful when thinking about national politics turns citizens away from protest actions. If we focus on the high-intensity angry group, we observe a positive, albeit not significant, coefficient. Non-electoral protest participation is only significantly larger in the high-intensity emotive group compared to the neutral group, with the value of the coefficient being much larger than that of any other category. In fact, the difference between apathetic and high-intensity emotive respondents, respectively those registering the lowest and highest probability of protest participation, is over two points. These results provide a relevant message: non-electoral protest participation is mostly driven by the joint' action of positive (hope) and negative (anger) emotions towards politics, thus corroborating our hypothesis H1. In other words, people participate most in protest actions if they feel high-intensity angry, but also high-intensity hopeful, and they might believe that political conditions may improve thanks to collective action. Our set of controls confirms that protest activity tends to be higher among younger, male citizens with higher levels of education, and from the more urban area of Brussels, which corroborates existing knowledge (Brady et al., 1995; Marien et al., 2010). Interestingly, protest participation is also driven by high levels of trust in politics, which goes against existing knowledge (Hooghe & Marien, 2013), higher levels of populism, and left-wing attitudes. This finding may be related to the specific context of the 2014–2019 legislature in Belgium led by a right-wing government. Protest actions may have been initiated by the left-wing opposition, which could explain this result.

Table 4.8 Regression results.

	(1)	(2)	(3)	(4)
	Protest	Mainstream vote	Exit vote	Populist vote
EMOTIONS (Ref: Neutral)				
Apathetic	-.7114*	.0744*	.0689***	-.0759***
	(.1753)	(.0386)	(.0069)	(.0132)
High-intensity hopeful	-.3437*	.1014***	-.0412**	-.068
	(.1034)	(.0245)	(.0171)	(.0465)
High-intensity angry	.2604	-.0686***	-.0031	.0555***
	(.1075)	(.0199)	(.0234)	(.0084)
High-intensity emotive	1.3597**	-.0395	.0194	.0387

	(.2201)	(.03)	(.0181)	(.0361)
CONTROLS				
Age (in years)	-.0095*	.0043***	.0001	-.0038***
	(.0028)	(.0007)	(.0001)	(.0006)
Gender (female)	-.6919***	.0071	.0033	-.0297**
	(.0593)	(.0147)	(.0065)	(.0117)
Higher level of education	.2595**	.0672***	-.0228***	-.0438***
	(.0415)	(.0092)	(.0058)	(.0116)
Populism index	.1397*	-.0033	-.0028	.0155**
	(.0445)	(.004)	(.0033)	(.0059)
Efficacy index	-.0564	.0196***	.0026	-.021**
	(.0542)	(.0035)	(.003)	(.0087)
Trust index	.2787***	.0596***	-.0208***	-.0373***
	(.0265)	(.0018)	(.0033)	(.0052)
Right-wing orientation	-.1358**	-.0146***	.0006	.0082
	(.0139)	(.0031)	(.004)	(.0089)
REGIONS (Reference: Brussels)				
Flanders	-.9567***	-.1091***	-.0633***	.1739***
	(.0136)	(.0044)	(.0014)	(.0056)
Wallonia	-.1726***	-.0404***	-.0166***	.0269***
	(.0101)	(.0028)	(.0011)	(.0028)
Observations	3,830	3,837	3,837	3,837
R^2	.114	.125	.124	.126

Note. Standard errors in parentheses, clustered by region. Model (1) has been estimated through OLS, and entries are coefficients. Models (2)–(4) have been estimated through Logit and entries are Average Marginal Effects.
*** $p<.01$, ** $p<.05$, * $p<.1$

In columns 2 to 4, we considered the results for our second dependent variable, protest voting. First, we expected that high intensities of hope would be positively related to voting for mainstream parties, but negatively related to voting for protest parties. Results indicate that higher intensities of hope are indeed positively associated with voting for mainstream parties, but this does not have a significant relationship with voting for protest parties, which means that H2a is only partly supported. Second, we expected high intensities of anger to have a positive relationship with voting for protest parties, but a negative relationship with voting for mainstream parties. The results support these associations, with higher intensities of anger being significantly related to a protest vote and negatively related to a mainstream vote. Finally, we expected apathy to mainly drive exit behaviour rather than voting for mainstream and protest parties. Again, results provide mixed support for the hypothesis: while apathy is positively associated with exit behaviour and negatively associated with protest voting, we also find apathy to have a significant positive relationship with voting for mainstream parties. Hence, H2c is only partly supported. All in all, these results show that the various emotional clusters (high hope, high anger, and the lack of hope and anger) are significant drivers of distinct types of behaviours (exit, loyalty, and voice). Our set of controls points to different protest dynamics among different demographics. Protest voting shares some characteristics with protest participation, as it is higher among young, male respondents with higher levels of populist attitudes. But protest voting differs from protest participation in that it is higher among citizens with lower levels of education, and lower trust and efficacy, which is more in line with existing studies (Hooghe & Marien, 2013). Exit behaviour is mainly driven by low trust and education, but we find that emotional clusters do offer an independent contribution on top of these sociodemographic factors.

Conclusion

This chapter has sought to investgate the affective complexity of resentment and its impact on protest participation. Using the RepResent Voter Panel Survey conducted around the 2019 elections in Belgium, we analysed whether specific combinations and intensities of anger and hope drive different choices in terms of protest behaviours, understood as non-electoral protest participation and protest voting. The results offer an excellent starting point to reflect on the implications of this affective complexity for protest behaviour and on its challenges and opportunities for representative democracy at large.

Our focus on resentment led us to conceive of emotions not as single discrete concepts, but rather as concepts that can be combined, leading to affective arrangements that we call 'emotional clusters'. More specifically, we have centred our analysis around the combination of various intensities of two core emotions: anger and hope. Our latent class analysis has revealed that citizens can be clustered in five distinct emotional clusters, based on their intensity on the anger and hope scales: apathetic, high-intensity angry, high-intensity hopeful, high-intensity emotive, neutral. This is the first important contribution made by this chapter: we show how emotions can combine simultaneously in diverse ways and 'produce' types of citizens who respond emotionally to politics in very different ways (exit, voice or loyalty). The socio-political consequences of these combinations deserve further attention.

Further, we demonstrated that these emotional clusters drive distinct protest behaviours, thereby connecting the affective/emotional dimension of resentment and the behavioural expression of resentment. We show that apathy drives citizens away from non-electoral protest participation, and increases their likelihood of exiting the electoral process. High intensities of hope deter people from non-electoral protest participation and from voting abstention, and increase the likelihood of voting for a mainstream party. High intensities of anger alone drive protest voting, but not non-electoral protest participation. Conversely, the combination of high intensities of anger and hope drive non-electoral protest participation, but not protest voting.

Overall, these findings attest to the idea that politics is not only rational and evaluative, but also involves a significant affective dimension that should be taken into account (Theiss-Morse et al., 1993). We show that different forms of protest result from different emotional clusters. How emotions combine is an important factor that can enable us to understand the choice between 'voice' or 'exit' on election day, but also the choice to engage in non-electoral protest behaviours. These are important results that help us to better grasp citizens' relations to politics, how they feel about it, and how they act as a result. They provide important insights for the functioning of representative democracy as a whole. If apathy drives citizens away from protest but also from the electoral process, it means that representative democracy may need to nurture emotions and affect to engage citizens. Yet hope benefits the status quo. Therefore, a certain level of anger may be beneficial, if not necessary, for the functioning of democracy: combined with hope, it can foster critical citizens who can articulate their concerns and initiate change. This finding supports Pippa Norris' claim that credulous trust alone may be detrimental to democracy, and that trust works best when combined with skepticism and verification (Norris, 2022). Similarly, our findings show that there is value in having hopeful citizens who able to feel angry and indignant when dissatisfied. While the broader ramifications for society as a whole need to be addressed in greater depth (and are being assessed elsewhere in this book), these findings invite us to reflect on the normative implications, prompting a reconsideration of what is often viewed as 'positive' (hope) or 'negative' (anger) emotions. This chapter offers insights into the complex dynamics of how distinct emotions interact with distinct behaviours and can act as drivers of 'agency' in a representative democracy.

References

Altomonte, C., Gennaro, G., & Passarelli, F. (2019). *Collective Emotions and Protest Vote* (SSRN Scholarly Paper ID 3315401). Social Science Research Network, https://doi.org/10.2139/ssrn.3315401

Aron, H., & Superti, C. (2022). 'Protest at the ballot box : From blank vote to populism.' *Party Politics*, 28(4), 638–650, https://doi.org/10.1177/1354068821999741

Balch, G. I. (1974). 'Multiple Indicators in Survey Research: The Concept "Sense of Political Efficacy".' *Political Methodology*, 1(2), 1–43, https://doi.org/ 10.2307/25791375

Blais, A., & Daoust, J-F. (2020). *The Motivation to Vote: Explaining Electoral Participation*. Vancouver: UBC Press.

Brader, T., Merolla, J., Cikanek, E., & Chin, H. (2019). 'Report on 2018 ANES Pilot: Discrete Emotions Batteries.' *ANES Board of Overseers*, 5.

Britt, L., & Heise, D. (2000). 'From shame to pride in identity politics.' In S. Stryker, T. J. Owens, & R. W. White (eds.). *Self, Identity, and Social Movements* (pp. 252–270). Minneapolis: University of Minnesota Press.

Capelos, T., & Demertzis, N. (2018). 'Political Action and Resentful Affectivity in Critical Times.' *Humanity & Society*, 42(4), 410–433, https://doi.org/10.1177/0160597618802517

Castells, M. (2012). *Networks of Outrage and Hope: Social Movements in the Internet Age*. Cambridge: Polity Press.

Celis, K., Knops, L., Van Ingelgom, V., & Verhaegen, S. (2021). 'Resentment and Coping with the Democratic Dilemma'. *Politics and Governance*, 9(3), 237–247, https://doi.org/10.17645/pag.v9i3.4026

Chadwick, A. E. (2015). 'Toward a theory of persuasive hope: Effects of cognitive appraisals, hope appeals, and hope in the context of climate change.' *Health Communication*, 30(6), 598–611, https://doi.org/10.1080/10410 236.2014.916777

Close, C., & van Haute, E. (2020). 'Emotions and vote choice: An analysis of the 2019 Belgian elections.' *Politics of the Low Countries*, 2(3), 353–379, https://doi.org/10.5553/plc/258999292020002003006

Cohen, D. (2019). 'Between strategy and protest: How policy demand, political dissatisfaction and strategic incentives matter for far-right voting.' *Political Science Research and Methods*, 662–676, https://doi.org/10.1017/psrm.2019.21

Cowen, A., Sauter, D., Tracy, J. L., & Keltner, D. (2019). 'Mapping the Passions: Towards a High-Dimensional Taxonomy of Emotional Experience an Expression.' *The Journal of Abnormal and Social Psychology*, 20(1), 60–90.

Davis, N. T. (2015). 'The role of indifference in split-ticket voting.' *Political Behavior*, 37(1), 67–86, https://doi.org/10.1007/s11109-013-9266-9

Dornschneider, S. (2020). *Hot Contention, Cool Abstention: Positive Emotions and Protest Behavior During the Arab Spring*. Oxford: Oxford University Press.

Ekman, P. (2016). 'What Scientists Who Study Emotion Agree About.' *Perspectives on Psychological Science*, 11(1), 31–34.

Flam, H., & King, D. (2007). *Emotions and Social Movements*. London: Routledge.

Fleury, C. (2020). *Ci-gît l'amer: Guérir du ressentiment* [Here lies the bitter: To heal resentment]. Paris: Editions Gallimard.

Gaffney, A. M., Hackett, J. D., Rast III, D. E., Hohman, Z. P., & Jaurique, A. (2018). 'The State of American Protest: Shared Anger and Populism.' *Analyses of Social Issues and Public Policy*, 18(1), 11–33, https://doi.org/10.1111/asap.12145

Gasper, K., Spencer, L. A., & Hu, D. (2019). 'Does Neutral Affect Exist? How Challenging Three Beliefs About Neutral Affect Can Advance Affective Research.' *Frontiers in Psychology*, 10(2476), 1–11.

Geurkink, B., Zaslove, A., Sluiter, R., & Jacobs, K. (2020). 'Populist attitudes, political trust, and external political efficacy: Old wine in new bottles.' *Political Studies*, 68(1), 247–267, https://doi.org/10.1177/0032321719842768

Hooghe, M., & Marien, S. (2013). 'A Comparative Analysis of the Relation Between Political Trust and Forms of Political Participationin Europe.' *European Societies*, 15(1), 131–152.

Hirschman, A. O. (1970). *Exit, Voice, and Loyalty.* Cambridge, MA: Harvard University Press.

Jasper, J. M. (1998). 'The Emotions of Protest: Affective and Reactive Emotions In and Around Social Movements.' *Sociological Forum*, 13(3), 397–424, https://doi.org/10.1023/A:1022175308081

Jasper, J. M. (2011). 'Emotions and Social Movements: Twenty Years of Theory and Research.' *Annual Review of Sociology*, 37(1), 285–303, https://doi.org/10.1146/annurev-soc-081309-150015

Jasper, J. M. (2014). 'Constructing Indignation: Anger Dynamics in Protest Movements.' *Emotion Review*, 6(3), 208–213, https://doi.org/10.1177/1754073914522863

Just, M. R., Crigler, A. N., & Belt, T. L. (2007). 'Don't give up hope: Emotions, candidate appraisals, and votes.' In W. R. Neuman, G. E. Marcus, A. N. Crigler, & M. MacKuen (eds.). *The Affect Effect: Dynamics of Emotion in Political Thinking and Behavior*. Chicago: The University of Chicago Press.

Knops, L., & Petit, G. (2022). 'Indignation as affective transformation: An effect-theoretical approach to the Belgian Yellow vest movement.' *Mobilization: An International Quarterly*, 27(2), 169–192, https://doi.org/10.17813/1086-671X-27-2-169

Ladd, J. M. D., & Lenz, G. S. (2008). 'Reassessing the role of anxiety in vote choice.' *Political Psychology*, 29(2), 275–296, https://doi.org/10.1111/j.1467-9221.2008.00626.x

Landmann, H., & Rohmann, A. (2020). 'Being moved by protest: Collective efficacy beliefs and injustice appraisals enhance collective action intentions for forest protection via positive and negative emotions.' *Journal of Environmental Psychology*, 71, https://doi.org/10.1016/j.jenvp.2020.101491

Marcus, G. E. (2000). 'Emotions in politics.' *Annual Review of Political Science*, 3, 221–250, https://doi.org/10.1146/annurev.polisci.3.1.221

Marcus, G. E., Valentino, N. A., Vasilopoulos, P., & Foucault, M. (2019). 'Applying the Theory of Affective Intelligence to Support for Authoritarian Policies and Parties.' *Political Psychology*, 40(S1), 109–139, https://doi.org/10.1111/pops.12571

Melucci, A. (1995). 'The Process of Collective Identity.' In B. Klandermans & H. Johnston (eds.). *Social Movements and Culture* (pp. 41–63). Minneapolis: University of Minnesota Press.

Mudde, C. (2004). 'The populist Zeitgeist.' *Government and Opposition*, 39(4), 541–563.

Nai, A. (2021). 'Fear and loathing in populist campaigns? Comparing the communication style of populists and non-populists in elections worldwide.' *Journal of Political Marketing*, 20(2), 219–250, https://doi.org/10.1080/15377857.2018.1491439

Niemi, R. G., Craig, S. C., & Mattei, F. (1991). 'Measuring Internal Political Efficacy in the 1988 National Election Study.' *American Political Science Review*, 85(4), 1407–1413.

Nikolayenko, O. (2022). '"I am tired of being afraid": Emotions and protest participation in Belarus.' *International Sociology*, 37(1), 78–96, https://doi.org/10.1177/02685809211023051

Norris, P. (2022). *In Praise of Skepticism: Trust but Verify*. Oxford: Oxford University Press.

Polletta, F., & Jasper, J. M. (2001). 'Collective Identity and Social Movements.' *Annual Review of Sociology*, 27, 283–305.

Rico, G., Guinjoan, M., & Anduiza, E. (2017). 'The emotional underpunnings of populism: How anger and fear affect populist attitudes.' *Swiss Political Science Review*, 23(4), 444–461, https://doi.org/10.1111/spsr.12261

Rooduijn, M. (2018). 'What unites the voter bases of populist parties? Comparing the electorates of 15 populist parties.' *European Political Science Review*, 10(3), 351–368, https://doi.org/10.1017/S1755773917000145

Roseman, I. J. (1991). 'Appraisal determinants of discrete emotions.' *Cognition & Emotions*, 5(3), 161–200.

Ryan, T. J. (2017). 'How do indifferent voters decide? The political importance of implicit attitudes.' *American Journal of Political Science*, 61(4), 892–907, https://doi.org/10.1111/ajps.12307

Salmela, M., & von Scheve, C. (2017). 'Emotional roots of right-wing political populism.' *Social Science Information*, 56(4), 567–595, https://doi.org/10.1177/0539018417734419

Snyder, C. R. (2002). 'Hope theory: Rainbows in the mind.' *Psychological Inquiry*, 13(4), 249–275, https://doi.org/10.1207/S15327965PLI1304_01

Valentino, N. A., Hutchings, V. L., Banks, A. J., & Davis, A. K. (2008). 'Is a Worried Citizen a Good Citizen? Emotions, Political Information Seeking, and Learning via the Internet.' *Political Psychology*, 29(2), 247–273.

Van Stekelenburg, J., & Klandermans, B. (2013). 'The social psychology of protest.' *Current Sociology*, 61(5–6), 886–905, https://doi.org/10.1177/0011392113479314

Vasilopoulos, P., Marcus, G. E., Valentino, N. A., & Foucault, M. (2019). 'Fear, Anger, and Voting for the Far Right: Evidence From the November 13, 2015 Paris Terror Attacks.' *Political Psychology*, 40(4), 679–704, https://doi.org/10.1111/pops.12513

Vasilopoulou, S., & Wagner, M. (2017). 'Fear, anger and enthusiasm about the European Union: Effects of emotional reactions on public preferences towards European integration.' *European Union Politics*, 18(3), 382–405, https://doi.org/10.1177/1465116517698048

Widmann, T. (2021). 'How emotional are populists really? Factors explaining emotional appeals in the communication of political parties.' *Political Psychology*, 42(1), 163–181, https://doi.org/10.2139/ssrn.3590265

Woods, M., Anderson, J., Guilbert, S., & Watkin, S. (2012). '"The country(side) is angry": Emotion and explanation in protest mobilization.' *Social & Cultural Geography*, 13(6), 567–585, https://doi.org/10.1080/14649365.2012.704643

5. Illustrations of political resentment among disadvantaged people

Ramon van der Does, Kenza Amara-Hammou & David Talukder

Abstract: People who face socio-economic disadvantages tend to be underrepresented in politics. Existing research suggests that this should make them particularly resentful towards politics. Yet, empirical studies on how resentment might express itself among them remains rare. This chapter seeks to address this gap in the literature through the analysis of survey data as well as focus groups conducted among socio-economically disadvantaged people in Brussels, Belgium. The survey results show that socio-economically disadvantaged people are generally more resentful, but also underline the difficulty to reach this population and the necessity to combine it with qualitative research methods. Our analyses of the focus groups show, first, that the objects of participants' resentment were mostly local actors and that expressions of resentment seemed tied to the experience of concrete problems. Second, even though resentment manifested itself in frustration, disappointment, and, at times, indifference towards politics, it also went hand in hand with at least some hope that politics could offer a solution to societal challenges. Most of all, participants wanted to be heard and they generally wanted local politicians and bureaucrats to just come to talk to them. We discuss the implications these findings have for the empirical study of political resentment among people experiencing socio-economic disadvantages.

https://doi.org/10.11647/OBP.0401.05

Introduction

People facing socio-economic disadvantages are often underrepresented in politics. They are underrepresented descriptively, in terms of not having representatives in office who share their physical features (Pitkin, 1967, p. 11) or lived experiences (Allen, 2022, p. 1114; Mansbridge, 1999, pp. 629, 644; Young, 1997, p. 366), and substantively, in terms of not having their interests represented and translated into policy outcomes and political decisions (Dovi, 2002; Phillips, 2020; Williams, 2000). In this chapter, socio-economic disadvantage refers to people who face particular difficulties in the labour market, such as unfavourable working conditions, not having a stable income, or receiving a low wage; in the housing market; and/or in education, due to limited access to formal schooling.

Existing research shows that these people's underrepresentation in politics tends to weaken their support for democracy and their trust in political institutions and politicians; undercuts the degree of legitimacy they award to decision-making; makes them support political reform; and, for instance, discourages them from participating in politics (Ceka & Magalhães, 2016, 2020; Dacombe, 2021; Mayne & Hakhverdian, 2017; McCormick, Hague, & Harrop, 2019; Phillips, 1998; Talukder & Pilet, 2021; van der Does & Kantorowicz, 2022; Williams, 2000). This structural lack of voice, both with regard to not being present and not being heard (Young, 2000), seems to fuel negative appraisals of politics and disengagement, suggesting resentment towards politics should be particularly pronounced among people experiencing socio-economic disadvantages.

Yet, so far, few studies have focused specifically on political resentment among people experiencing socio-economic disadvantages. They often fall outside of the scope of empirical studies on political resentment, mainly because they are considered to belong to a vulnerable and hard-to-reach population (cf. Ellard-Gray, Jeffrey, Choubak, & Crann, 2015). It follows that empirical evidence regarding how they feel about politics is therefore sparse (Behrens, Freedman, & McGuckin, 2009; Miscoiu & Gherghina, 2021; Wojciechowska, 2019), and a specific focus on their potential resentment towards politics remains wanting too. Our study aims to fill this gap in the literature.

We use a combination of survey data on the Belgian population and focus group data on people living in socio-economically disadvantaged neighbourhoods in the municipality of Molenbeek, Brussels. This chapter thereby further expands and deepens the literature on political resentment by uncovering how the expression of resentment captured through survey questions manifests itself in a variety of ways among participants in these neighbourhoods, as communicated in their own discourses produced during a series of focus groups. We conducted the latter in a typical European city: Brussels. Brussels is typical in that, as in many other European cities, socio-economic disadvantage is highly concentrated geographically in specific municipalities and neighbourhoods (Nieuwenhuis, Tammaru, Van Ham, Hedman, & Manley, 2019; Van Hamme, Grippa, & Van Criekingen, 2016). Zooming in on the experiences of people living in one such municipality (Molenbeek) thereby allows us to provide insights that could help us to begin understanding resentment among similar groups of people in other cities too.

Supplementing survey research with focus group data on people in Brussels who experience socio-economic disadvantages allows us to add more depth and nuance to the assumption that people experiencing such disadvantages are unequivocally politically resentful, in three ways. First, zooming in on this population enables us to take a closer look at how resentment manifests itself, adding substance to the claim made in the introduction to and prior chapters of this book that resentment is a multi-layered concept and a complex emotion. Second, it allows us to show how day-to-day experiences shape political emotions like resentment, as other scholars have suggested (Cramer & Toff, 2017; Knops, 2021; Rosanvallon, 2021). Third, it enables us to demonstrate how socio-economic forms of discrimination can intersect with other types of discrimination, such as xenophobia, racism, or religious discrimination.

Our results thereby offer a more nuanced view of how these people experience politics and on their possible resentment towards it. Our analyses show: (a) that resentment was fuelled by people's everyday experiences, (b) that the objects of participants' resentment were mostly local actors, and (c) that feelings of resentment were often accompanied by expressions of hope that politics could still change and offer a solution to the societal problems that people identified, pointing towards what Celis et al. (2021) have called the 'democratic dilemma.'

In the following, we first describe the political attitudes of socio-economically disadvantaged people associated with resentment, based on survey data from the first cross-sectional survey carried out by the RepResent team in May 2019. Then, we provide an account of how resentment possibly manifests itself among people experiencing socio-economic difficulties in neighbourhoods in Molenbeek. We examine how 'resentment' manifested itself in discussions about societal problems and how those might be resolved. Specifically, we study what the objects of resentment are and how its three dimensions (that is, emotional complexity, morality, and temporality) come to the fore in relation to those identified targets of resentment. We end with a discussion about the 'democratic dilemma' and the implications of these findings for the wider study of political resentment.

Survey data on resentment

This section aims first to situate the analyses by means of survey data on indicators commonly associated with resentment. In the following, we compare respondents who, according to their self-reports, were in a socio-economically disadvantaged situation compared to the rest of the sample on several proxies for political resentment. We measure political resentment based on five items that we expect to be associated with resentment as conceptualized in Chapter 2 of this book. The items are reported in Table 5.1 and have been re-coded to a 0-1 scale, where higher scores represent more negative (and, by approximation, more resentful) attitudes toward politics.

Table 5.1 Items used to measure political resentment.

Item	Min	Max	Name
To what extent are you satisfied with the policies implemented by the following political decision-making entities in the past few years?* [The federal government]	0 (very unsatisfied)	10 (very satisfied)	Policy dissatisfaction

When you think of Belgian politics in general, to what extent do you feel each of the following emotions? [anger]	0 (not at all)	10 (to a great extent)	Anger
Voting is pointless because parties do what they want anyway.	1 (totally disagree)	5 (totally agree)	Election is useless
In general, politics reflect rather well the people's preferences*	1 (totally disagree)	5 (totally agree)	People's preferences not reflected
In general, our political system functions in an efficient way*	1 (totally disagree)	5 (totally agree)	System is inefficient

Notes: Reports the original scales. All the items were recoded to a 0-1 scale.
* Items for which we reversed the scale.

In order to obtain an overview of disadvantaged people's attitudes in relation to political resentment, Figure 5.1 compares disadvantaged people (respondents who are either unemployed/unqualified workers and have not completed secondary education) to the other respondents ($N = 7433$). Despite a sample of 7609 respondents, only a few of them ($N = 184$) are socio-economically disadvantaged. The small sample size reflects the limits of general-population-based surveys to reach this group of people and underlines the value of combining the results with qualitative data to get an accurate picture of their potential political resentment. The results show that the distributions for disadvantaged people on the five items are much more tilted towards the higher end of the scale compared to other people. These results are in line with the common observation that underrepresentation in politics tends to weaken public support for democracy.

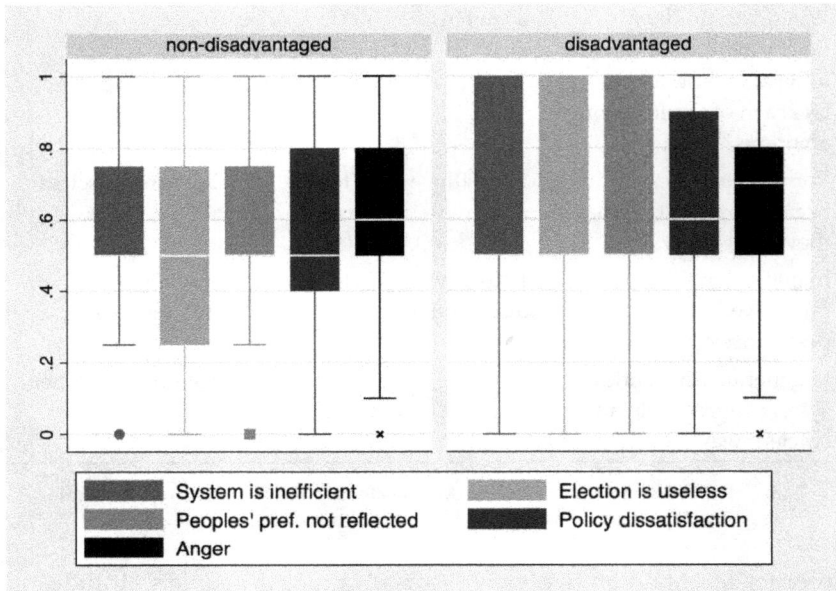

Fig. 5.1 Boxplots of five items measuring resentment by socio-economic (dis) advantage.

To move a step further, we conducted several t-tests and Figure 5.2 provides a 95% confidence interval plot which compares disadvantaged and non-disadvantaged people. The results of the t-tests tend to show that disadvantaged people do hold significantly more negative attitudes than people who do not experience socio-economic disadvantages on four[1] of the five items. There are no significant differences between disadvantaged and non-disadvantaged people on the perception that politics reflect people's preferences rather badly ($t = -0.88$, $p = .81$). Nevertheless, as with the other items, the score is still higher for disadvantaged people (*Mean* = .633, *SD* = .020) than for others (*Mean* = .617, *SD* = .003).

However, the fact that—according to the survey data—there are differences between people experiencing socio-economic disadvantages and those who do not in terms of attitudes associated with resentment does not tell us much about *how* political resentment expresses itself.

---

1   The respective t-values are the following: -2.06 (Anger); -2.47 (Elections is useless); -2.48 (System is inefficient); -4.99 (Policy dissatisfaction).

More specifically, we do not know how people *experience* political resentment and how they talk about it. In order to move one step further and to have an in-depth view of what political resentment looks like, we recommend focusing on the analysis of several focus groups conducted among disadvantaged people in the next section of this chapter.

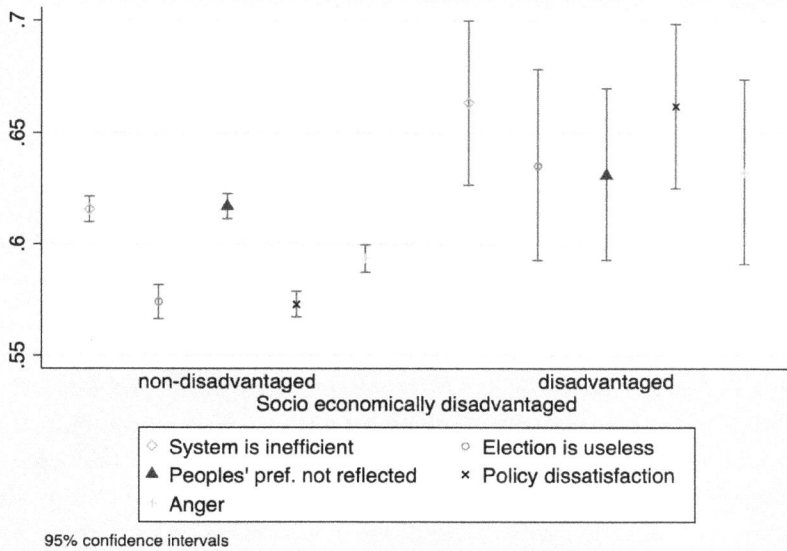

Fig. 5.2 Average scores on the five resentment items with 95% confidence intervals.

A study of resentment through focus groups

To provide qualitative insight into how these people express resentment towards politics, we draw on four focus groups that the RepResent team conducted in the fall of 2019. The team recruited the participants via door-to-door canvassing in a socio-economically challenged municipality in Brussels: Molenbeek. Molenbeek is part of the former industrialized area in Brussels. While the area used to house workers, today mainly people with a migration background live in the area. Molenbeek is also one of the poorer, more densely populated municipalities in Brussels and is characterized by low household income and lower levels of employment, manifesting itself especially in a high youth unemployment rate (Van Hamme et al., 2016).[2]

We used this spatial proxy to recruit people who would be likely to experience socio-economic disadvantages. Table 2 provides the background characteristics of the 22 participants based on a short survey they were asked to fill out. Most participants had completed, at most, secondary education (15 out of 22) and did not have paid work (16 out of 22).[3]

The focus group format allowed participants to use their own words to express themselves, focus on the problems they themselves considered important, and challenge each other's formulations and arguments (cf. Van Ingelgom, 2020). The analyses reported in this chapter draw on the first set of questions posed in each of the four focus groups. These questions addressed what participants considered to be the most important societal problems (i.e., 'In your opinion, what are the most important societal challenges that Belgium is facing today?'), what they thought were potential solutions to those problems (i.e., 'How should these societal challenges be resolved?'), and whom they thought was responsible for these challenges and should take care of solving them (see Appendix 1, Chapter 2 of this volume for a simplified version of the topic guide). These questions offered a way to tap into participants' thinking about societal problems and the role various actors and institutions do and should play in resolving those problems. The focus groups allowed us to inquire into the varying ways in which people in socio-economically difficult situations connect the societal problems they deem important to their evaluations of relevant actors and institutions.

We conducted a thematic analysis of the parts of the focus group transcripts that deal with the aforementioned questions, providing a summary per group with accompanying quotes to substantiate our

---

2   As with other municipalities in Brussels like Anderlecht, Saint-Josse-ten-
     Noode and Schaerbeek, it is not uncommon for households to have a total
     disposable income falling below the poverty line (i.e., €1,284 per month for a
     single person). For details, see STATBEL at https://statbel.fgov.be/en/news/
     poverty-risks-belgium-2020
3   For education: not counting missing data or ongoing education.

interpretations (cf. Kvale & Brinkmann, 2009).[4] We started by cataloguing what participants viewed as (a) the most important problems, (b) potential solutions, and (c) the actors and institutions involved in creating and solving the identified problems. After this descriptive exercise, we then moved to a more detailed reading of the materials, in which we focused on participants' understandings and evaluations of the actors and institutions they identified. To underpin the accuracy of our interpretations of the materials, we relied on discussion to share our understandings of the transcripts as well as to settle any remaining disagreements (Mason, 2013).

In line with the conceptual discussion in Chapter 1, we focused in the second stage of coding on the three dimensions of resentment: morality, emotional complexity, and temporality. To capture its moral dimension, we looked for statements regarding unfairness, injustice, and moral wrongs. We specifically looked into references that participants made to experiences, interactions or events that caused a sense of injustice or of being treated unfairly or badly (Améry, 1980; Fassin, 2013; Russell & McKenna, 2012). These included experiences such as being discriminated against on the job market, not being listened to or consulted and not being responded to. We also examined comparisons participants made between how different social groups are treated and how different people within social groups are treated (e.g., residents of a certain municipality, minorities, and people who experience socio-economic disadvantages).

Subsequently, we looked into the complexity of feelings (Strawson, 2008) that participants expressed when talking about these experiences, interactions or events. Viewing resentment as a complex constellation of feelings with anger at its core, we took note of expressions of anger, disappointment, and fear but also, conversely, of positive feelings such as hope and satisfaction. Finally, we captured the temporal dimension by looking into references that participants made to the past, present and future and comparisons that participants made between different points in time. We paid specific attention to experiences, interactions

---

4   We conducted the analyses based on the original transcripts in French. For transcripts partly in Arabic, we based our coding on a translation to French provided by one of the authors.

or events that seemed to have a long-lasting effect on participants and impact their present-day feelings and attitudes (Améry, 1980).

Taken together, we thereby seek to complement the description drawn from the survey data by providing qualitative insight into *how* resentment manifests itself when people discuss politics. Further, by providing a contextualized analysis of people's expressions of resentment, we can also point towards potential reasons *why* people feel resentful.

Table 5.2 Overview of focus group participants.

Group	Pseudonym	Sex	Age	Education	Employment
Molenbeek1	Moussa	Male	45–54	None or primary	Unemployed
	Sonia	Female	45–54	None or primary	Incapable of work
	David	Male	45–54	None or primary	Permanent contract
	Emma	Female	65–74	Post-sec. vocational	Retired
Molenbeek2*	Jamal	Male	35–44	None or primary	Unemployed
	Rayane	Female	55–64	None or primary	Retired
	Malik	Male	35–44	Secondary	Student
	Chayma	Female	35–44	Secondary	Housekeeper
	Younes	Male	45–54	None or primary	Incapable of work
	Malory	Female	35–44	None or primary	Housekeeper
Molenbeek3	Walid	Male	18–24	Ongoing	Student
	Tais	Male	25–34	Post-sec. vocational	Permanent contract
	Mehmet	Male	25–34	University (short)	Unemployed

	Abbou	Male	25–34	Secondary	Permanent contract
	Adil	Male	25–34	NA	Permanent contract
Molenbeek4**	Abdelkrim	Male	45–54	None or primary	Unemployed
	Ayman	Male	45–54	Post-sec. vocational	Permanent contract
	Asma	Female	35–44	Secondary	Housekeeper
	Anabelle	Female	25–34	Post-sec. vocational	Permanent contract
	Hamid	Male	45–54	Post-sec. vocational	Incapable of work
	Abdellah	Male	55–64	None or primary	Unemployed
	Soukaina	Female	25–34	None or primary	Unemployed

Note: * = In this group, three social workers were present too. The participants at the time of the focus group lacked legal documentation to reside in Belgium. ** = For this group, we focused the analyses on the participants who faced socio-economic difficulties: Abdelkrim, Asma, Hamid, Abdellah, and Soukaina. NA = Missing data. All names are pseudonyms.

Concrete problems

Participants' discussions generally focused on concrete, local problems. In terms of space, these problems varied from a lack of services provided by the management of their own social housing unit to a variety of issues in their neighbourhood, including theft, drug use and traffic, and a lack of public transport services and childcare. If not tied to their direct surroundings, participants often discussed concrete issues encountered in their daily lives, such as difficulties paying taxes or obtaining legal documentation as well as experiences of discrimination. Nevertheless, at times, they did connect these everyday issues to wider trends and problems. For example, participants in Molenbeek3 linked their discussion of discrimination against Muslims on the job market to the recognition of Islam as a religion in Belgium (Adil), the many koranic schools in the country (Mehmet), and the representation of the Muslim community in Brussels (Abbou). To give another example, in Molenbeek1, David and Sonia suggested that politicians are just 'marionettes' and everything is settled behind the scenes. Besides linking this to freemasonry and the Illuminati, they also sparked a discussion on (former) world leaders, such as Obama and Chirac.

Notwithstanding these exceptions, the predominant focus on concrete problems meant that participants also concentrated their discussions mostly on local actors, most notably street-level bureaucrats and local politicians, such as public welfare employees, police officers, and the mayor of Molenbeek. The solutions participants had in mind often focused on a stronger presence of these actors in the neighbourhood, and on enhanced efforts to consult residents before taking any decisions.[5] We recognize that the focus on local, concrete problems and solutions is in part the result of our methodological choices, singling out people in a single socio-economically challenged neighbourhood and asking them to discuss together what societal challenges they deem most important. At the same time, the findings echo the relevance of local circumstances and interactions to how these people think about politics, as also identified in prior studies (Dacombe, 2021; Rosanvallon, 2021; van Wessel, 2017). This underlines the need to move beyond generic, decontextualized statements about how these groups relate to politics if we are to understand their resentment towards it. In the following section, we show how resentment towards politics surfaced during the focus group discussions, being closely tied to the concrete problems and solutions participants had in mind.

Morality

In all focus groups, participants expressed a feeling of being treated unfairly and unequally compared to others. This often pertained to discrimination on the basis of one's migrant, and, sometimes, religious background. Participants signalled general prejudice towards them, such as the stereotyping of Muslims as terrorists: 'Ah, it's the Arabs,

---

5   After that, solutions focused on people themselves, including proposals to
     improve education (Molenbeek3) and to unite in order to be heard by local
     administrators (Molenbeek1), as well as on substantive policy reforms, such as a
     revision of the tax return system (Molenbeek3).

it's the Arabs. They are terrorists' (Malik, Molenbeek2). In addition, they linked it to direct and indirect personal experiences. For instance, in Molenbeek2, Malik expressed his frustration with the way people without legal documentation are discriminated against based on their country of origin: '[...] No, not even the fact that they don't obtain [required documents] [...] The fact that not regulating individuals without legal documentation promotes criminality among people coming from Morocco or North Africa who are obliged to steal to survive. You know?' In another example, David (Molenbeek1) linked this to encounters with the police: 'Immediately when a police officer sees a man of Moroccan origin, well, then it's he who did it.' Similarly, in an account that resonated with the other participants in Molenbeek3, Abbou expressed his feeling of being discriminated against on the job market based on his foreign, Muslim name and appearance:

> I had all the competencies for the job for which I had applied. I had it all. And so, they had to make a choice. They had to make a decision. There was me, my name is Abbou, and next to me there was a mister Jean-Marie, and on the other side there was another girl. You see? And so, they immediately saw my face and they didn't even look at my competencies that were on my CV, and said: 'Mister is called Abbou...' I felt it like that, they didn't say that to me, but it felt like that: 'He is called Abbou, so we remove him directly from the list.'
>
> (Molenbeek3)

At times, participants also compared their own situation in Brussels to other places in Belgium to underscore their relative deprivation. For example, in Molenbeek3, they emphasized the stronger presence of the police and better public services in other Belgian cities, such as Antwerp, and in Molenbeek1, participants discussed how a former mayor of the municipality did more for 'the rich' than for them.

However, the most prevalent theme related to fairness, encountered in all of the focus groups, was procedural rather than substantive: participants time and again expressed their lack of voice and linked this to the ineffectiveness of public policies aimed at addressing the problems in their community. This pertained both to street-level bureaucrats as well as to local politicians. Regarding the former, David (Molenbeek1) described, for example, how police officers tend to make a lot of fuss in the neighbourhood but do not tackle the actual problems:

But there is [...] a lot of incompetence. Here, there is a lot of laxity. We're going to do, they're going to do the Lucky Luke thing because quickly, [...] there's something coming out of, I don't know, out of a garbage can or something like that, then they're going to come quickly and make a row, put on the flashing lights, [...] pissing everyone off.

(Molenbeek1)

When participants turned to solutions concerning safety and the police, they indicated that they not only wanted a stronger presence from the police but specifically police officers who 'don't hesitate to come and find people, asking whether it is going all right or not' (Emma, Molenbeek1). The idea that street-level bureaucrats are out of touch with people and with the actual problems that participants experience could also be seen in complaints about the local housing agency not solving the 'real' problems and failing to listen to residents.

We find a similar view on local politicians. In Molenbeek4, Abdelkrim pointed out that he started a petition together with other residents to counter noise nuisance at night in Molenbeek. He had already been to the town hall and the mayor of Molenbeek twice but did not receive a response:

Abelkrim: They didn't do anything. So how does that happen?

Hamid: [in a loud voice] They have seen the petition! 15 or 20 people, [and] nobody responded.

Abdelkrim: [outraged] There you go! Nothing!

Hamid: That is what he wanted to say. They filed a petition! But, there you go. There, on Léopold II, it's rotten.

(Molenbeek4)

In the other focus groups, we find comparable accounts of participants that express their frustration with not being listened to by local politicians. In line with their description of street-level bureaucrats, participants in Molenbeek1 linked their frustration with the local mayor to her failure to take concrete actions or to demonstrate a physical presence in the neighbourhood:

David: [mockingly] She does social things. She says 'No but we will try to do something, we will do social things. We will help them, we will roll out a red carpet.' Well...

[...]

Moussa: But do you see her? Since the elections, I have never seen her.

David: [in a firm tone] I have never seen her! I have never seen her
               and I haven't even crossed her.

Sonia: She had to come, uhm, to the building. A month ago, the new
               management [of the building] presented itself. And she
               had to be introduced.

[...]

Moussa: But she wasn't there.

Sonia: Everyone, well, everyone was outraged because she wasn't
               there.

                                                          (Molenbeek1)

Participants in Molenbeek3 also mentioned that the current mayor did
not consult residents before making decisions about public facilities in
Molenbeek, such as the removal of parking lots. According to Abbou,
for example, she should have discussed this first with the inhabitants:

> The mayor hasn't made the effort to come to the residents of that place
> [...] So, what do we do, what is negative, what is positive, right, and after
> that we take a decision together. But according to her, taking decisions by
> herself like that without talking to residents, I don't think that's normal,
> you see?
>
>   (Molenbeek3)

Finally, what also tended to generate frustration among participants was
the lack of accountability from the people whom participants presumably
held responsible for the problems they experience. In Molenbeek1 for
instance Sonia discussed the mismanagement of the social housing
services, suggesting that neither social housing agencies nor politicians
at the local level want to claim responsibility. Instead 'they point their
finger at each other' when a problem presents itself. This also meant that
Sonia was confused about who is actually responsible:

Sonia: When you have a problem, they tell you to go the housing
               department at the town hall, to the mayor.

David: No! That's because what they are trying to say is 'Listen
            carefully, sort it out yourself. Try and talk to the
            management' [...]

Sonia: They point their finger at each other!

David: [Simultaneously] They point their finger at each other!
                                                    (Molenbeek1)

Overall, then, we observe across the focus groups that participants feel
discriminated against in their encounters with government officials
and generally think that local politicians are out of touch with reality.
Importantly, they feel ill-served by government officials and politicians
who do not try to truly listen to them linking it to their physical absence
in the neighbourhood. In the next section, we discuss how these elements
play into to their feelings towards politics.

Emotion

The previous section has illustrated participants' frustration and
disappointment with politics and how those feelings generally centred
on local actors. Another emotion that is linked to interaction with local
authorities and voiced by participants was fear. In Molenbeek2, this
revolved around the problem that the participants did not have the
requisite documentation and were therefore afraid to ask for it, scared
of being evicted. In Molenbeek4, fear manifested itself in relation to
problems of crime in the municipality. As Abdellah explained, that is
because one cannot trust the judicial system: '...the judiciary is implied
in it as well, right. Even if I report, if I report him, for example. He will
go by the police, he will arrive at a judge and [he will] set him free. Who
is being humiliated? It's me.'

Sometimes participants' disappointment with politics and local
administrations because of their deficient delivery of services or
poor attempts to listen to residents was accompanied by statements
signalling indifference. To illustrate, Moussa (Molenbeek1) did not see
any difference between successive mayors in terms of addressing local
problems: 'And they say that it was a MR [French-speaking liberal party]
project before and Schepmans [the previous mayor] she has finished and
that now PS [French-speaking socialist party] will take over. In reality,

it's... It's the same thing. For us it's the same thing.' Indifference also manifested itself when—exceptionally—participants in the same group connected their problems to global-level conspiracy theories. As Sonia made clear: '...we know very well that everything is settled in advance. Whether it's the United States or whatever other country, everything is arranged among them.'

Nevertheless, in two of the focus groups (Molenbeek1 and Molenbeek3), participants also offered a series of solutions to address problems in their community, suggesting that they neither despaired nor rejected local politics. Even participants such as David and Sonia, who expressed indifference towards politics, also suggested ways forward. Sonia, for example, pushed fellow residents in her building to unite and express themselves towards the management; argued that it was important that police officers should be 'neutral, above all, correct'; and proposed that the previous mayor should return because she 'beautified the community and made the Belgians return a bit.' Such signs of hope that politics could still resolve the societal problems that participants identified is also reflected in the suggestions made by participants in Molenbeek3 to consult residents before making decisions, and the need for the state and even the prime minister to address social problems. In fact, participants stated that such consultations and the opportunity to interact with politicians would make them feel more positive and optimistic about politics. Consider for instance the sequence below, which took place during the Molenbeek 3 focus group. Adil said he felt hopeful and positive about the future, after which Mehmet said he felt listened to. He added that this is what he and the other participants want from the government: to be listened to.

> Adil: I'm positive. When I see all the youngsters present here. That gives... [...]. That gives hope for the future. [...] I'm very happy about this evening, I learned a lot of things and I am leaving here with a lot of hope and a big smile on my face.
>
> [...]
>
> Mehmet: Me too. Because at least someone listened to us, wrote to us, gave us... You were here to listen to us. That is what we want actually. We want the government to listen to us and take good decisions.
>
> (Molenbeek3)

Temporality

These feelings associated with local politicians and bureaucrats were generally tied to long-lasting problems. In Molenbeek3, for instance, participants emphasized the recurring nature of problems of insecurity in their neighbourhood due to the enduring lack of police interventions. In Molenbeek2, Jamal's disappointment provides a potential example of resentment stemming from an enduring lack of response from the local administration: 'almost now, almost four years, I have deposited my files for social housing, there's nothing like a response, there's nothing. That's it too, you see. Waiting for almost ten years.'

The relevance of temporality also showed in participants' feelings towards local politicians. Abbou (Molenbeek3) remarked, for example, that he prefers to cast a blank vote because of the repeated empty messages coming from politicians:

> These politicians, it's only empty words. You see? For me politicians, I consider them as people that put the money into their pockets, that's all. I consider them like that and I don't believe what they say anymore. Every time they say 'Yes, we will do that, we will do this...' That's empty words.
>
> (Molenbeek3)

Abbou then goes on to describe how current problems can be traced back to the previous mayor. This resonates with a similar frustration expressed by Moussa in Molenbeek1 regarding the incompetence of successive mayors. Yet it is worth pointing out that the other participants in the same group were instead nostalgic about the past, providing a potential source of hope rather than bitterness towards politics. To illustrate, Sonia and David agreed that the previous mayor had a stronger social agenda and Emma added that she brought more security to the municipality. Similarly, in terms of micro politics, Sonia and Emma pointed out that while the management of their building now fails to listen to them, they had a different relationship with the management twenty years ago when they also had meetings with them.

Discussion

This chapter focused on socio-economically disadvantaged people's resentment toward politics in Belgium. Our analysis of population-based survey data show that these people tend to hold more negative political attitudes than people not experiencing socio-economic disadvantages. However, based on an analysis of focus groups conducted in the Belgian capital, we demonstrate that such resentment is not clear-cut, manifesting itself as a complex cluster of emotions (cf. Capelos & Demertzis, 2018). Indeed, even though decision-making via established democratic institutions seems to be experienced as something that is imposed on them—that is, as something that they do not choose, but have to accept—they realize that in order to solve many of the societal problems they experience, contact with and support from politicians are necessary. At the same time, they know that such contact and support are simply missing in practice. This makes for what we call an 'imposed' democratic dilemma.

These varied expressions of resentment among the disadvantaged participants were tied closely to local, concrete experiences, including deficient facilities and services in the municipality, (a lack of) interactions with street-level bureaucrats and local politicians, and other everyday experiences in their neighbourhood. Focus group participants generally underlined the absence of politicians and the inadequacy of institutions related to their everyday experiences and struggles. For some of our participants, the persistence of such a situation brewed resentment, echoing the findings in Chapter 8 related to the temporality of resentment.

These findings also feed back into survey-based research on political resentment. In contrast to what prior research and our own description based on the survey items suggest, the focus group discussions show that disadvantaged people cannot simply be portrayed as (particularly) resentful people. Among this population too, resentment expresses itself as a complex emotion that can go hand in hand with more positive feelings. Future research should therefore be careful not to draw overly simplistic conclusions about these people's resentment towards politics. What is more, our qualitative findings draw attention to the relevance of taking a micro-perspective and focusing on people's personal experiences to study manifestations of resentment as well as other emotions. The analyses of the different focus groups underlined the fact that disadvantaged people's attitudes are closely tied to their personal experiences with the state and local politics, something the existing survey items did not allow us to tease out. Integrating questions about such personal experiences, on the one hand, and political resentment, on the other, could provide a way to gain a more nuanced view of resentment in future survey research. Finally, we wish to emphasize the need to adequately include disadvantaged people in survey research to be able to make well-informed statements about the population under discussion.

Our study nonetheless has several limitations. One possible limitation is the question format we adopted in the focus groups. That is to say, by asking participants to identify societal challenges or problems, we might have prompted more negative appraisals. However, despite the many problems that participants identified, at least some of them also shared positive appreciations of political actors and challenged other participants for being too pessimistic. In addition, we also asked how societal challenges might be resolved. To this question, as our findings show, participants gave answers that signalled hope.

Another limitation is our small and diverse sample. We focused on data from four focus groups and one of the focus groups, unlike the others, consisted almost exclusively of participants without legal documents.[6] Nevertheless, our goal was to look into the many ways in which resentment manifests itself during conversations about political topics by listening to people who are hardly reached by surveys and are rarely asked to give their opinion about politics. Our goal therefore was not to give a representative assessment of their political attitudes but rather to provide some initial qualitative insights into what resentment might look like in this understudied population.

Despite these limitations, our study sheds light on how political resentment manifests itself among disadvantaged people, specifically among those living in socio-economically challenged neighbourhoods similar in many ways to those in other European cities. We have shown

---

6   We also admit that while we were careful to communicate the aims of our study
     and put participants at ease, they might still have been fearful or reluctant to talk
     openly about politics.

that although disadvantaged people hold negative political attitudes and are dissatisfied with their everyday experiences, they do not fully reject politics and have not given up hope on politics or politicians as a means to solve their problems. However, contrary to people not experiencing socio-economic hardships, they experience this as an *imposed* democratic dilemma in that they do not have alternative means or channels to tackle the problems they experience.

The number of people in Europe experiencing socio-economic problems in their daily lives is growing as a result of a spike in food and energy insecurity in the wake of the COVID-19 pandemic, climate-change-induced droughts and floods, and conflicts such as the war in Ukraine and the war and ongoing occupation in Palestine. As policymakers continue to struggle with tackling these problems, these resentments toward politics might become increasingly pronounced. This makes it urgent for future studies to improve our understanding of resentment among people experiencing socio-economic disadvantages as well as how it influences them in the short and long term, using both qualitative and survey data.

References

Allen, P. (2022). 'Experience, knowledge, and political representation.' *Politics & Gender,* 18(4), 1112–1140.

Améry, J. (1980). *At the Mind's Limits: Contemplations by a Survivor of Auschwitz and its Realities.* Trans. by S. Rosenfeld & S. P. Rosenfeld. Bloomington, IN: Indiana University Press.

Behrens, R., Freedman, M., & McGuckin, N. (2009). 'The challenges of surveying "hard to reach" groups: Synthesis of a workshop.' In *Transport Survey Methods: Keeping up with a Changing World.* (145-152). Emerald Group Publishing Limited.

Capelos, T., & Demertzis, N. (2018). 'Political action and resentful affectivity in critical times.' *Humanity & Society,* 42(4), 410-433.

Ceka, B., & Magalhães, P. C. (2016). 'How people understand democracy: A social dominance approach.' In M. Ferrín & H. Kriesi (eds.). *How Europeans View and Evaluate Democracy* (pp. 90–110). Oxford: Oxford University Press.

Ceka, B., & Magalhães, P. C. (2020). 'Do the rich and the poor have different conceptions of democracy? Socioeconomic status, inequality, and the political status quo.' *Comparative Politics,* 52(3), 383–412.

Celis, K., Knops, L., Van Ingelgom, V., & Verhaegen, S. (2021). 'Resentment and coping with the democratic dilemma.' *Politics and Governance,* 9(3), 237–247.

Cramer, K. J., & Toff, B. (2017). 'The fact of experience: Rethinking political knowledge and civic competence.' *Perspectives on Politics,* 15(3), 754–770.

Dacombe, R. (2021). 'Doing democracy differently: How can participatory democracy take hold in deprived areas?' *Representation,* 57(2), 175–191.

Dovi, S. (2002). 'Preferable descriptive representatives: Will just any woman, black, or Latino do?' *American Political Science Review,* 96(4), 729–743.

Ellard-Gray, A., Jeffrey, N. K., Choubak, M., & Crann, S. E. (2015). 'Finding the hidden participant: Solutions for recruiting hidden, hard-to-reach, and vulnerable populations.' *International Journal of Qualitative Methods,* 14(5), 1609406915621420.

Fassin, D. (2013). 'On resentment and ressentiment: the politics and ethics of moral emotions.' *Current Anthropology,* 54(3), 249–267.

Knops, L. (2021). *Political Indignation: A conceptual and empirical investigation of indignant citizens (Belgium 2017-2020).* PhD Thesis. Brussels: Vrije Universiteit Brussels.

Kvale, S., & Brinkmann, S. (2009). *InterViews: Learning the Craft of Qualitative Research Interviewing.* Thousand Oaks, CA: Sage.

Mansbridge, J. (1999). 'Should blacks represent blacks and women represent women? A contingent "yes".' *The Journal of Politics,* 61(3), 628–657.

Mason, J. (2013). *Qualitative Researching* (2nd ed.). London: Sage.

Mayne, Q., & Hakhverdian, A. (2017). 'Ideological congruence and citizen satisfaction: Evidence from 25 advanced democracies.' *Comparative Political Studies,* 50(6), 822–849.

McCormick, J., Hague, R., & Harrop, M. (2019). *Comparative Government and Politics: An Introduction.* London: Bloomsbury Publishing.

Miscoiu, S., & Gherghina, S. (2021). 'Poorly designed deliberation: Explaining the banlieues' non-involvement in the Great Debate.' *Innovation: The European Journal of Social Science Research,* 1–18.

Nieuwenhuis, J., Tammaru, T., Van Ham, M., Hedman, L., & Manley, D. (2019). 'Does segregation reduce socio-spatial mobility? Evidence from four European countries with different inequality and segregation contexts.' *Urban Studies,* 1–12, doi:10.1177/0042098018807628

Phillips, A. (1998). *The Politics of Presence.* Oxford: Oxford University Press.

Phillips, A. (2020). 'Descriptive representation revisited.' In R. Rohrschneider & J. Thomassen (eds.). *The Oxford Handbook of Political Representation in Liberal Democracies* (pp. 174–191). Oxford: Oxford University Press.

Pitkin, H. F. (1967). *The Concept of Representation*. Berkeley/Los Angeles, CA: University of California Press.

Rosanvallon, P. (2021). *Les épreuves de la vie: comprendre autrement les Français*. Paris: Editions du Seuil.

Russell, P., & McKenna, M. (eds.). (2012). *Free Will and Reactive Attitudes: Perspectives on P. F. Strawson's 'Freedom and Resentment'*. Burlington, VT: Ashgate Publishing.

Strawson, P. F. (2008). *Freedom and Resentment and Other Essays*. London: Routledge.

Talukder, D., & Pilet, J.-B. (2021). 'Public support for deliberative democracy. A specific look at the attitudes of citizens from disadvantaged groups.' *Innovation: The European Journal of Social Science Research*, 34(5), 656–676.

Van der Does, R., & Kantorowicz, J. (2022). 'Political exclusion and support for democratic innovations: Evidence from a conjoint experiment on participatory budgeting.' *Political Science Research and Methods*, 1–9, https://www.doi.org/10.1017/psrm.2022.3

Van Hamme, G., Grippa, T., & Van Criekingen, M. (2016). 'Migratory movements and dynamics of neighbourhoods in Brussels. Brussels Studies.' *La revue scientifique pour les recherches sur Bruxelles/Het wetenschappelijk tijdschrift voor onderzoek over Brussel/The Journal of Research on Brussels*, 97.

Van Ingelgom, V. (2020). 'Focus groups: From qualitative data generation to analysis.' In L. Curini & R. Franzese (eds.). *Sage Handbook of Research Methods in Political Science and International Relations* (pp. 1190–1210). London: Sage.

Van Wessel, M. (2017). 'Citizens as sense-makers: Towards a deeper appreciation of citizens' understandings of democratic politics.' *Political Studies*, 65(1_suppl), 127–145.

Williams, M. S. (2000). *Voice, Trust, and Memory: Marginalized Groups and the Failings of Liberal Representation*. Princeton, NJ: Princeton University Press.

Wojciechowska, M. (2019). 'Towards intersectional democratic innovations.' *Political Studies*, 67(4), 895–911.

Young, I. M. (1997). 'Deferring group representation.' In I. Shapiro & W. Kymlicka (eds.). *Ethnicity and Group Rights* (pp. 349–376). New York, NY: New York University Press.

Young, I. M. (2000). *Inclusion and Democracy*. Oxford: Oxford University Press.

6. Congruent, yet resentful? Issue incongruence, resentment and party position knowledge

Jonas Lefevere, Patrick van Erkel, Stefaan Walgrave, Isaïa Jennart, Pierre Baudewyns & Benoît Rihoux

Abstract: This chapter investigates the relation between a voter's policy incongruence and resentment. Incongruence refers to the mismatch between voters' and parties' preferences: we hypothesize that incongruence will be positively related to resentment. The more incongruent voters are with either their own preferred party (egotropic incongruence) or the whole party system (sociotropic incongruence), the less likely voters can expect policy that aligns with their preferences, and thus benefits them. Such incongruence likely fosters resentment. We further hypothesize that the relation between incongruence and resentment is moderated by voters' party issue positions knowledge. Using the 2019 RepResent survey data, we find no support for the hypothesized relation between incongruence and resentment. Rather, we find strong indications that citizens' party position knowledge moderates the relation between incongruence and resentment. This indicates that it does not just matter that citizens *are* incongruent with their preferred party and/or the party system, but also that they *know* they are incongruent.

  https://doi.org/10.11647/OBP.0401.06

Introduction

Contemporary democracies face a growing divide between political elites and the people they represent. Amongst other signs, this is borne out by the rise of populist and radical parties that thrive by channelling people's resentment towards politics (Capelos & Demertzis, 2018). As is discussed in greater detail in the first two chapters of this book, resentment is a multidimensional concept with anger as a core emotion, and is a key factor in understanding the broader crisis of representation (Fukuyama, 2018). In recognizing that resentment is a multidimensional concept, in this chapter we investigate a variety of factors that constitute core aspects of resentment or that closely relate to it (see Chapter 1): emotions, cynicism, trust and voting abstention.

In this chapter, we investigate to what extent resentment can be connected to a more traditional aspect of representative democracy: policy incongruence. Policy incongruence refers to the mismatch between the policy preferences of the public, on the one hand, and the policy preferences of elites on the other hand (Miller & Stokes, 1963; Stimson et al., 1995; Thomassen, 1994). We propose that this mismatch may partially explain the growing sense of resentment amongst the public. After all, incongruence can result in policies that are not responsive to public expectations, fostering perceptions of unfair treatment and anger. Moreover, when people's preferences do not match with those of the parties that should represent them, they are unlikely to see their demands represented by any of the competing parties. We are not the first to study the link between (in)congruence and people's disappointment with politics and democracy (Mayne & Hakhverdian, 2017; Reher, 2016). The message emanating from prior studies is that greater congruence results in more satisfied citizens. So, we consider the flipside: greater *in*congruence fosters resentment. We move beyond prior research, however, by considering the role of knowledge, and argue that it is not just about people mismatching with parties, but people knowing they mismatch with parties. In other words, the connection between resentment and incongruence may only come about when people also have knowledge of that incongruence. Thus, the central query of this study is: To what extent does issue incongruence impact citizens' democratic resentment, and how does knowledge of a party's position moderate this effect?

Our chapter makes three contributions. First, we acknowledge the inherently multifaceted nature of resentment, and consider how incongruence affects a variety of indicators (see also Chapters 1 and 2). Second, following Golder and Stramski (2010), we assess the impact of two types of incongruence—egotropic incongruence, which is the extent to which individual citizens mismatch with their preferred party (one-to-one), and sociotropic incongruence, or the extent to which they mismatch with the party system as a whole. The latter, in particular, may foster resentment, through the feeling that the political system as a whole fails to represent one's policy preferences and is therefore unjust. Third, we examine whether the (possible) link between incongruence and resentment is conditional on citizens' political knowledge. Being able to correctly assess whether one is (in)congruent with one's preferred political party and the party system as whole asks a lot of citizens: they need to know parties' positions, clearly understand their own position, and be able to connect both (Mayne & Hakhverdian, 2017; Thomassen, 1994). Knowledge of parties' policy positions is a key requirement for this, so we hypothesize that the link between incongruence and resentment is moderated by citizens' knowledge of party positions. When citizens are more aware of parties' positions, they are increasingly cognizant of their own incongruence with their preferred party and/or the whole party system. Consequently, we expect the relationship between resentment and incongruence to be especially pronounced amongst more knowledgeable citizens, who are aware of the mismatch between their own policy preferences and that of their party and/or the political system.

We begin our chapter with a discussion of resentment, before turning our attention to incongruence and theorizing our hypotheses on the link between resentment, incongruence, and knowledge. We then discuss our methodological approach and results, and end with a conclusion in which we reflect on the broader implications of our findings.

Incongruence and resentment of the political system

Resentment

In line with the broader perspective of this book, we define resentment here as a multi-layered emotional state in response to (perceived) unfair treatment (Moruno, 2013). For brevity, we limit our discussion of the concept here to the aspects we investigate empirically, and refer to the opening chapters of the book for a more elaborate discussion. We conceptualize resentment through four indicators that are central to, or that are associated with, resentment: emotions towards politics, political cynicism, political trust, and vote abstention. We briefly discuss each in turn.

People's emotions towards politics are most directly connected to resentment: resentment is typically referred to as a state of anger. Beyond emotions themselves, however, political cynicism is also clearly connected to the notion of resentment: Capella and Jamieson define cynicism as being a 'bitter or resentful attitude' (Cappella & Jamieson, 1997, p. 142). Political cynicism is a negative view towards politics and political actors, which are held in disregard and are seen to only serve their self-interest (Agger et al., 1961). While trust is not a core component of resentment as such, resentment is strongly linked to, and often follows from, a lack of trust in the political system. Citrin and Stoker (2018) posit trust as the opposite of cynicism, so it follows that a lack of trust brings one closer to cynical attitudes. Resentful feelings thus may arise in response to a preceding breach of trust (Kasperson et al., 1992; Van Der Meer, 2010) particularly including social distrust. Finally, although resentment is mostly described as an emotional state, we also consider an obvious behavioural consequence of political resentment: vote abstention. Abstention has been linked to political alienation, with the assumption being that when citizens feel alienated from or indifferent towards politics, they will feel that participation in the political system is of no use and therefore refrain from voting (Adams et al., 2006; but see Capelos & Demertzis, 2018). While feelings of anger may motivate people to act to 'right the wrong', we argue that it is unlikely that they will do so through voting: the electoral mechanism of representation has, in the eyes of resentful citizens, proven ineffective in bringing about the expected returns. Moreover, the compulsory voting system in Belgium also dampens the potential for resentment to result in more participation: turnout rates are historically above 90% in Belgium, suggesting that the vast majority already turn out—and thus a ceiling effect may take place, making it unlikely that resentment might drive turnout further upwards. As such, especially in the Belgian context, it seems likely that resentment increases electoral abstention.

Incongruence and resentment

Our key expectation is that these four indicators—emotions, political trust, cynicism, and abstention—are affected by the level of incongruence between voters and parties. We consider two types of incongruence. Egotropic incongruence refers to the policy preference 'match' between voters and their preferred party: it points to the extent to which the party for which a citizen voted holds dissimilar policy preferences to that person (Mayne & Hakhverdian, 2017). Egotropic incongruence can either be the fault of the party, which no longer represents its voters, or that of the voters themselves, when they vote for a party that does not share similar policy preferences. Sociotropic incongruence, on the other hand, refers to the mismatch between a voter and the whole party system. It indicates that the different political parties in the system, on average, do not share the same policy positions as the citizen. A consequence of sociotropic incongruence is that the citizen's policy preferences are unlikely to be translated into actual policy, no matter who gets into power after the elections (Golder & Stramski, 2010).

For our indicators of resentment, we expect that the worse voters' opinions match with their preferred party (egotropic incongruence) or with the whole party system (sociotropic incongruence), the more their level of resentment increases. The argument is straightforward: increased levels of opinion incongruence suggest that voters are less likely to expect policy that aligns with their preferences, and thus benefits them. At the system level, evidence suggests that higher levels of congruence lead citizens to express greater satisfaction with democracy (Mayne & Hakhverdian, 2017; Reher, 2016), although Andeweg (2011) found a negative correlation between congruence and trust. Still, the disadvantages posed by greater incongruence are important: less congruent groups are less likely to have their interests represented in the legislature (low egotropic congruence), and by extension in the enacted policies (low sociotropic congruence) (Lesschaeve, 2017). Consequently, it is unlikely they will feel that policy is just and fair to them—ultimately resulting in feelings of resentment.

The above argument hinges on the assumption that voters consider issue positions when they cast their vote (egotropic congruence) or when they evaluate the whole party system (sociotropic congruence). In that regard, it is important to acknowledge that non-issue-related factors, such as candidate traits, religion, and so on, also affect electoral choice (Nyhuis, 2016; Raymond, 2018). Yet, these other determinants of electoral choice notwithstanding, the empirical evidence for spatial voting, including within the 2019 Belgian context, is quite robust (see, e.g., Flavin & Law, 2022; Jessee, 2009; Lachat, 2012; Shor & Rogowski, 2018; Walgrave et al., 2020). This suggests that while voters' electoral appraisal of parties is not solely driven by the similarity of issue positions, it does remain an important element in electoral choice. Consequently, it seems reasonable to expect that when voters do not have a good match with their party or the party system, this may lead to resentment.

This basic argument readily translates to all of our four indicators of resentment. Given that resentment is defined as an emotional state to begin with (Moruno, 2013), the expectation for emotions is straightforward: greater incongruence leads people to experience greater anger, fear, bitterness and anxiety towards politics as these voters will be less likely to see their interests represented in the legislature, and observe policy progress in their desired direction. So, we hypothesize that:

H1a: Voters with greater incongruence with their preferred party experience more anger, fear, bitterness and anxiety about politics than voters with lower incongruence.

H1b: Voters with greater incongruence with the party system in general experience more anger, fear, bitterness and anxiety about politics than voters with lower incongruence.

Regarding trust, issue incongruence should negatively impact the commitment and care dimensions of political trust. When the preferences of citizens and the party they voted for do not align, citizens may feel that this party is not committed to their cause, or in the worst case simply does not care about them. Hence, the relationship of trust with this party will be broken: if anything, these voters might be pushed to distrust all parties, because the policies that are pursued by such parties do not match their own preferences. For those voters with high levels of sociotropic incongruence, there is no feasible policy option within what the parties offer, further augmenting feelings that the political system does not care about them and is not committed to their cause, breaking the relationship of trust. As such, we expect that:

> H2a: Voters with greater incongruence with their preferred party have less political trust than voters with lower incongruence.

> H2b: Voters with greater incongruence with the party system in general have less political trust than voters with lower incongruence.

Cynicism lies at the opposite end to political trust: cynical voters display a disdain for politics and politicians (Agger et al., 1961). That said, compared to political trust, the expectations of cynical voters may be less straightforward: opinion incongruence is mainly concerned with the lack of parties' utility to voters, whereas cynicism has an inherent emotional component that may be only loosely affiliated with the utility that voters gain from parties. Still, it seems likely that a voter who is not well represented substantively may grow suspicious of the party (egotropic congruence) or the party system (sociotropic congruence). When the policy preferences of a voter and the party they voted for do not correspond, the voter will observe that the party takes differing policy positions compared to her own. This further drives the feeling that politicians do not know what is going on in people's lives and are breaking their promises. As such, we expect that:

> H3a: Voters with greater incongruence with their preferred party have greater political cynicism than voters with lower incongruence.

> H3b: Voters with greater incongruence with the party system in general have greater political cynicism than voters with lower incongruence.

Finally, we expect that incongruence will result in a higher likelihood that the person will abstain from voting: why bother turning out to vote if the utility gained from this vote is minimal at best (egotropic incongruence), or is unlikely to be reflected in actual policy, due to having low congruence with the whole party system (sociotropic incongruence)?

> H4a: Voters with greater incongruence with their preferred party are more likely to abstain from voting than voters with lower incongruence.

H4b: Voters with greater incongruence with the party system in general are more likely to abstain from voting than voters with lower incongruence.

Incongruence and resentment: the role of party position knowledge

In line with prior research, we focus on what we call 'objective' incongruence: a mismatch between the actual policy positions taken by voters and parties. Yet, that voters are objectively incongruent does not automatically mean that voters also *know* they mismatch with their party and/or the whole party system. Rational voting places a high demand on voters' knowledge of politics, and we know that many voters are unaware of parties' policy positions (Adams et al., 2011; Delli Carpini & Keeter, 1996). Knowing what parties stand for on a wide range of issues and then being able to link these positions to one's own policy preferences as well is a daunting task (Mayne & Hakhverdian, 2017). In practice, most citizens will not be able to succeed in this exercise, or only to a limited extent at best. Therefore, we expect that the link between issue incongruence and resentment is conditional on voters' knowledge of parties' issue positions: the hypothesized effects should be strongest for more knowledgeable voters who are better able to assess what the party positions are, and thus whether they are congruent or incongruent with their preferred party and/or the party system as a whole. This results in our final hypothesis:

H5: Voters' party position knowledge moderates the impact of incongruence on resentment, with the relationships of H1–H4 being stronger for more knowledgeable voters compared to less knowledgeable voters.

Methods

To test our expectations, we relied on several data sources. The first dataset is the RepResent panel survey that was fielded in the context of the 2019 Belgian general elections, and that is explained in more detail in Chapter 2. In addition, to calculate the various measures of issue incongruence, we need measurements of party positions. For this, we rely on the national party chair survey, which surveyed all party chairmen on their party's position on all statements that were included in the RepResent survey (see below). The fact that this survey of party chairmen occurred in the context of a large Voting Advice Application (Stemtest/Test Electoral 2019), which was organized and publicized by the public broadcasters in both Flanders and Wallonia (RTBF/VRT), ensures that parties' positions were scrutinized in the public eye. Therefore, as argued in prior publications, this highly visible survey of party positions ensures a binding and valid position being taken by the party (Walgrave et al., 2009).

Our key dependent and independent variables were all measured in the post-electoral survey. Detailed measures are available in Chapter 2; we limit ourselves here to a basic description of the scales used in the analysis. We use a reliable 0 to 10 scale to track emotions based on the 8 measured emotions, with higher values indicating more anger, fear, bitterness and anxiety–and less hope, relief, happiness and contentment (alpha=0.83). We use a 0 to 30 scale to measure political trust based on the items tracking trust in political parties, the federal parliament, and politicians, with higher values indicating greater trust (alpha=0.95). Political cynicism is measured on a reliable 0 to 35 scale based on the seven related items in the survey (alpha=0.78), with higher values indicating greater levels of cynicism. Finally, we track respondents' probability to abstain from voting through a 0 to 12 sum scale, based on the survey question tracking probability to vote in federal, national and local elections if voting was no longer mandatory. Higher values indicate a greater chance of abstention (alpha = 0.96).

Our key independent variables are the measures of sociotropic and egotropic incongruence. The RepResent survey contained 18 specific policy proposals, for which voters could indicate whether they agreed or disagreed. The proposals were selected to cover a wide range of policy domains, and to ensure that parties actually offered divergent opinions, thus excluding valence proposals on which all parties agreed/disagreed. Of course, any selection of issues is likely to be only a partial representation of the relevant policy space, but we contend the sheer number of statements allows us to go beyond extant approaches such as the overarching left-right position of voters and parties. Moreover, the selection maximizes our ability to incorporate positions on a wide number of policy domains. Appendix 1 includes an overview of the 18 policy statements.

As discussed at the beginning of this section, we also obtained the parties' positions on the same statements. The parties include CD&V, Groen, N-VA, Open VLD, PVDA, sp.a and Vlaams Belang for Flanders, and CDH, DéFI, Ecolo, MR, Parti Populaire, PS and PTB for Wallonia. A voter's egotropic incongruence is then the number of proposals on which they hold a different position to the party they voted for in the federal elections of 2019, and ranges from 0 (congruent on all proposals) to 18 (incongruent on all proposals). In contrast, sociotropic incongruence refers to incongruence with the system in general and is therefore operationalised as the average incongruence with the seven parties in the party system (as calculated above). Given that parties take different positions from each other, respondents will always have some incongruence with at least one of the parties in the system and therefore never achieve full incongruence (18) on this measure. Moreover, they can never be perfectly congruent with all seven parties at the same time either. In practice, this measure therefore takes a value between 4.6 and 12.6. A low score indicates that the respondent is, on average, well represented by the party system, and a high score indicate that the policy preferences of a respondent large fail to match the average party. Note that the party 'offer' in Flanders and Wallonia is different, with the Flemish parties as a group offering more right-wing policies and the Walloon parties offering more left-wing policies (so that a right-wing voter would have a lower sociotropic incongruence in Flanders and a higher in Wallonia, and vice versa). Comparing results across both regions therefore generates a good robustness test for our findings.

To assess H5, we track respondents' knowledge of party positions. We asked respondents to describe the position of all seven major parties in their region in relation to the same 18 statements used to measure incongruence.[1] The measure tracks the proportion of correct assessments

---

1   Flanders: CD&V, Groen, N-VA, Open VLD, sp.a, PVDA, VB. Wallonia: CDH, Ecolo, MR, PS, PTB, PVDA, PP. For Flanders, the measure is based on 126 positions (18 statements * 7 parties). For Wallonia it is based on 124 positions, because for two statements the MR did not present a unified position. We further checked for straight lining: some respondents simply ticked all boxes for a given party (i.e., indicating it agreed with all 18 statements) as a means to bypass the knowledge question. If respondents straight-lined one or more parties on this question, they were removed from the analysis. We also removed respondents who did not

of party positions, ranging from 0 (none correct) to 1 (all correct). We also include a number of controls in the analyses, which were measured in the first wave of the survey: these include a respondent's Gender (0=Male, 1=Female); Age; Education (1=No or elementary education, 2=High school (reference), 3=Higher education); Ideological extremity (rescaling of the left–right question so that 0 means 'centre' and 5 means 'extreme' on either the left or right); Political interest; Political sophistication; and Satisfaction with income (see Chapter 2 for the exact formulation of these questions). Finally, given that the Belgian political system is split along linguistic lines, we control for the Region of the respondent (0=Flanders, 1=Wallonia), as the different party constellations might result in systematic differences between the regions. We also add fixed effects for respondents' self-reported vote choice in 2019 (measured in wave 2) to account for systematic differences between party electorates.

Results

To assess our hypotheses, we conducted a linear regression analysis in which we included additional controls for both socio-demographic factors as well as general political attitudes. For brevity, we only report the key coefficients in the main document (Tables 6.1 and 6.2) and relegate the full model results to the Appendix (Tables A1 and A2).

Table 6.1 Egotropic incongruence regressions.

	Emotions (H1a)		Political Trust (H2a)		Political Cyn. (H3a)		Abstention (H4a)	
	Coef.	S.E.	Coef.	S.E.	Coef.	S.E.	Coef.	S.E.
Egotropic incongruence	-0.05*	(0.02)	0.15*	(0.06)	-0.06	(0.03)	0.03	(0.03)
Party position knowledge	2.80**	(0.70)	-7.84**	(1.94)	0.48	(2.00)	-6.79***	(0.84)
Controls	See appendix							
R²	0.19		0.29		0.22		0.29	
N	2,476		2,476		2,476		2,476	

tick any of the answer options for any party on any statement, as this suggests non-response.

Bitter-Sweet Democracy?

Table 6.2: Sociotropic incongruence regressions.

Variable	Emotions (H1b)		Political Trust (H2b)		Political Cyn. (H3b)		Abstention (H4b)	
	Coef.	S.E.	Coef.	S.E.	Coef.	S.E.	Coef.	S.E.
Sociotropic incongruence	-0.11**	(0.03)	0.17	(0.12)	-0.21*	(0.09)	0.12**	(0.03)
Party position knowledge	3.00***	(0.67)	-8.89***	(1.65)	0.54	(2.00)	-6.77***	(0.84)
Controls	See appendix							
R^2	0.19		0.28		0.22		0.29	
N	2,476		2,476		2,476		2,476	

First, we consider the impact of egotropic incongruence. Even controlling for other determinants, the results for emotions, trust and cynicism lead us to reject H1a, H2a and H3a: increasing egotropic incongruence does not result in more feelings of anger, lower trust or higher cynicism. In fact, our data suggest the reverse. Incongruence leads to significantly fewer such emotions (-0.05, $p<.05$) and more trust (0.15, $p<.05$). For cynicism, the coefficient does not reach significance, but the direction of the effect once more goes against our expectations, with more incongruent voters becoming *less* cynical (-0.06, $p=0.06$). For abstention, we do not find a significant effect—but no support for our hypothesis either. In sum, the evidence leads us to reject H1a, H2a, H3a and H4a.

Next, we turn to the impact of sociotropic congruence (H1b through H4b). Once again, the evidence leads us to reject our expectations for H1b (Emotions), H2b (Trust), and H3b (Cynicism): sociotropic incongruence correlates to fewer emotions such as anger, anxiety, bitterness and fear (-0.11, $p<.01$); it does not lead to lower trust (0.17, $p=.189$); and results in less cynicism (-0.21, $p<.05$). Only for abstention (H4b) do the results show a pattern consistent with our expectation: more sociotropic incongruence leads to a greater propensity to abstain from voting (0.12, $p<.01$).

However, we hypothesized that the link between incongruence and resentment might be contingent upon voters' knowledge of party positions (H5); incongruence may only impact (indicators of) resentment when people also have the knowledge that they are incongruent. We therefore ran interaction models to assert whether the impact of egotropic and sociotropic congruence was moderated by voters' knowledge of party positions. Following the recommendation of Brambor, Clark and Golder (2006) we plot the marginal effect of egotropic and sociotropic congruence for the various values of the moderating variable (knowledge of party positions). We report the full interaction models in tables A3 and A4 in the Appendix. Figure 6.1 shows the results for egotropic congruence: the graph shows the marginal effect of egotropic incongruence for varying levels of position knowledge on the x-axis (ranging from 45% correctly placed party positions to 75%).

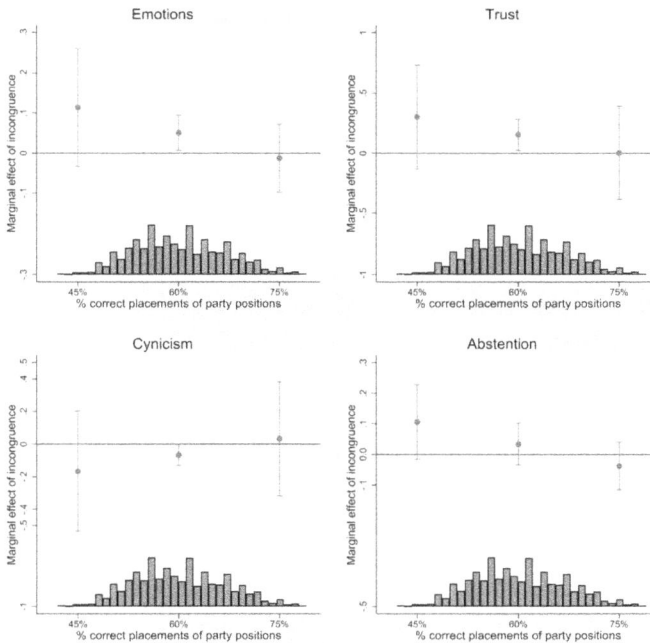

Fig. 6.1 Marginal effect of egotropic incongruence on respondents' emotions, political cynicism, trust and abstention, for varying levels of knowledge of party positions.

We expected a stronger effect for incongruence among more sophisticated respondents, but we based this expectation on the assumption of different effect directions for the direct impact of incongruence on trust, cynicism and abstention for H1 to H4. Given our earlier findings, the moderation patterns for egotropic incongruence are quite sensible—though they fail to meet statistical significance. For emotions, we find that the unexpected negative relationship between incongruence and emotions such as anger, anxiety, fear and bitterness only manifests itself amongst respondents with low levels of knowledge. As knowledge increases, the negative relation shifts in the hypothesized direction, although it fails to reach statistical significance. For trust, we find a similar pattern: the unexpected positive relation between incongruence and trust disappears at higher levels of knowledge. We see a similar pattern for cynicism, although the marginal effects do not reach significance at any level of knowledge (as visualized by the 95% confidence interval not separating from the horizontal zero line). The negative effect of incongruence on cynicism, which runs counter to our expectation, manifests amongst the less knowledgeable citizens, and becomes slightly positive amongst highly knowledgeable respondents. Finally, for abstention no marginal effect reaches significance.

Figure 6.2 presents the moderation findings for sociotropic incongruence. The patterns show a high degree of similarity, and moderation is stronger. For emotions, trust, and cynicism, the graphs show that the unexpected direction of the relation with incongruence manifests amongst respondents with low levels of positional knowledge. When knowledge increases, however, the relation turns in the expected direction—although the marginal effect itself is not significant among the highly knowledgeable. For example, we find a slight positive relation between emotions, cynicism and incongruence, and a negative one between trust and incongruence. So, it appears important to acknowledge that while citizens may *be* incongruent with the party system, they do not necessarily *know* they are. For abstention, finally, we find no pattern of moderation—but the overall effect of sociotropic incongruence on abstention generally falls in line with our hypothesis H4b. Overall, H5 is accepted.

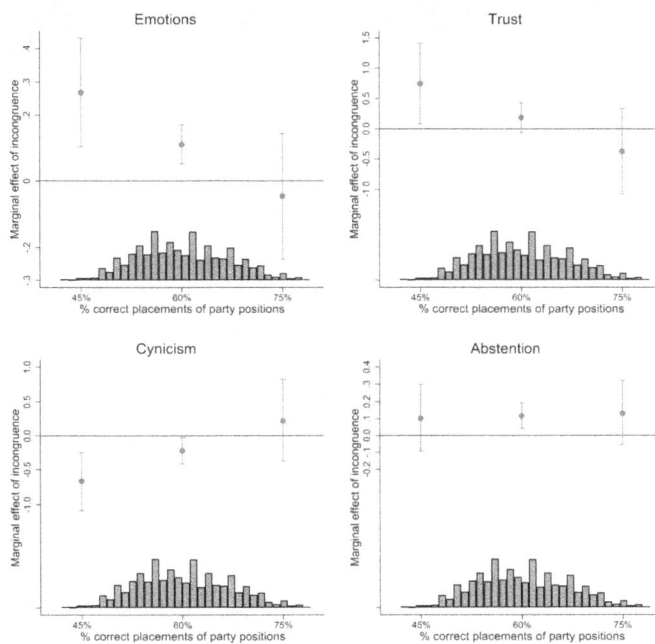

Fig. 6.2 Marginal effect of sociotropic incongruence on respondents' emotions, political cynicism, trust and abstention, for varying levels of knowledge of party positions.

To assert the robustness of the findings, we executed two checks. First, we estimated the models for Flanders and Wallonia separately. The evidence, presented in appendix tables A5 and A6, shows that the direct impact of incongruence (H1—H4) is similar in both regions. We also ran the interaction models for each region separately. Because the patterns are similar in both regions, we do not present all 12 models, but briefly recap the main findings. For egotropic incongruence, in both regions we find the same pattern for emotion and trust: the unexpected association between incongruence and trust / emotions weakens as knowledge increases. For cynicism, the patterns are also similar in Flanders and Wallonia, with a stronger moderation in Wallonia, where for low levels of knowledge incongruence significantly decreases cynicism ($p<.05$), whereas amongst highly knowledgeable citizens we find the expected positive relation: more incongruence breeds more cynicism ($p=.05$). For abstention, finally, we do not find evidence of moderation in either region. Regarding sociotropic incongruence, once again the findings of moderation are identical across the two regions, but moderation tends to be stronger. For trust, cynicism and emotions, the unexpected findings only manifest amongst less knowledgeable respondents and disappear or even turn in the hypothesized direction for knowledgeable voters. For abstention, we do not find evidence of moderation in either Flanders or Wallonia.

Second, we ran the main analysis again using an alternative operationalization of incongruence, in which we account for the salience of the issues: in the second wave of the survey, respondents were asked to indicate between three and five statements they considered especially important. The alternative incongruence scale gives a greater weight for a match on these salient statements (2 instead of 1). As such, the incongruence measure varies between 0 and 23. Tables A7 and A8 present these models, which show that once again, our findings regarding H1 through H4 hold up.

Conclusion

Democracies are increasingly challenged by declining levels of political trust, higher levels of political cynicism, and lower turnout rates in elections. This has resulted in a surge of studies that examine the factors that drive democratic resentment. One potential factor is that the system of representative democracy is in fact no longer working adequately: what drives resentment is the system's inability to provide the public with the policies it demands. This chapter set out to investigate to what extent democratic resentment is the result of a failure in substantive representation. Does incongruence with the political system drive the feelings of resentment that many citizens have? Specifically, we focused on four indicators that constitute, or are closely related to, resentment: citizens' emotions towards politics, political cynicism, political trust, and vote abstention. Moreover, we focused on two types of issue congruence: egotropic congruence, the extent to which voters are congruent with their preferred party, and sociotropic congruence, the extent to which voters match with the offer of the entire party system. We hypothesized that incongruent voters would display more emotions such as anger, anxiety, fear and bitterness, have lower levels of political trust, higher levels of political cynicism, and a higher likelihood to abstain from voting. However, the link between incongruence and resentment hinges on strong assumptions that incongruent voters know their own position on policy issues, know where the parties stand on these issues, and understand their overall levels of incongruence with the party offer. This is often not the case. Therefore, we further hypothesized that the impact of incongruence on resentment would be moderated by voters' knowledge of party positions: amongst knowledgeable voters, we would expect a stronger link between incongruence and resentment compared to less knowledgeable voters.

Our general expectations about the link between incongruence and resentment were not met. On the contrary, our findings demonstrate that more incongruent voters display less anger, bitterness, anxiety and fear, higher levels of political trust, lower levels of political cynicism and are thus less resentful towards the democratic system. This finding holds for both egotropic and sociotropic congruence. Only regarding the impact of sociotropic incongruence on abstention do we find that, in line with our expectation, greater incongruence results in a greater propensity to abstain from voting.

In contrast, we find that knowledge has moderating effects on the impact of both egotropic and sociotropic voting on emotions, trust and cynicism, with sociotropic incongruence in particular being contingent on knowledge. In simple terms, whereas we find a counterintuitive relation between incongruence and resentment overall, when this is moderated by knowledge, the conclusion becomes more nuanced. Incongruence indeed reduces anger and similar emotions, increases trust and lowers cynicism—but only amongst voters with low levels of knowledge, i.e., those voters who are not aware of the mismatch between their own positions and what their party and the parties in general want (see also Chapter 3 about the description of resentful people). This suggests that these voters may be 'blissfully ignorant' of the fact that they are incongruent. Amongst those voters who do know party positions—and thus are aware they are incongruent—the connection between incongruence and emotions, trust, and cynicism turns in the direction we hypothesized, although the effect of incongruence is not always significant.

Although further research is necessary, the results regarding moderation suggest that the paradoxical findings when we consider the electorate at large may be explained by a difference between perception and reality. One element that should therefore be further investigated is the role of feeling subjectively represented. While incongruent voters may objectively be poorly represented, they may not feel so subjectively. It could be that such feelings of being represented, even in the absence of actual substantive representation, alter the impact of incongruence on resentment (see also Chapter 7, which delves deeper into the matter of feeling represented). Of course, feeling represented—or not—can have many causes, and is not solely driven by incongruence. We leave it to future studies to disentangle this puzzle further, but it does raise questions regarding the long-term relationship between incongruence and resentment: we were unable to examine the back-and-forth dynamic between incongruence and resentment over time. If citizens lack information on party positions, they may not realize they are incongruent with party positions. Yet, we consider it likely that over time, such incongruent citizens may realize their incongruence as they see the (lack of) policy they desire coming to fruition. As a result, it may be that the moderating effect of knowledge only temporarily dampens the relation between incongruence and resentment. If that is the case, we might expect citizens with lower levels of knowledge to experience a steeper increase in resentment as they age. To disentangle such a puzzle, however, would entail a longitudinal design that tracks citizens over prolonged periods of time.

There are still several shortcomings to our study. First, we cannot be certain whether the 18 statements we use for our congruence measures are representative for the full population of potential policy statements. Although we aimed to maximize policy domains when selecting the statements, it is possible that our selection biases congruence towards certain parties. That our findings hold even when we adjust our incongruence scale for issue salience, however, bolsters our confidence that we would find similar patterns with other statements that may carry different importance amongst voters. Second, the egotropic measure is somewhat endogenous as certain voters are more likely or better able to cast a vote for a party that matches their political policy preferences than others. However, the fact that we find similar results when using the more exogenous sociotropic measure convinces us that the findings are not driven by this endogeneity. Third, Belgium is a peculiar case, as it has compulsory voting. This, of course, means that the findings regarding abstention may not readily generalize to other contexts. Beyond abstention, it may be that the connection between incongruence, on the one hand, and trust, cynicism and emotions on the other, varies as a function of the political system.

The takeaway is that knowledge matters when we consider the relation between resentment and incongruence. Incongruent but unaware citizens do not become resentful, presumably because they do not realize they are in fact incongruent with parties' positions. Amongst those citizens with high levels of knowledge, the paradoxical impact of incongruence on resentment disappears and the more expected pattern of incongruence effectively driving resentment emerges. This raises important questions for follow-up research. For example, while 'ignorance is bliss' applies to some extent, in an age of disinformation we need to consider adverse effects of the knowledge moderation mechanism. If those citizens that are congruent become misinformed and mistakenly assume they are incongruent, they may begin to subjectively feel misrepresented—even if their interests are represented in the political system. We leave it to future studies to tackle these questions. For now, we have shown that incongruence affects levels of resentment—but mainly amongst those citizens that actually know they are incongruent with their party and/or the system as a whole.

References

Adams, J., Dow, J., & Merrill, S. (2006). 'The political consequences of alienation-based and indifference-based voter abstention: Applications to Presidential Elections.' *Political Behavior*, 28(1), 65–86, https://doi.org/10.1007/s11109-005-9002-1

Adams, J., Ezrow, L., & Somer-Topcu, Z. (2011). 'Is Anybody Listening? Evidence That Voters Do Not Respond to European Parties' Policy Statements During Elections.' *American Journal of Political Science*, 55(2), 370–382, https://doi.org/10.1111/j.1540-5907.2010.00489.x

Agger, R. E., Goldstein, M. N., & Pearl, S. A. (1961). 'Political Cynicism: Measurement and Meaning.' *The Journal of Politics*, 23(3), 477–506, https://doi.org/10.2307/2127102

Andeweg, R. B. (2011). 'Approaching Perfect Policy Congruence. Measurement, Development, and Relevance for Political Representation.' In M. Rosema, B. Denters, & K. Aarts (eds.). *How Democracy Works. Political Representation and Policy Congruence in Modern Societies* (pp. 39–52). Pallas Publications. https://doi.org/ 10.1017/9789048513369

Brambor, T., Clark, W. R., & Golder, M. (2006). 'Understanding Interaction Models: Improving Empirical Analyses.' *Political Analysis*, 14(1), 63–82, https://doi.org/10.1093/pan/mpi014

Capelos, T., & Demertzis, N. (2018). 'Political Action and Resentful Affectivity in Critical Times.' *Humanity & Society*, 42(4), 410–433, https://doi. org/10.1177/0160597618802517

Cappella, J. N., & Jamieson, K. H. (1997). *Spiral of Cynicism: The Press and the Public Good*. Oxford: Oxford University Press.

Citrin, J., & Stoker, L. (2018). 'Political Trust in a Cynical Age.' *Annual Review of Political Science*, 21(1), 49–70, https://doi.org/10.1146/ annurev-polisci-050316-092550

Delli Carpini, M., & Keeter, S. (1996). *What Americans Know about Politics and Why It Matters* (Map Political Knowledge). New Haven: Yale University Press.

Flavin, P., & Law, W. (2022). 'Ideological proximity, issue importance, and vote choice.' *Electoral Studies*, 75, 102422, https://doi.org/10.1016/j. electstud.2021.102422

Fukuyama, F. (2018). *Identity: The Demand for Dignity and the Politics of Resentment* (1st Edition). Farrar, Straus and Giroux.

Golder, M., & Stramski, J. (2010). 'Ideological Congruence and Electoral Institutions.' *American Journal of Political Science*, 54(1), 90–106, https://doi. org/10.1111/j.1540-5907.2009.00420.x

Jessee, S. A. (2009). 'Spatial Voting in the 2004 Presidential Election.' *American Political Science Review*, 103(1), 59–81, https://doi.org/10.1017/ S000305540909008X

Kasperson, R. E., Golding, D., & Tuler, S. (1992). 'Social Distrust as a Factor in Siting Hazardous Facilities and Communicating Risks.' *Journal of Social Issues*, 48(4), 161–187, https://doi.org/10.1111/j.1540-4560.1992.tb01950.x

Lachat, R. (2012). Issue Ownership and the vote: Salience or competence? [Unpublished manuscript].

Lesschaeve, C. (2017). 'Inequality in Party-voter Opinion Congruence: A Matter of Choices Made or Choices Given?' *Representation*, 53(2), 153–166, https://doi.org/10.1080/00344893.2017.1333034

Mayne, Q., & Hakhverdian, A. (2017). 'Ideological Congruence and Citizen Satisfaction: Evidence From 25 Advanced Democracies.' *Comparative Political Studies*, 50(6), 822–849, https://doi.org/10.1177/0010414016639708

Miller, W. E., & Stokes, D. E. (1963). 'Constituency Influence in Congress.' *The American Political Science Review*, 57(1), 45–56, https://doi. org/10.2307/1952717

Moruno, Olorès M. (2013). 'On Resentment. Introduction. Past and Present of an Emotion.' In *On Resentment. Past and Present.* Cambridge: Cambridge Scholars Publishing, https://archive-ouverte.unige.ch/unige:85227

Nyhuis, D. (2016). 'Electoral effects of candidate valence.' *Electoral Studies*, 42, 33–41, https://doi.org/10.1016/j.electstud.2016.01.007

Raymond, C. D. (2018). 'Electoral Choice and Religion: An Overview.' In C. D. Raymond, *Oxford Research Encyclopedia of Politics.* Oxford: Oxford University Press, https://doi.org/10.1093/acrefore/9780190228637.013.672

Reher, S. (2016). 'The Effects of Congruence in Policy Priorities on Satisfaction with Democracy.' *Journal of Elections, Public Opinion and Parties*, 26(1), 40–57, https://doi.org/10.1080/17457289.2015.1064436

Shor, B., & Rogowski, J. C. (2018). ,Ideology and the US Congressional Vote.' *Political Science Research and Methods*, 6(2), 323–341, https://doi. org/10.1017/psrm.2016.23

Stimson, J. A., Mackuen, M. B., & Erikson, R. S. (1995). 'Dynamic Representation.' *The American Political Science Review*, 89(3), 543–565, https://doi.org/10.2307/2082973

Thomassen, J. (1994). 'Empirical Research into Political Representation: Failing Democracy of Failing Models.' In M. K. Jennings & T. Mann (eds.). *Elections at Home and Abroad: Essays in Honor of Warren E. Miller* (237-265). University of Michigan Press.

Van Der Meer, T. W. G. (2010). 'In what we trust? A multi-level study into trust in parliament as an evaluation of state characteristics.' *International Review of Administrative Sciences*, 76(3), 517–536, https://doi. org/10.1177/0020852310372450

Walgrave, S., Nuytemans, M., & Pepermans, K. (2009). 'Voting Aid Applications and the Effect of Statement Selection.' *West-European Politics*, 32(6), 1161–1180.

Walgrave, S., Van Erkel, P. F. A., Jennart, I., Lefevere, J., & Baudewyns, P. (2020). 'How Issue Salience Pushes Voters to the Left or to the Right.' *Politics of the Low Countries*, 2(3), 320–353, https://doi.org/10.5553/ PLC/258999292020002003005

Appendix 1: Overview of policy proposals

Note: parties that agreed with the statement are indicated using square brackets.

1. Hosting transit migrants must be a punishable offence. [N-VA, Vlaams Belang; PP]

2. Situation tests must be put in place to detect discrimination in employment. [CD&V, Groen, Open VLD, PVDA, sp.a; cdH, Defi, Ecolo, MR, PS, PTB]

3. There must be a test on the European values in order to obtain the Belgian nationality. [CD&V, N-VA, Open VLD, sp.a, Vlaams Belang; cdH, Defi, MR,PP]

4. If the request for asylum of families with children is rejected, these families can be placed in detention pending their repatriation. [CD&V, N-VA, Open VLD, Vlaams Belang; MR, PP]

5. By 2024, the company cars that run with petrol or diesel must be banned. [CD&V, Groen, PVDA, sp.a; cdH, PS, PTB]

6. The VAT on electricity must be reduced from 21 to 6%. [PVDA, sp.a, Vlaams Belang; cdH, Defi, PP, PS, PTB]

7. There must be a tax on plane tickets in order to raise their price. [CD&V, Groen; cdH, Defi, Ecolo, PS]

8. Nuclear power plants must remain operational after 2025. [N-VA, Vlaams Belang; PP]

9. We cannot drive while having drunk alcohol. [PVDA, sp.a; cdH, Defi, Ecolo, MR, PS, PTB]

10. Abortion must be allowed beyond the 12th week of a pregnancy. [Groen, Open VLD, PVDA, sp.a; Defi, Ecolo, PS, PTB]

11. Sperm donation must no longer be anonymous. [CD&V, Groen, N-VA; PP]

12. Great fortunes must be more taxed. [CD&V, Groen, PVDA, sp.a; cdH, Ecolo, MR, PS, PTB]

13. Wages must no longer be automatically indexed. [N-VA]

14. The fingerprints of all citizens must be kept in a central database. [N-VA; cdH]

15. Shops must be able to choose when to do sales. [Open VLd, sp.a; PP]

16. A retirement pension of at least 1500€ per month must be put in place. [CD&V, Groen, Open VLD, PVDA, sp.a, Vlaams Belang; Ecolo, PP, PS, PTB]

17. The government should be composed of an equal number of men and women. [Groen, Open VLD, PVDA, sp.a; Defi, Ecolo, PS, PTB]

18. Important political decisions must be handled by citizens via a referendum. [Groen, Open VLD, PVDA, sp.a, Vlaams Belang; cdH, Defi, Ecolo, PP, PS, PT

Appendix 2: Full model results

Tables 6A.1–6A.8 may be viewed online at
https://doi.org/10.11647/OBP.0401#resources

7. Dissatisfied partisans and the unrepresented: how feeling represented by at least some representatives matters

August De Mulder

Abstract: This chapter sheds new light on citizens' resentment towards politics by looking at what may be part of the problem: citizens may feel unrepresented. Using data from the 2021 Belgian election survey and drawing on an innovative measure of feeling represented, this chapter first examines how well citizens in Belgium feel represented. The results show that, while the majority of citizens feel represented by at least some representatives, more than 1/3 does not feel represented by anyone. Second, I find that not feeling represented by any politician or party goes together with a disengaged political resentment: having low trust, anger, hopelessness and being more likely to abstain. In contrast, citizens who feel unrepresented by most representatives, yet who do feel represented by at least some of them, are associated with a more engaged kind of resentment as they are no longer likely to abstain nor likely to feel hopeless. The results also suggest that populist parties can play a key role by keeping discontented citizens politically engaged. Lastly, I find that feelings of being unrepresented by all politicians and parties are especially prevalent among historically disadvantaged groups, which is additional cause for concern from a political equality perspective.

Introduction

This chapter concentrates on what is arguably one of the underlying causes of political resentment among citizens; many citizens simply do not feel represented by their representatives. Thereby, this chapter shifts focus to an underexposed, yet particularly relevant aspect of the democratic crisis. Whether or not citizens feel represented by their representatives is indicative of how politically legitimate citizens perceive their rule to be (Thomassen and Van Ham, 2017). From an ideal democratic standpoint, where political equality is a key value (Dahl, 2006), we would hope that most (if not all) people feel represented and that differences between societal groups are minimal (Holmberg, 2020). In contrast, when feelings of being unrepresented are prevalent among the citizenry, it threatens democracy's very being: if a majority of citizens no longer feel represented, then 'where is democracy'? (Miller and Listhaug, 1990, p. 385). Using an innovative multidimensional measure of feeling represented, the first question this chapter aims to answer is how well (or how badly) citizens in Belgium feel represented by their political representatives.

Second, this chapter aims to explore how feeling represented is correlated with resentment towards politics. Several studies have linked feelings of (not) being represented to emotions of political resentment (Smith et al., 2012), political trust (Dunn, 2015) and even satisfaction with democracy (Muller, 1970). The mechanism behind this is simple: citizens have certain ideas about what their preferences and interests are, and they have certain perceptions about whether or not their political representatives look after those interests. Logically, we can expect that people who do not feel that their preferences and interests are looked after will have more resentful emotions about—and less trust in—politics, and vice versa. However, in this chapter, I argue that the relationship might be more complex. Specifically, I expect that depending on how well and in what ways citizens feel represented, they will experience different kinds of political resentment.

Third, this chapter also explores how societal inequality impacts citizens' feeling of being represented. Previous studies have found that people who belong to historically underrepresented groups, such as women, low-income citizens, less educated people and young people tend to feel badly represented compared to groups such as men, high-income citizens, better educated or older people (Giger et al., 2009; Holmberg, 2020). However, these studies all approached the feeling of being represented as a dichotomy—you either feel represented or you do not. Taking into account different dimensions of feeling represented, this chapter aims to offer a more nuanced analysis of how well citizens feel represented and how this differs between societal groups.

The results show that going beyond a dichotomous notion of the feeling of being represented can lead to more nuanced insights into the apparent democratic crisis. While the results show that the majority of citizens feel represented in some way by at least some representatives, more than one third of Belgian citizens do not feel represented by anyone. Furthermore, the results show that these citizens who do not feel represented by any representatives experience what can be described as a 'disengaged' resentment, involving low political trust, emotions of anger and hopelessness and a greater likelihood of abstention. In contrast, when citizens do feel represented by at least some representatives (whilst feeling badly represented by most of them), they are no longer likely to abstain nor likely to feel hopeless. In other words, these citizens generally have experience a more engaged kind of political resentment (see also, Capelos and Demertzis, 2018). Interestingly, these citizens are also more likely to vote for populist parties, which suggests that these parties can play a role by keeping dissatisfied citizens engaged. A comparison between Wallonia (where no populist radical right party is active) and Flanders also supports this finding. Lastly, this chapter shows that feeling unrepresented by all representatives (and the associated disengaging resentment) is especially prevalent among historically disadvantaged groups, which is an additional cause for concern from a political equality perspective (Dahl, 2006).

Using data from the 2021 RepResent Belgian election study, I combine different methodological approaches. First, I identify different subgroups of citizens by identifying how well or badly they feel represented, using Latent Profile Analysis (LPA). The next steps build upon these latent profiles. First, I explore how the profiles are associated with different kinds of political resentment by performing bivariate correlations with emotions of resentment, political trust and voting preference. Lastly, I perform multinomial regressions in order to examine whether certain socio-demographic traits are associated with some of the profiles.

Capturing various dimensions of feeling represented

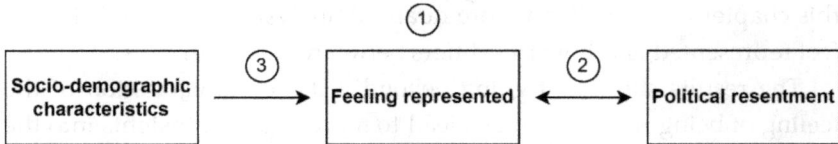

Fig. 7.1 Theoretical framework.

This chapter has three main research aims (see Figure 7.1). The first aim of this chapter is to explore how well citizens in Belgium feel represented by their representatives, using a multidimensional measure of feeling represented. Although most empirical accounts on representation generally examine whether or not people *are* represented (Minta, 2009; Vega and Firestone, 1995, Peress, 2013; Stimson et al., 1995), some studies have recently started to look at whether or not citizens *feel* represented as well. Specifically, since 2001, the Comparative Study of Electoral Systems (CSES) included a yes-or-no-question to measure whether or not citizens feel that a party 'represents their views reasonably well' and this question has since been adopted by several other studies (e.g., Blais et al., 2014; Dunn, 2015; Giger et al., 2009; Holmberg, 2020). Among other things, these studies provide meaningful insight in the number of citizens that feel represented across countries (Holmberg, 2020), how this differs between societal groups (Giger et al., 2009; Holmberg, 2020) and how it relates to other variables such as the intention to vote (Blais et al., 2014), being substantively represented (Giger et al., 2009) and political trust (Dunn, 2015).

One downside to the measures used in these studies, however, is that they reduce feeling represented to a yes-or-no-question: you either feel represented or you do not. By taking this approach, we lose a lot of information about how well people feel represented, which might obscure some of the differences that exist between groups in society. Recent studies have demonstrated that citizens can feel well represented in some respects while feeling badly represented in others (see De Mulder, 2022 or Lavi et al., 2021, for more elaborate discussions on the multidimensionality of feeling represented). In this chapter, I therefore take into account in what way (the representative behaviour), by whom (the representative actor) and how well (the intensity) citizens feel represented by their political representatives.

First, representative behaviour refers to the kind of substantive representation that citizens may perceive. As Pitkin (1967) explains, substantive representation involves 'acting in the interests of the represented, in a manner responsive to them' (p. 209). Yet, some citizens might feel that representatives are responsive in the sense that they are listening to them or know what they need, but at the same time believe that they are not really acting in response to their views and interests (Esaiasson et al., 2015). Similarly, some people might feel that representatives do listen, know and act, but at the same time feel unrepresented in the sense that they are perceived to be unsuccessful in translating these views into policy (De Mulder, 2022). For instance, this is something that might differentiate people who vote for a party that is elected into government (governmental winners) from people who support a party that is not (governmental losers) (Singh et al., 2012). This chapter therefore takes into account whether or not citizens feel represented on these four distinct aspects of representation (listen vs. know vs. act vs. succeed).

Second, as citizens can be represented by a variety of political actors within the political system, their perceptions of how well they are represented will probably depend on who the representative actor in question is (Lavi et al., 2021). As Norris (1999) points out, citizens' feeling of being represented may differ depending on whether we are thinking about most representatives, or only about some representatives. For instance, it is consistent for citizens 'to disparage most politicians but to continue to support a particular leader' (Norris, 1999, pp. 7–8). Some fervid partisans or voters of populist parties might, for example, feel very well represented by some particular representatives, while at the same time being very dissatisfied about representation by politicians and parties more generally. This chapter differentiates between whether citizens feel represented by most, some or no representatives.

Third, I also take into account the intensity of one's feeling of being represented. Research has shown that attitude extremity, which relates to how much an object is liked or disliked, has important consequences for human behaviour (Bergman, 1998). Likewise, we can imagine that there may be differences in how strongly one feels (un)represented and that these differences might be relevant for explaining one's political behaviour (e.g., political participation, voting preference etc.). For instance, someone who feels completely neglected by his or her representatives might be a lot less likely to participate politically than someone who feels only slightly unrepresented.

By combining these three dimensions—the representative behaviour, the representative actor, and the intensity—this chapter aims to identify more nuanced types or 'profiles' of feeling represented, going beyond a dichotomous classification.

Feeling represented and (dis)engaging resentment

After having identified different subgroups of people in terms of feeling represented, the second aim of this paper is to explore how feeling represented (in a certain way) relates to political resentment (see point 2 in Figure 7.1). Previous studies have found that not feeling represented by any representatives is generally associated with negative attitudes towards politics (e.g., Dunn, 2015; Muller, 1970; Smith et al., 2012). This is not a very surprising finding. That is, citizens have certain policy views and certain ideas about what their interests are, and they have perceptions about whether or not politicians and parties properly represent these views and interests (Holmberg, 2020). Such cognitive perceptions about how well one is represented, although not always grounded on correct information or knowledge (Giger et al., 2009), can be a driver of other, more general attitudes towards politics such as political resentment. In turn, citizens' resentment towards politics might also affect how well or badly they perceive themselves to be represented, resulting in a kind of circular relationship (hence the arrow in Figure 7.1 runs both ways).

In this chapter, I theorize that the relationship is more complex. As Chapter 4 demonstrates, citizens may experience different 'clusters' of emotions, simultaneously combining emotions such as 'hope' and 'anger' in diverse ways. People who are very angry when thinking about politics can, for example, still be hopeful that politics may ultimately solve their problems. In this chapter, I expect that depending on whether citizens feel represented by no, some or most representatives, citizens will also have different 'clusters' of emotions of hope and anger, different levels of political trust and a different propensity to vote.

Specifically, citizens who feel represented by no representatives at all probably have negative attitudes and emotions about politics overall. As Dunn (2015) previously showed, citizens who do not feel represented by any party generally have lower political trust. Similarly, we can expect that these citizens experience anger when thinking about politics, with little hope of change to come (see also Capelos and Demertzis, 2018; Celis et al., 2021). Furthermore, in line with Blais et al. (2014), I expect that these citizens will also be less likely to vote compared to other citizens. Not feeling politically represented by anyone, in this sense, is expected to be associated with a disengaged kind of resentment, which is characterized by political passivity (i.e., vote abstention), less political trust and largely negative emotions towards politics (i.e., anger and hopelessness) (see also Capelos and Demertzis, 2018).

> H1: Citizens who feel represented by no representatives are more likely to have a disengaging kind of political resentment.

Arguably less problematic are the citizens who do feel represented by some politicians or parties, for which they can vote and who might win in future elections, even when these feelings coincide with the belief that most representatives are not representing them properly. While these people might reasonably experience emotions of anger when thinking about politics, and generally have low trust in political actors and institutions (after all, they perceive themselves to be poorly represented by most of their representatives), they might still be hopeful that tides will turn if the right representatives gain power (Celis et al., 2021). These citizens are unlikely to 'exit' the system, as they can 'voice' their discontent and frustration by voting for the political representative they do like (Hirschman, 1970). These citizens are more likely to experience an engaged kind of resentment, a moral indignation (Capelos and Demertzis, 2018), that may be channelled in a political manner by voting for the representatives by which one does feel represented e.g., a populist politician or party (Havlík and Voda, 2018). In this regard, it has been suggested that populist parties can be 'good' for the long-term stability of a political system as they allow dissatisfied citizens to voice their discontent via the system (Hooghe et al., 2011). In this chapter, I will also explore whether populist parties can indeed help to keep (some) dissatisfied citizens engaged. In sum, I expect citizens who do feel represented by some representatives, but not by most, to experience an engaged kind of political resentment, characterized by less political trust and more anger compared to other citizens, yet similar levels of hope and being unlikely to abstain.

> H2: Citizens who feel represented by some, but not by most, are more likely to have an engaged kind of political resentment.

Lastly, citizens who feel well-represented by most politicians and parties will probably have positive attitudes and emotions about politics overall, and are likely to engage in the political system. In other words, these citizens are unlikely to be resentful towards politics.

> H3: Citizens who feel represented by most representatives are unlikely to be resentful towards politics.

Feeling represented and societal inequality

Lastly, taking into account the different dimensions of feeling represented, the third aim of this chapter is to explore which factors explain variation in feeling represented among citizens. Particularly, I examine how societal inequality may play a role (see point 3 in Figure 7.1). From an ideal democratic standpoint, we would desire that most (if not all) citizens feel well represented by their political representatives (Holmberg, 2020). Obviously, this is quite a demanding scenario—not least because studies have often demonstrated that many citizens are simply not always well represented (Bernauer et al., 2015). Although people's perception of being represented might not always correspond with reality (Holmberg, 2020), we would think that people who are badly represented will generally also feel so, and vice versa. Specifically, we would expect that citizens who belong to societal groups that have been found to be substantively underrepresented—such as women (Wängnerud and Sundell, 2012), citizens with lower income levels (Bernauer et al., 2015), the less well educated (Lesschaeve, 2016) and younger age groups (Tsabari et al., 2005)—will more often feel badly represented compared to citizens in more privileged positions. If these citizens are also less likely to vote, as Blais et al. (2014) have found, this is concerning from a democratic equality perspective (Dahl, 2006).

Giger et al. (2009) find that across 23 countries, citizens who are less well educated, have a lower income, young people and women are indeed less likely than average to feel represented by a party. Similarly, while Holmberg (2020) finds that in a clear majority of the 46 examined countries (70%) more than half of its citizens feel represented by at least one party, his results also point to some societal inequality. In most countries, historically 'privileged' groups such as men, older people, the university educated and the middle class more often tend to feel represented than women, younger people, less well educated people and the working class. I expect to find similar results.

> H4: Men, higher-income citizens, more highly educated and older age groups feel better represented than women, lower-income citizens, less well educated and younger age groups.

Methods

I made use of survey data collected in October/November 2021 among Belgian citizens. A representative sample of Belgian citizens (based on age, gender and level of education) was surveyed online (for more information about this, see Chapter 2). After removing 'straight-liners', the dataset included 1825 respondents.

The Belgian context provides a good case to analyse the three research questions. First, based on Holmberg's (2020) comparative study, we know that Belgium is comparable to most other western European countries in terms of the share of people that feel represented by at least one party. Second, Belgium has strong populist parties (a national left-wing and Flemish regional right-wing party) gaining rising support based on the most recent 2019 election results (Pilet, 2021). This rising electoral support for populist parties points to rising political discontent among large portions of the population, making Belgium a particularly relevant case to study citizens' feeling of being represented. Lastly, the Belgian case is somewhat unique as it allows us to compare two quasi-autonomous party systems. With the exception of the national radical left party PvdA-PTB, citizens in Flanders can only vote for exclusively Flemish parties, and voters in Wallonia can only vote for exclusively

Walloon parties (De Winter et al., 2006). As Wallonia does not have a populist radical right party, this allows us to test whether discontented voters in Wallonia are more likely to 'exit' the system compared to voters in Flanders as they have less opportunity to express their discontent by voting for a populist radical right party (Hirschman, 1970; Hooghe et al., 2011).

The survey contained a number of relevant variables for the analyses I conducted. First and foremost, I designed a 16-item measuring instrument (see Appendix 1) to capture the extent to which citizens feel represented (for more information on the measure and its validity, see De Mulder, 2022). The intensity of these feelings was measured on a five-point Likert-type scale ranging from 1 = strongly disagree to 5 = strongly agree. Furthermore, these items varied with regards to the representative behaviour (listen vs. know vs. act vs. succeed) and the representative actor (some vs most), with every item having a positively and negatively phrased equivalent. By taking into account the intensity, the representative behaviour and the representative actor, the measure allows us to perform a nuanced examination of the extent to which citizens feel represented, going beyond a simplistic dichotomy.

The survey also included questions regarding respondents' socio-demographic traits (gender, age, education, income satisfaction, region) and political preferences (voting preference). Furthermore, I calculated respondents' political trust based on four questions about trust in, respectively, political parties, the federal parliament, politicians and the federal government (Cronbach's alpha = .955). Lastly, the survey contained a large battery of questions to measure citizens' political resentment (for more information, see Chapter 2). The question on anger ('If I think about politics, I get angry') and hope ('I believe politics is capable of solving the problems that people have') are used in this chapter to analyse the complex cluster of emotions people may experience when thinking about politics.

Building on this dataset, analyses were run in three steps. The first goal of this chapter was to identify subgroups of citizens in terms of how well or badly they feel represented. Therefore, Latent Profile Analysis (LPA) was used. Thereafter, I explore the relation of the 'types' with political resentment. Specifically, I performed bivariate correlations of the profiles with voting preference (intention to abstain, to vote radical or to vote moderate), emotions of anger and hope and political trust. Lastly, I performed multinomial regressions in order to examine whether certain socio-demographic traits explain membership of the profiles.

Results

Can we find different profiles in terms of feeling represented?

In this section, I make use of a Latent Profile Analysis (LPA) to identify latent subgroups (profiles) of respondents based on how well they feel represented. The idea behind LPA is that respondents fall, with varying degrees of probability, into one of a finite number of discrete classes, and that the classes differ with regard to the values of the indicators (Pilet et al., 2020). As I mentioned, the survey included 16 items, with each item having a positively and negatively phrased equivalent. Together, the questions thus tapped into eight distinct aspects of feeling represented—that is, the feeling that some representatives 1) listen, 2) know, 3) act, 4) succeed, and the feeling that most representatives 5) listen, 6) know, 7) act, 8) succeed. Instead of using the single items to input into the LPA, I use the mean scores of the eight aspects, which showed acceptable internal consistency (Cronbach's alpha above .66). Although using single items may lead to more detailed descriptions in terms of subgroups, the mean score approach is preferable to avoid overly detailed subgroups and higher complexity (Nielsen et al., 2016).

To determine the number of profiles to be extracted, I ran multiple models going from one to ten profiles extracted and then compared them in terms of goodness-of-fit statistics. Specifically, a model is considered to have the best fit when the Bayesian Information Criterion (BIC) is at its smallest value (Nylund et al., 2007). However, as is not uncommon (Pilet et al., 2020), in our data the BIC keeps decreasing the more latent profiles are extracted. In such cases, one should explore when the marginal gains in BIC becomes less significant. In this respect, a five-profile model is the best solution as the BIC only marginally diminishes going from five to six extracted profiles (see Table 7A.2, Appendix 2).

Figure 7.2 reports the value of the eight aspects of feeling represented for the five identified profiles. To interpret the profiles, I pay attention to two elements. First, I examine differences between profiles in their score on the different aspects of feeling represented. More concretely, I look at whether certain profiles have significantly higher or lower scores on certain aspects of feeling represented than other profiles. Second, I compare the scores on the different aspects of feeling represented within each profile, for example, if a group feels significantly better represented on one aspect (e.g., feeling represented by some) than it does on another (e.g., feeling represented by most). In Appendix 2, I provide an overview of the values on the eight aspects of feeling represented for the five latent profiles with 95th percent confidence intervals. As the original items were measured on scales from 1 to 5, and negatively phrased items were recoded prior to creating the mean scores, low scores reflect feeling badly represented and high scores reflect feeling well represented, with 3 as the neutral score.

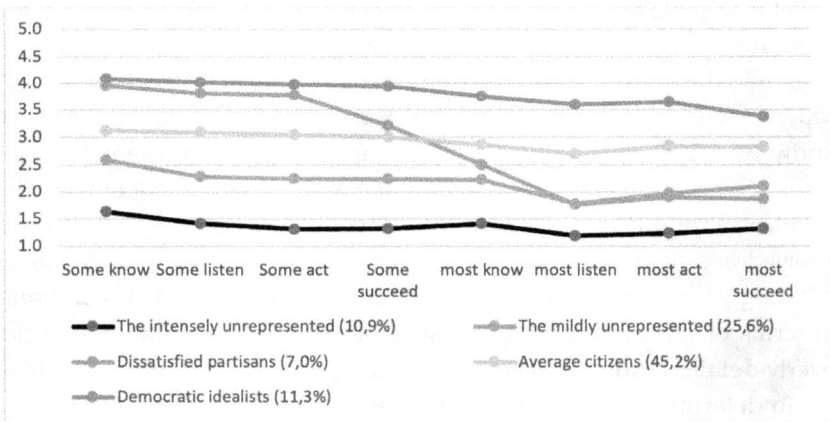

Fig. 7.2 Latent Profile Analysis with five extracted profiles.

I interpret the five profiles as follows. First, there is the largest profile (45.2% of the sample) which is composed of citizens who scored just above the neutral option of 3 for the aspects about feeling represented by some, and just below 3 for representation by most. These voters thus have very neutral scores about the extent to which they are represented, feeling slightly positive about representation by some representatives, and slightly negative about representation by most representatives. With almost half of the sample belonging to this neutral group, the profile could be regarded as representing the average citizen.

The second profile (11.3% of the sample) consists of citizens who feel very well-represented by some representatives (around 4 on a scale of 1–5), whilst also being quite content about representation by most representatives (clearly above 3). I refer to these citizens as democratic idealists, as these citizens have very 'ideal' perceptions of how their representative democracy works in practice: they believe that most politicians and parties represent their interests.

While respondents in the third profile (7.0% of the sample) also have very high scores on the feeling of being represented by some (also approaching 4), they score very low on feeling represented by most (between 1.7 and 2.5). Furthermore, while these respondents feel very well represented by at least some representatives in terms of listening, knowing and acting, they indicate that they are less satisfied with the extent to which these representatives also successfully weigh in on policy (predicted score of 3.2). This result makes sense as, in contrast to the first three aspects of feeling represented, whether or not a representative succeeds in having an impact on policy is not entirely in control of the representative in question, but depends to a large part on external factors, such as election results and whether other representatives are willing to cooperate. I refer to respondents in this group as dissatisfied partisans, as these people feel very well-represented by some representatives but are dissatisfied about representation by most.

The fourth profile (10.9% of the sample) is composed of respondents who have very low scores (below a score of 1.7) on all aspects of feeling represented. I refer to them as the intensely unrepresented, as citizens belonging to this type perceive that there are no representatives that represent them in any way: they intensely believe that all representatives do not listen, do not know their interests, do not act in their interests and do not succeed in translating their interests into policy. They feel completely neglected. Lastly, the respondents in the fifth profile (25.6% of the sample) also score quite low on all aspects of feeling represented, yet not as low as the intensely unrepresented, with scores between 1.7 and 2.6. In other words, while these people also feel badly represented by all representatives, these feelings are significantly less intense. I refer to them as the mildly unrepresented.

My first conclusion from the five profiles is that they illustrate that citizens who feel well represented in one respect can feel very badly represented in another, and vice-versa. Such differences between groups in terms of feeling represented are obscured by previous dichotomous approaches to feeling represented. Specifically, citizens belonging to the average citizen profile, the democratic idealists and the dissatisfied partisans all feel represented by some representatives. Yet, these profiles differ significantly with regards to other aspects of feeling represented. As the analyses in the next section will demonstrate, these differences are crucial for understanding variation in citizens' political resentment.

Second, the profiles echo Holmberg's (2020) finding that the majority of citizens do feel represented by at least some representatives. However, overall, they do not paint a very optimistic picture. Specifically, two profiles do not feel represented by any representatives: the intensely and mildly unrepresented, together comprising 36.5% of the sample. In other words, more than one third of Belgian citizens do not feel represented by anyone. Furthermore, while the three other profiles, the dissatisfied partisans, the average citizens and the democratic idealists, or 63.5% of the sample, do feel that at least one politician or party represents them reasonably well, this should come with some nuance. Only the democratic idealists (11.3%) and the dissatisfied partisans (7%) clearly indicate that they feel well represented by at least some representatives, with scores well beyond the neutral score of 3. For the average citizen (45.2% of the sample), the scores reflect a neutral or rather unconvinced feeling of being represented.

How do the profiles relate to political resentment?

The second aim of this chapter is to explore how feeling represented in a certain way relates to political resentment. My first expectation (H1) was that feeling unrepresented by all representatives (i.e., the intensely and mildly unrepresented) would go hand in hand with a disengaged kind of political resentment. The results of bivariate correlations (see Table 7.1) show that citizens who belong to the intensely and mildly unrepresented groups indeed experience significantly more anger, less hope, less political trust and are more likely to abstain from voting.[1] In other words, citizens who feel represented by no representatives at all

---

1   In the Belgian context of compulsory voting, I consider voting blank and
     abstaining as equivalent.

tend to be characterized by a disengaged kind of political resentment, confirming Hypothesis 1.

Table 7.1 Correlations between the five latent profiles and resentment, trust, vote and abstention.

	Intensely unrepresented	Mildly unrepresented	Dissatisfied partisans	Average citizen	Democratic idealists
Anger	,274***	,177***	,087**	-,162**	-,329**
Hope	-,274**	-,183**	-,007 (ns)	,190**	,230**
Trust	-,370***	-,260***	-,105***	,271***	,381***
Moderate vote	-,133***	-,098***	-040 (ns)	,074**	,182***
Populist vote	,006 (ns)	,064**	,158***	-,072**	-,108***
Abstain	,137***	,070**	-,081***	-,052*	-,083***

Note: *** sig. at < .001 level, ** sig. at .01 level, * sig. at 0.05 level, ns = non-significant.

Furthermore, I hypothesized that citizens who feel badly represented by most, but who do feel well represented by some (i.e., dissatisfied partisans), would be associated with an engaged kind of political resentment, characterized by more anger and less political trust compared to other citizens, yet experiencing similar levels of hope as well as being unlikely to abstain (H2). Confirming the hypothesis, bivariate correlations show that belonging to the dissatisfied partisans is indeed associated with more anger and low trust in politics, while it does not significantly correlate with hope and is negatively correlated with abstention (see Table 7.1). Note, however, that these citizens are less hopeful compared to the 'average citizen' profile, which does correlate significantly and positively with hope.

Interestingly, the results also show that being a dissatisfied partisan is strongly correlated with the intention to vote for a populist party, while the mildly and intensely unrepresented respectively have a weaker and non-significant correlation with populist voting. These results give an initial indication that populist parties may play a 'positive' role in the political system by making some citizens feel well represented, thereby keeping them engaged in the political system (Havlík and Voda, 2018).

In the next section, I further explore this finding by comparing Wallonia (a region with no populist radical right party) with Flanders.

Lastly, citizens who feel well represented by most politicians and parties (i.e., democratic idealists) tend to have very little (if any) resentment towards politics. These democratic idealists show strong negative correlations with anger and abstention (instead, they tend to vote for moderate parties), and strong positive correlations with political trust and hope (confirming H3). While these citizens are very similar to the dissatisfied partisans in terms of some dimensions of feeling represented (they both feel very well-represented by some representatives in terms of listening, knowing and acting, see Figure 7.2), their differences in terms of other aspects of feeling represented leads them to have very different relationship with political resentment. This underpins the reasons why we need to go beyond dichotomously classifying citizens as either feeling represented or not.

Who belongs to the profiles?

Having identified these different profiles in terms of how well citizens feel represented and exploring how these profiles relate to political resentment, I analyse how the profiles differ with regards to their socio-demographic characteristics. Specifically, I examine whether the results point to societal inequality as a factor in feeling represented, as the results of previous studies indicate (e.g., Giger et al, 2009; Holmberg, 2020). To test this, I ran a multinomial logistic regression to see whether individual-level characteristics predict the likelihood of belonging to one of the profiles. The predictor variables include: level of education, income satisfaction, gender, being a student, being a pensioner and region of residence.

Table 7.2 presents the results of the model. As the 'average citizen profile' is the reference category, the model shows the effect of each independent variable on belonging to one latent profile, rather than to the 'average citizen'. The Relative Risk Ratio (RRR) is presented instead of the raw coefficients to facilitate interpretation. A relative risk ratio higher than 1 means that one unit increase in the independent variable increases the likelihood of belonging to that latent profile, instead of to the average citizen profile, by the value of the RRR. Conversely, a RRR smaller than one indicates that one unit increase in the independent variable decreases the probability of belonging to the latent profile in question.

Table 7.2 Multinomial logistic regression of latent profiles by socio-demographics and political interest and region (ref. 'average citizen profile').

	Intensely unrepresented	Mildly unrepresented	Dissatisfied partisans	Democratic idealists
Relative risk ratio (RRR) coefficient with standard errors in parenthesis				
Education (low to high)	0.957 (0.087)	0.982 (0.62)	0.977 (0.099)	**1.474*** (0.085)**
Income satisfaction	**0.788*** (0.035)**	**0.831*** (0.027)**	**0.862*** (0.043)**	**1.266*** (0.049)**
man (=1)	0.893 (0.168)	**0.763* (0.123)**	0.996 (0.198)	0.799 (0.167)
Student (=1)	**0.171** (0.605)**	**0.409** (0.302)**	0.453 (0.535)	1.478 (0.298)
Pensioner (=1)	1.076 (0.179)	1.270 (0.133)	1.373 (0.207)	**1.918*** (0.179)**
Flanders (=1)	**0.676* (0.170)**	1.092 (0.121)	**2.607*** (0.210)**	1.274 (0.164)

Note: Bold values highlight significant effects, *** sig. at < .001 level, ** sig. at .01 level, * sig. at .05 level.

I hypothesized that citizens who belong to historically disadvantaged groups would generally feel more badly represented than more privileged groups (H4). For most variables, this was confirmed. Specifically, in line with my expectations, I found that citizens who are more satisfied with their income are less likely to belong to a profile that feels badly represented by most representatives (i.e., the intensely unrepresented, the mildly unrepresented or dissatisfied partisans) and more likely to belong to a profile that does (i.e., democratic idealists). Similarly, I found that people who are better educated are more likely to belong to the democratic idealists, while men are less likely than women to belong to the mildly unrepresented. With regards to age, however, the findings are mixed. Specifically, while I found that older age groups (pensioners) are more likely to belong to the democratic idealists, the results also indicate that younger age groups (students) are unlikely to belong to the intensely or mildly unrepresented. Descriptive statistics reveal that feelings of not being represented are actually most prevalent among citizens of middle age—particularly around the age of 50. If we disregard age, I conclude that the results indicate that historically disadvantaged groups tend to feel more badly represented compared to more privileged citizens.

Lastly, region of residence (Flanders or Wallonia) was also included as a predictor variable, in order to further test whether populist parties could play a 'positive' role in the political system by providing the opportunity for dissatisfied citizens to voice their discontent, thereby keeping them politically engaged. As Wallonia uniquely does not have a populist radical right party, while Flanders does (both regions have the same radical left party, PVDA-PTB), it provides an interesting case to examine whether the presence of a populist radical right party increases the likelihood of feeling represented by at least some representatives (i.e., dissatisfied partisans) and therefore of voting, and decreases the likelihood of feeling represented by no one (i.e., the mildly and intensely unrepresented). The results suggest that this is the case. Specifically, controlling for other socio-demographic variables, the results show that citizens in Flanders are significantly less likely to belong to the intensely unrepresented (which is highly correlated with abstention) and instead are more likely to belong to the dissatisfied partisans (which is highly correlated with voting populist). An additional Chi-Square test also shows that citizens in Flanders are significantly less likely to abstain from voting compared to citizens in Wallonia, X^2 (1, N =1825) = 29,362 p < .001. In other words, the presence of a populist radical right party appears to increase the likelihood that citizens feel represented by at least one politician or party (and thus belong to the dissatisfied democrats) thereby keeping (some) dissatisfied citizens from abstaining.

Conclusion

This chapter aimed to shed new light on the apparent 'crisis of representative democracy' by looking at a somewhat neglected aspect: that citizens may not feel adequately represented. Specifically, this chapter examines 1) how well (or badly) citizens in Belgium feel represented, 2) how the feeling of being represented relates to political resentment and 3) whether there are differences between societal groups. Overall, the results indicate that feeling represented by at least some political representatives matters a lot, not only from a legitimacy standpoint, but also for the functioning of representative democracy.

Specifically, using data from the 2021 RepResent election survey among Belgian citizens and drawing on an innovative multidimensional measure of feeling represented, I undertook a latent profile analysis (LPA) and identified five types of citizens. While I found that the majority (63.5%) of citizens feel represented by at least some representatives, the results do not warrant much optimism. Specifically, the largest group of citizens (45.2%), which I called the average citizen, feel only slightly positive about representation by some representatives, whilst having slightly negative perceptions about representation by most. Only a small portion of Belgian citizens clearly indicate that they feel well represented: the democratic idealists (10.3%), who feel well represented by most representatives, and the dissatisfied partisans (7.0%), who feel well represented by only some of them. Most problematic is that one third of Belgian citizens do not feel represented by anyone. This is the case for the intensely and mildly unrepresented, who have negative perceptions about the extent to which they are represented by all of their political representatives. From a legitimacy standpoint, the prevalence of these feelings of being unrepresented is in itself concerning.

In addition, I found that not feeling represented by any politician or party (i.e., the mildly and intensely unrepresented) goes together with a disengaged political resentment: having low trust, anger, hopelessness and being more likely to abstain. Also, in line with previous studies, the results show that these feelings of being unrepresented are especially prevalent among historically disadvantaged groups. Considering that feeling unrepresented goes hand in hand with a disengaged form of resentment, this is not a welcomed finding from a democratic equality standpoint: historically disadvantaged citizens are more likely to feel unrepresented, and are consequently more likely to 'exit' the political system entirely (i.e., to no longer vote).

In contrast, citizens who do feel represented by at least some representatives (i.e., dissatisfied partisans) are associated with a more engaged kind of resentment, as they are unlikely to abstain nor likely to feel hopeless. Instead, these citizens are more likely to vote for a populist party. An additional analysis comparing Wallonia and Flanders suggests that populist parties can play a 'positive' role in the political system by keeping dissatisfied citizens politically engaged. Although populist parties can negatively influence citizens' political attitudes and engagement with their rhetoric (Hameleers et al., 2018), their presence in the political system does allow some dissatisfied citizens to voice their discontent in a political manner by voting for the party or politician they like (Capelos and Demertzis, 2018; Havlík and Voda, 2018; Hirschman, 1970).

This chapter has some limitations. First, the chapter does not provide evidence for a causal link between feeling represented on the one hand and political resentment on the other, but merely demonstrates an association. Experimental research could help to disentangle the relationship between these variables further. Second, although Holmberg's (2020) study shows that the number of citizens in Belgium that feel represented is comparable to other western European countries, the analyses would benefit from a comparative approach that would enable more generalizable claims about the apparent democratic crisis. Examining survey data over different points in time would also strengthen the generalizability of the chapter.

Nevertheless, the chapter does bring forward a number of findings that help us to better understand the so-called crisis of representation. The chapter highlights that feeling represented by at least some representatives matters a lot, not only from a normative point of view, but also for the functioning of representative democracy. Specifically, citizens who feel represented by at least some representatives generally do not feel hopeless, and thereby stay engaged and politically active. Further, as in Chapter 4—which demonstrates that citizens may show different 'clusters' of emotions beyond a simplistic binary distinction between 'positive' and 'negative' emotions—this chapter indicates that feeling represented is also not a dichotomous matter of yes or no. Citizens may feel well represented in some respects while feeling badly represented in others, and can do so with varying intensities. Most importantly, this chapter shows that a multidimensional approach to studying citizens' feeling of being represented helps us to better understand negative attitudes and emotions about politics and may even predict and explain (unwelcome) political behaviour, such as abstaining from voting.

References

Bergman, M. M. (1998). 'A theoretical note on the differences between attitudes, opinions, and values.' *Swiss Political Science Review*, 4(2), 81–93, https://doi.org/10.1002/j.1662-6370.1998.tb00239.x

Bernauer, J., Giger, N., and Rosset, J. (2015). ,Mind the gap: Do proportional electoral systems foster a more equal representation of women and men, poor and rich?' *International Political Science Review*, 36(1), 78–98, https://doi.org/10.1177/0192512113498830

Blais, A., Singh, S., and Dumitrescu, D. (2014). 'Political institutions, perceptions of representation, and the turnout decision.' In J. Thomassen (ed.). *Elections and Representative Democracy: Representation and Accountability* (pp. 99–112). Oxford: Oxford University Press, https://doi.org/10.1093/acprof:oso/9780198716334.003.0006

Capelos, T., and Demertzis, N. (2018). 'Political action and resentful affectivity in critical times.' *Humanity and Society*, 42(4), 410–433, https://doi.org/10.1177/0160597618802517

Celis, K., Knops, L., Van Ingelgom, V., and Verhaegen, S. (2021). 'Resentment and coping with the democratic dilemma.' *Politics and Governance*, 9(3), 237–247, https://doi.org/10.17645/pag.v9i3.4026

Dahl, R. A. (2006). *On Political Equality*. New Haven: Yale University Press.

De Mulder, A. (2022). 'Making Sense of Citizens' Sense of Being Represented. A Novel Conceptualisation and Measure of Feeling Represented.' *Representation*, 1–25.

De Winter, L., Swyngedouw, M., and Dumont, P. (2006). 'Party system (s) and electoral behaviour in Belgium: From stability to balkanisation.' *West European Politics*, 29(5), 933–956, https://doi.org/10.1080/01402380600968836

Dunn, K. (2015). 'Voice, representation and trust in parliament.' *Acta Politica*, 50(2), 171–192, https://doi.org/10.1057/ap.2014.15

Esaiasson, P., Kölln, A. K., and Turper, S. (2015). 'External efficacy and perceived responsiveness—Similar but distinct concepts.' *International Journal of Public Opinion Research*, 27(3), 432–445, https://doi.org/10.1093/ijpor/edv003

Giger, N., Kissau, K., Lutz, G., and Rosset, J. (2009). 'Explaining the variance of subjective and substantive representation.' In *ECPR General Conference 2009*. Potsdam, Germany.

Hameleers, M., Bos, L., Fawzi, N., Reinemann, C., Andreadis, I., Corbu, N., & Weiss-Yaniv, N. (2018). 'Start spreading the news: A comparative experiment on the effects of populist communication on political engagement in sixteen European countries.' *The International Journal of Press/Politics*, 23(4), 517–538.

Havlík, V., and Voda, P. (2018). 'Cleavages, protest or voting for hope? The rise of centrist populist parties in the Czech Republic.' *Swiss Political Science Review*, 24(2), 161–186, http://dx.doi.org/10.1111/spsr.12299

Hirschman, A. O. (1970). *Exit, Voice, and Loyalty: Responses to Decline in Firms, Organizations, and States* (Vol. 25). Cambridge, MA: Harvard University Press.

Holmberg, S. (2020). 'Feeling Represented.' In R. Rohrschneider and J. Thomassen (eds.). *The Oxford Handbook of Political Representation in Liberal Democracies* (pp. 413–434). Oxford: Oxford University Press.

Hooghe, M., Marien, S., & Pauwels, T. (2011). 'Where Do Distrusting Voters Turn if There is No Viable Exit or Voice Option? The Impact of Political Trust on Electoral Behaviour in the Belgian Regional Elections of June 2001.' *Government and Opposition*, 46(2), 245–273.

Lavi, L., Treger, C., Rivlin, N., Sheafer, T., Waismel-Manor, I., Shenhav, S., Harsgor, L., and Shamir, M. (2021). *The Pitkinian Public: Representation in the Eyes of Citizens.* Available at SSRN: https://ssrn.com/abstract=3835506

Lesschaeve, C. (2016). 'Naar een voorwaardelijk model van ongelijkheid in vertegenwoordiging: Een onderzoek naar het moderatie-effect van beleidsdomeinen op ongelijkheid in beleidscongruentie.' *Res Publica*, 58(1), 59–80.

Miller, A. H., and Listhaug, O. (1990). 'Political parties and confidence in government: A comparison of Norway, Sweden and the United States.' *British Journal of Political Science*, 20(3), 357–386, https://doi.org/10.1017/S0007123400005883

Minta, M. D. (2009). 'Legislative oversight and the substantive representation of Black and Latino interests in Congress.' *Legislative Studies Quarterly*, 34(2), 193–218, https://doi.org/10.3162/036298009788314336

Muller, E. N. (1970). 'The representation of citizens by political authorities: Consequences for regime support.' *American Political Science Review*, 64(4), 1149–1166, https://doi.org/10.2307/1958363

Nielsen, A. M., Vach, W., Kent, P., Hestbaek, L., and Kongsted, A. (2016). 'Using existing questionnaires in latent class analysis: should we use summary scores or single items as input? A methodological study using a cohort of patients with low back pain.' *Clinical Epidemiology*, 8, 73, https://doi.org/10.2147/CLEP.S103330

Norris, P. (1999). 'Introduction: The growth of critical citizens?' In P. Norris (ed.). *Critical Citizens: Global Support for Democratic Government* (pp. 1–30). Oxford: Oxford University Press, https://doi.org/10.1093/0198295685.001.0001

Nylund, K. L., Asparouhov, T., and Muthén, B. O. (2007). 'Deciding on the number of classes in latent class analysis and growth mixture modeling: A Monte Carlo simulation study.' *Structural Equation Modeling: A Multidisciplinary Journal*, 14(4), 535–569, https://doi.org/10.1080/10705510701575396

Peress, M. (2013). 'Candidate positioning and responsiveness to constituent opinion in the US House of Representatives.' *Public Choice*, 156(1-2), 77–94, https://doi.org/10.1007/s11127-012-0032-z

Pilet, J. B. (2021). 'Hard times for governing parties: the 2019 federal elections in Belgium.' *West European Politics*, 44(2), 439–449, https://doi.org/10.1080/01402382.2020.1750834

Pilet, J. B., Talukder, D., Sanhueza, M. J., and Rangoni, S. (2020). 'Do citizens perceive elected politicians, experts and citizens as alternative or complementary policy-makers? A study of Belgian citizens.' *Frontiers in Political Science*, 2, 10, https://doi.org/10.3389/fpos.2020.567297

Pitkin, H. F. (1967). *The Concept of Representation*. Berkeley: University of California Press.

Singh, S., Karakoç, E., and Blais, A. (2012). 'Differentiating winners: How elections affect satisfaction with democracy.' *Electoral Studies*, 31(1), 201–211, https://doi.org/10.1016/j.electstud.2011.11.001

Smith, H. J., Pettigrew, T. F., Pippin, G. M., and Bialosiewicz, S. (2012). 'Relative deprivation: A theoretical and meta-analytic review.' *Personality and Social Psychology Review*, 16(3), 203–232, https://doi.org/10.1177/1088868311430825

Stimson, J. A., MacKuen, M. B., and Erikson, R. S. (1995). 'Dynamic representation.' *American Political Science Review*, 89(3), 543–565, https://doi.org/10.2307/2082973

Thomassen, J., and Van Ham, C. (2017). 'A legitimacy crisis of representative democracy?' In C. van Ham, C., J. Thomassen, K. Aarts, and R. Andeweg (eds.). *Myth and Reality of the Legitimacy Crisis: Explaining Trends and Cross-National Differences in Established Democracies* (pp. 3–16). Oxford: Oxford University Press, https://doi.org/10.1093/oso/9780198793717.001.0001

Tsabari, O., Tziner, A., and Meir, E. I. (2005). 'Updated meta-analysis on the relationship between congruence and satisfaction.' *Journal of Career Assessment*, 13(2), 216–232, https://doi.org/10.1177/1069072704273165

Vega, A., and Firestone, J. M. (1995). 'The effects of gender on congressional behavior and the substantive representation of women.' *Legislative Studies Quarterly*, 20(2), 213–222.

Wängnerud, L., and Sundell, A. (2012). 'Do politics matter? Women in Swedish local elected assemblies 1970–2010 and gender equality in outcomes.' *European Political Science Review*, 4(1), 97–120, https://doi.org/10.1017/S1755773911000087

Appendix 1

Table 7A.1 Items to measure the feeling of being represented.

Variables	Items
Listen_1–Listen_4	**Now we would like to ask you some questions about the extent to which you feel represented by politicians and political parties.** **First, we would like to present a number of statements about the extent to which politicians and parties listen to you. Can you indicate to what extent you agree with the following statements?** 1. There is not a single politician or party who listens to people like me. 2. There are politicians and parties who take note of what people like me have to say. 3. Most politicians and parties ignore the opinions of people like me. 4. Most politicians and parties usually pay attention to the opinions of people like me.
Know_1–Know_4	**Now, we present a number of statements about the extent to which politicians and political parties know your interests and preferences. Can you indicate to what extent you agree with the following statements?** 1. There is not a single politician or party who knows what goes on among people like me. 2. There are politicians and parties who are informed about what people like me want. 3. Most politicians and parties do not have a clue about what is important for people like me. 4. Most politicians and parties do know the interests and preferences of people like me.

Act_1–Act_4	**Now, we present a number of statements about the extent to which politicians and political parties act in your interests and according to your preferences. Can you indicate to what extent you agree with the following statements?**
	1. There is not a single politician or party who really takes action to defend to interests and preferences of people like me.
	2. There are politicians and parties who do act in the interest and according to the preferences of people like me.
	3. Most politicians and parties neglect the interests and preferences of people like me when they take action.
	4. Most politicians and parties do try to act in line with what is important for people like me.
Succ_1–Succ_4	**Lastly, we present a number of statements about the extent to which politicians and political parties also succeed in translating your interests and preferences into policy. Can you indicate to what extent you agree with the following statements?**
	1. There is not a single politician or party who succeeds in realizing the things that are important for people like me.
	2. There are politicians and parties who do manage to make policy reflect the preferences of people like me.
	3. Most politicians fail to translate the preferences of people like me into policy.
	4. Most politicians and parties generally succeed in making policy that addresses the issues that are important to people like me.

Appendix 2

Table 7A.2 Bayesian Information Criterion (BIC) scores for Latent Profiles Analyses with 1-10 profiles extracted.

Number of profiles extracted	BIC	Difference in BIC
1	38648,99	
2	33778,55	4870,44
3	32211,15	1567,4
4	31426,04	785,11
5	30770,43	655,61
6	30686,34	84,09
7	30368,56	317,78
8	30290,72	77,84
9	30094,69	196,03
10	30060,26	34,43

Appendix 3

Table 7A.3 may be viewed online at https://doi.org/10.11647/OBP.0401#resources

8. Resentment and time: clashing temporalities in citizens' relation to politics

Louise Knops, Heidi Mercenier & Eline Severs

Abstract: Drawing on the affective turn in social sciences and increasing scholarly attention for political temporalities, our chapter investigates the entanglement between feelings of injustice, resentment, and time in citizens' discourses on politics. Our research is based on a qualitative analysis of focus groups with activists (in the Yellow Vests and Youth for Climate movement) and with individuals interviewed during the COVID-19 pandemic (employees of the cultural sector and students). Our findings highlight different temporal facets of citizens' resentment and situate their discontent as the result of clashing temporalities: between the temporalities of capitalism and human societies, and between different temporalities that structure politics within the boundaries of representative democracy. Our chapter sheds light on the relevance of adopting an affective-temporal lens to understand citizens' resentment within the broader context of the crisis of representative democracy.

Introduction

In the current context of the crisis of representative democracy, citizens are said to be not simply critical towards their political authorities (Norris, 2011) but also angry, indignant, and resentful (Fleury, 2020). Politics, in general, seems characterised by increasing affective explicitness (Webster and Alberston, 2022) and affective polarisation; as testified, for example, by the increasing force exerted by populist emotional appeals

https://doi.org/10.11647/OBP.0401.08

(Cossarini and Vallespin, 2019), and the explicit emotionality of salient debates, such as migration, climate change or the COVID-19 pandemic.

This increasing explicitness of emotions and affective expressions has encouraged scholars to pay a renewed attention to emotions and affects in citizens' relationships to politics; something which is often coined as an 'affective turn' in social sciences. Concomitantly to this affective turn, scholars are also increasingly attentive to the ways in which citizens' attitudes towards politics reflect different accounts of time and temporality. Politicians are regularly conceived as being 'out-of-sync' with the everyday struggles of citizens (Valgarössen et al., 2020; Noordzij et al., 2020) and representative democracy's myopia (its bias towards the short term) is seen as undermining its ability to take long-term action and secure the interests of future generations (McKenzie, 2021). In a similar vein, discussions about the functioning of representative democracy have focused on whether democratic decision-making processes are too slow or, alternatively, would benefit from further distancing from the high speed of social media (Fawcett, 2018; Aubert, 2010). Scholars have, in addition, problematised the temporal clashes between democracy and capitalism, anchored in the now and fast-paced tempo of consumerism (Tomba, 2014); or between the modern conception of time geared towards infinite progress, and the argument that societal development should fit within ecological boundaries (Chakrabarty, 2018; Bensaude-Vincent, 2021).

This chapter draws on the growing scholarship of the affective turn and the increasing attention paid to temporality to analyse the distinctive conceptions of time that underlie citizens' expressions of resentment. We argue that applying a temporal lens to citizens' discourses on politics helps us uncover the temporal dimensions of resentment itself and the temporalities which shape citizens' relations to political institutions. Explicit attention to temporality in our analysis of citizens' resentment is important for a number of reasons. First, it deepens our understanding of resentment itself, by unveiling some of the macro-contextual conditions that may explain its emergence (inequalities, capitalism, climate change, etc). Second, at the normative level, it extends our understanding of resentment and democratic reform. By paying attention to how citizens experience and view the world around them, and how these experiences translate into an affective evaluation of politics (here, resentment), we extend the scholarly discussion on democratic reform beyond an institutional perspective only (including elements such as participatory budgeting, improving the transparency of decision-making). Our study brings into the conversation the way macro-level political transformations (e.g., globalised market economies, climate change, health pandemics) affect citizens' everyday lives and relationships to politics–and the different ways this might be responded to, beyond institutional responses only.

Resentment is a political affect that is situated at the crossroads of both the affective and the temporal dimensions of the crisis of representative democracy. It is a key emotion that characterises citizens' broken relationships with democratic institutions (Fleury, 2020) and an emotion that emerges in the context of protest and contestation against these political institutions (Capelos and Demertzis, 2018). Resentment, in addition, embodies a distinctive temporal dimension. Resentment can be thought of as an incremental emotion that builds over time (cf. Chapter 1): it displays a distinctive bitterness that emerges from the accumulation of fears, frustrations, and grievances. It is a complex, moral emotion that is expressed in reaction to recurring or structural situations of injustice and unfairness (Capelos and Demertzis, 2018; Celis et al., 2021; Hoggett et al., 2013).

To capture the articulation between resentment and time, we rely on the EoS-RepResent focus groups dataset (cf. Chapter 2) and analyse how resentment, feelings of unfairness, and time are articulated in the discourses of different groups of citizens. We draw specifically on focus groups organised with citizens active in the Belgian Yellow Vests movement, the Youth for Climate movement, and on focus groups organized during the COVID-19 health pandemic with students and workers from the cultural sector. Importantly, whilst our analyses draw on empirical data collected in the Belgian context, our discussion is not restricted to temporalities that would be distinctive to Belgian politics. Our analysis of the temporal dimensions of resentment and the entanglement between affect and temporality may, instead, offer pathways for reflection applicable to other Western democratic contexts and be a starting point for further conceptual and normative innovation.

Indeed, our findings shed light on different temporal facets of citizens' resentment towards politics. They highlight the way that feelings of injustice and unfairness expressed by citizens can be interpretated as 'clashes' between different temporalities: between the temporalities imposed by capitalism and the economisation of society, and the rhythm of human lives and lived experiences; or between the temporality of politics and politicians and the temporality of one's everyday struggle; between the emergency of the COVID-19 pandemic, climate change and the temporalities of decision-making within representative democracy. Finally, our findings also point towards the contours of 'new futures', in which demands for fairness and a 're-synchronisation' of politics with the lives of ordinary citizens feature prominently.

The chapter is structured as follows. First, we review the extant literature on time and political affect to clarify the advantages of including a temporal lens when studying citizens' resentment. Next, we elaborate on the focus group discussions we conducted and present our findings. The chapter concludes by reflecting on the limitations of the study and by identifying avenues for future research.

Resentment and clashing temporalities

Affect and time

In this chapter, we treat affect and time as two vantage points to produce more nuanced understandings of the crisis of representative democracy. We argue that affect and time are crucial to unpack the tensions and contradictions that characterise citizens' evaluations of contemporary politics and their embedding within the broader power structures and belief systems underpinning society.

Whilst affect has long been overlooked in political science, scholars are increasingly recognising the importance of emotions in shaping citizens' ability to judge and reflect (Marcus, 2002, pp. 77–78). Thanks to neuroscience, we know that emotions serve as mental representations of bodily states which allow us to perform functions of self-regulation. As heuristics or cognitive short-cuts, our emotions allow us to respond to situations of stress, seek a new balance (Damasio, 2000), and sometimes trigger more effective reactions than 'rational' calculations would allow for. Overall, emotions should therefore neither be conceived as an inherently negative quality of politics nor as factors that undermine 'rationality'.

On the contrary, they play a crucial role in the formation of judgments and beliefs about the world around us, in the construction of collective identities (Mouffe, 2018) and normative positions (Marcus, 2002, p. 76).

This is adequately captured by the concept of 'affect': it underscores how individuals' personal investment in politics and their (ability to form) political judgment is embodied. To be affected by something, as Sara Ahmed (2010, p. 23) notes, is to be grounded in individuals' distinct experiences, and involves the ways emotions make bodies turn toward things and make collective identities and subjectivities 'stick'. Affect, in this sense, refers to a bodily and indeterminate level of experience, fusing both 'emotion' (as *felt* experiences that have undergone qualification as they enter a more discursive level) and 'reason' (as cognitive processes that identify causes and provide explanations and justifications for concrete experiences and beliefs). A turn to political affect not only helps us make sense of the high emotional saturation of contemporary politics and political language, it also accounts for the indeterminate and sometimes paradoxical character of citizens' evaluations of politics.

The concept of time provides the second vantage point from which we study citizens' narratives about contemporary politics. From mobilisation studies, we know that citizens who engage in protest and collective action often invoke a sense of urgency to underscore the need for government action (Houdek and Phillips, 2002, pp. 370–371). More broadly, beyond moments of mobilisation, we also know that individual and collective practices of sense-making are rooted in a conception of time: our ability to define the present and set it apart from past and future depends on a capacity for remembering. It is the activity of remembering the near to far past that interrupts the everyday and creates a break-away from the grip of repetition that allows for cognitive reflections on 'the now' (Merleau-Ponty, 2012, p.167).

According to the French sociologist Henri Lefebvre (2004), time— understood here as a mental representation of the 'present'—is produced by the way in which people relate to each other and to their experiences. This view challenges the dominant, abstract or mathematical conception of time as days or minutes passing by. Instead, time is here conceived as, first and foremost, a human and social construct (Smith, 2015, p. 974). It is therefore both a result of and a precondition to the production of society: while 'time' emerges from the ways in which people relate to each other and their environment, particular accounts of 'time', when they gain dominance, also impose limitations on individuals and their agentive capacities (e.g., when entering adulthood 'the time for folly has passed') (Alhadeff-Jones, 2019, p. 168).

This signals four important things. First, as a social construct, time has its own historicity and contextuality, implying that a particular account of time can only arise in a particular spatial-temporal context. Time is, thus, fundamentally historical in that it reflects the specific characteristics and constellations of the societies, their power structures, and the dominant and subordinate belief systems in which activities of sense-making take place. Second, and reflecting its bearings as social construct, time does not exist universally, implying that competing and contradictory accounts of time are likely to co-exist and that these conceptions of time are unequally distributed across society. Third, and relatedly, how we engage with 'time', especially what we describe as being in the past, is bound up with social constellations, power relations, and conflicts relevant to a particular group or a particular society (Schmid, 2008, p. 29). Fourth, our accounts of time are also tied up with the social organisation of time, and the rhythms of our everyday life. The distinct temporalities of our personal lives (e.g., working 9 to 5 versus being permanently on call, financial abundance versus worries about making ends meet) are likely to affect how we perceive others and the world around us.

Against this backdrop, applying a temporal lens to the study of political resentment allows us to expand our focus from political institutions to citizens' broader experience of today's times and the conflicts they see emerging as the result of major societal and economic transformations, like globalisation, climate change, and the dismantling of the welfare state (cf. Delanty, 2021).

Political imaginary, evolving timescapes, and clashing temporalities

A growing body of research highlights that citizens' relationships to politics are continuously shaped by clashing temporalities and evolving timescapes (Adam, 1998). For the post-war generation in Western societies the future was characterised by the prospects of economic growth and welfare for increasing numbers of citizens, economic and political stability, and a growing attachment to principles of democratic inclusion. In contrast, the present generation is more astutely aware of the dangers of climate catastrophe and the increasing uninhabitability of the Earth (de Moor, 2021; Kenis, 2021). In addition, the dismantling of the welfare state has triggered a critique of the 'neoliberal timescape' that holds individuals responsible for their failures as much as their successes and that defines personal worth based on economic metrics (Gillan, 2020). Reflecting these trends, the future is increasingly imagined as catastrophic or doomed, especially among the youth where climate anxiety and fear for the future has reached record levels across the globe (Hickman et al., 2021). Social protests, and broader feelings of anxiety cutting across society, for example because of the COVID-19 health pandemic, give expression to citizens' experiences of breakdown, collapse, and cataclysmic end (Gentile, 2020, p. 657).

Increasingly, scholars (Clark and Teachout, 2012; Tomba, 2014) also argue that we are witnessing a clash 'of political, economic, and juridical temporalities in the globalised world that is destabilising the form of advanced Western democracies' (Tomba, 2014, p. 354). While capitalism is organised around short-term profits, permanent consumption and the fast tempo imposed by ideals of productivity and efficiency, climate change unveils the conflict that this creates with the Earth's geological temporalities and our collective story as a dominant species (Chakrabarty, 2018; Knops, 2023). Similarly, the fast pace of capitalism is thought of as being out of sync with the temporalities and rhythms of governance (Giroux, 2004). Not only are processes of citizen participation typically slow, but the very logic of parliamentary democracy is founded on a spatial-temporal distance (between citizens and sites of deliberation) that is meant to facilitate reflexivity and enable citizens to (re)consider how their personal needs and interest link up to the 'general interest' (Severs, 2020, p. 64–5).

Taking a different perspective to political time, some scholars have also argued that democracy can (and should) accelerate its pace via the technocratisation of decision-making (e.g., Connoly, 2002). At the same time, the myopia (or short-termism) of representative democracy is critiqued for delaying political action on climate change and for producing unsustainable policies (McKenzie, 2021; Blühdorn, 2013).

Others still consider attempts at synchronising or, rather, of subjecting the pace of democratic politics to capitalism as a form of violence and call for a deceleration and a decoupling of politics from the speed of globalisation (Tomba, 2014).

Lastly, scholars, have suggested that we live in a context of hypermodernity that is marked by a constant sense of urgency and instantaneity which risks confining us to the present (Chesneaux, 2000; Aubert, 2010) while foreclosing the possibilities of political action to the language of 'forecast' and 'predictions' and 'probabilities'. This hyper-realism is judged to undermine the quality of decision-making. Scholars problematise how the confinement to the present, reinforced by the hyperconnectivity and immediacy of social media, disables reflexive dialogue between the present, past, and future (Chesneaux, 2000; Aubert, 2010), and undermines our ability to reclaim utopian thinking (Giroux, 2004).

In the midst of this patchwork of political temporalities, recent events have also added new layers to our Western relationship to time. This is particularly true for the effects of the COVID-19 pandemic and the restrictive measures adopted in its wake. The suspended moments of 'lockdowns' represented a welcome invitation to slow down for some. Meanwhile, for others, it triggered an unwelcome acceleration of time and a simultaneous reduction of life to an endless repetition of intense tasks (e.g., those working in the healthcare sector or parents juggling childcare and working from home). For still others (e.g., the elderly, the youth, or single people), lockdowns were experienced as an endless wait marked by solitude, isolation, and desperation, or as a rapid fall into precarity (e.g., those working in shut-down sectors, squeezed between bank loans, rents and no income)

These changing timescapes and clashing temporalities have implications for our understanding of politics. They add, more specifically, to long-standing tensions in our political imaginary; understood as 'a more or less subconscious set of meanings, symbols values, narratives and representations of the world that influence the way in which people experience their political world' (Bottici, 2010, p. 686 in Diehl, 2019, pp. 413–4). Since the 19th century, we have come to embrace the democratic imaginary of popular sovereignty. This imaginary, Paula Diehl (2019, p. 411) argues, sets a normative horizon that allows society to imagine the future in terms of an emancipatory space that is characterised by ever greater inclusion in processes of decision-making. Meanwhile, our social and political practices reveal important incongruences to this normative horizon, of which citizens' resentment is just one expression. Citizens increasingly contest the institutions underpinning representative democracy and question the democratic character of long-standing practices and institutions that have come to characterise Western political systems (see Chapters 10 and 11 of this book). Recent protests as well as a general form of 'hate and disdain' towards politics (Hay, 2007) have become increasingly explicit in the overall contestation expressed against the institutions and the dominant political imaginary underpinning society.

In this chapter, we apply these temporal lenses to the study of political resentment and the accounts of politics that emerge in citizens' discourses and conversations. As well captured by Capelos et al. (2021), resentment has its distinctive temporality, in the sense that it builds over time, and over a sense of accumulated angers and frustrations. It also expresses itself in reaction to structural or perceived situations of injustice and unfairness, which are experienced in a repetitive and continuous way (Hoggett et al., 2013); feeling systematically deprived or discriminated vis-à-vis other groups, feeling envious or jealous, but also perceiving oneself as the victim of systemic forms of discrimination and injustice which have evolved over time (Pettigrew, 2016).

Design and methodology

Our analysis focuses on citizens' discourses and narratives of politics as they emerged during focus group discussions. We draw on a selection of eight focus group discussions from the EoS-RepResent focus group dataset where we expect citizens to express resentment (see Chapter 1). The data have been selected to capture a diversity of narratives of resentment linked to feelings of injustice or unfairness across the political spectrum: being activists in recent contentious movements which denounce different facets of representative democracy and belonging to groups who may have experienced situations of unfairness and injustice in the context of the pandemic.

From these eight groups, there are two focus groups with activists from the Yellow Vests movement (FG1/FG2, YV) in Belgium (see Knops and Petit, 2022; Petit, 2022), two focus groups with Youth for Climate activists (FG1/FG2, YfC), the Belgian branch of the global movement Fridays for Future (Knops, 2021). These groups are relevant for our discussion for a number of reasons. On the one hand, the YV movement denounced primarily fiscal and social injustice, and the temporalities of capitalism which have resulted in rising structural socio-economic inequalities in Western countries. The movement quickly morphed into a much broader contestation that denounced a form of political betrayal by the elites and feelings of being abandoned and 'left behind'. On the other hand, the YfC denounced another type of injustice with an explicit temporal dimension: a new form of intergenerational injustice where those who have contributed the least to global warming (the younger generations) will suffer disproportionally from its catastrophic impacts.

The four other groups participated in discussions we organised in December 2020 and January 2021, during the second lockdown of the COVID-19 health pandemic. We organised focus groups with sets of individuals who were depicted in the public debate as severely affected by the health crisis and the measures taken to combat it: two focus groups with workers from the cultural sector who were forced to stop their professional activities on the grounds that these were 'not essential'(FG1/FG2, cultural sector), and two focus groups with young university students in the first years of their studies (FG1/FG2, students) who were frequently vilified in the public debate. During the COVID-19 pandemic, young people were frequently criticized for breaching the social distancing and isolation protocols imposed by the government. Their actions were seen as unnecessarily putting other, more vulnerable and often older segments of society at risk. Meanwhile, young people also felt disproportionality affected by the ongoing crisis and argued that their 'future had been stolen'.

The focus groups conducted with the Yellow Vests and Youth for Climate activists were organized face-to-face and comprised of seven participants each. The discussions were conducted in French and lasted about three hours. In contrast, and because of COVID-19 restrictions, the focus groups with university students and cultural sector employees were conducted online, in French, with four to six participants in each group. The focus group transcripts ensure anonymity and pseudonyms are used to present participants' statements.

Our method of analysis followed an iterative, interpretative logic and was built on several distinctive steps. We started with a review of individual empirical observations of the field and focus group analyses presented elsewhere (Knops, 2021; Knops and Petit, 2022; Mercenier, 2023). We then re-engaged with the empirical material we had collected and coded it in a series of multiple rounds of interpretative analysis. We paid attention to themes (i.e., the moments citizens refer to politics, policies, and polity), evaluations (in particular when citizens express dissatisfaction, negative evaluations, feelings of injustice or unfairness), and affective connotations that belong to resentful affectivities (these include, amongst others, anger, fear, disgust, but also hope, see Celis et al., 2021; Capelos and Demertzis, 2018).

From these analyses, we drew the important insight that, amongst other things, time, and temporality feature as important elements in citizens' discourses on politics, especially when they express resentment towards politicians and political institutions. On that basis, a second round of analysis was conducted, at a more interpretative level, to identify precisely how time, resentment and feelings of unfairness were articulated in the way citizens make sense of politics and political institutions. We focused on the identification of 'clashing temporalities' in the discourses, referring to the moments when citizens bring together different types of temporalities—e.g., the everyday and the temporality of political institutions, the temporality of capitalism with the temporalities of climate change—and interrogate whether these clashes may cause tension, feelings of injustice and resentment in the way citizens conceive of and relate to political institutions. Finally, we also paid attention to different types of 'rhythm' in the empirical material to identify possible instances of '(a)synchronisation' between people's lived experiences and their experiences of representative democracy.

Resentment and clashing temporalities

Our analysis sheds light on different temporal facets of citizens' resentment towards politics and highlights the way that feelings of injustice and unfairness expressed by citizens can be interpretated as three different types of 'clashing temporalities': (1) the temporalities imposed by capitalism and the economisation of society, (2) the temporality of politics, and (3) emergency politics related to climate change and the emergency of the COVID-19 pandemic.

The pressure of capitalist temporalities

The first clash of temporalities we identified across the focus groups involved citizens' denunciations of the primacy of capital over all aspects of social and political life; the ways in which capitalism, as an economic system, has superimposed itself on politics and society and is defining both its temporality of action, and guiding norms and values. Whilst this critique is most outspoken among the Yellow Vests activists, respondents from the other focus groups concurred with the argument that capitalism imposes violent 're-synchronsisations' onto politics; implying that politics is in a subordinated position compared to the power of capital and this is to the detriment of ordinary citizens, their everyday life, needs and aspirations (cf. Tomba, 2014).

In this context, participants, like the Yellow Vests activist Antoine, problematise the dismantling of the welfare state and the austerity policies that followed in response to the 2008 financial and economic crisis. Invoking the Greek austerity crisis, Antoine states:

> You want to know the answer? It's all the capitalists behind all of this. They have the power, the money; they are the rulers. You've got lobbyists by thousands [...]. The problem is the capital. Look at what happened to Greece. They had left-wing ideas, but they got muzzled because of their debt. Austerity, debt, that's how they tie us.
>
> (FG1, YV, 2019)

In the same focus group, Ismael conceives of politics as fully consumed by capitalism; what he describes as a 'purely capitalist system' that 'chains' individuals and robs them of intrinsic human qualities, like solidarity, compassion, and feelings of belonging to a community or group. This is a critique that also explains why many Yellow Vests activists found in the movement, not just a place of contestation, but also a place of care and togetherness (Knops and Petit, 2022).

> The enemy number one is not politics, it's not the banks, it's not finance... it is the system we have conceived as a purely capitalist system. You let

capitalism fall and we all become free again, we lose our chains and we become human beings again.

(FG1, YV, 2019)

Central to the respondents' critique of the entanglement of politics and capitalism is the dismantling of social welfare provisions, and its effects on the decrease of purchasing power and the increasing levels of precarity. During one of the focus groups, Jeremy expresses outrage over the fact that '25% of the homeless in France have a job' but still cannot afford rent (FG1, YV, 2019). Participants treat this as symptomatic of the general and structural trends towards increasing socio-economic inequalities across society.

Jeremy:	25% of the homeless in France have a job. 25%. 25% of the homeless in France have a job (Jeremy repeats his sentence)
Jeremy:	When I read that... [as if to imply: 'I was outraged']
Thomas:	What, they work on the streets?
Jeremy:	No, no, they have a proper job, they simply don't have enough to pay rent!
Julien:	They sleep in their car...

(FG1, YV 2019)

Yellow Vests activists describe this situation as being 'squeezed like lemons', here in reference to the injustice of calling on the charity and solidarity of the working and middle-classes—who are already struggling—to help those who are in even greater need.

Alex:	Every year the RTBF does a thing...The Viva for Life action. We are told that a fourth of all children–a fourth of all children [he repeats to insist on the idea]–lives below the poverty line. [...].
Pierre:	Don't you think it's a bit strange that we are being squeezed like lemons, but still, they come to us to get money?
Julie:	Yes, exactly [....]
Pierre:	But the amount of money in the pot keeps going up and it's not normal that we should be the ones supporting this system.

(FG2, YV 2019)

The feeling of being exploited aptly captures the structural character of socio-economic inequalities from which resentment—as an emotion that emerges over repeated experiences and situations of injustice—may emerge. It also evokes images of bitterness that are characteristic of resentment (an emotion that builds over time). However, in contrast to other findings on the politics of resentment (e.g., Cramer, 2016), in the quotes above, feelings of unfairness are primarily directed at capitalist and political institutions, not towards other groups in society.

Similar denunciations of capitalism are also expressed among the activists of the YfC movement. Here, the critique of a 'money-driven' society features prominently in the discussions among climate activists which target the profit-oriented economy as one of the main causes of mass pollution, environmental destruction, and climate change. Strikingly, respondents signal here the need to slow down the frenetic pace of life that is imposed by capitalism and its related global competition:

> Felix: About the system, I am really against the capitalist system,
>   and the liberalism that is linked to capitalism. The
>   profit of big companies, the rich who take advantage
>   of globalisation [...]. All this is then justified based on
>   'merit' which is an invented notion to justify this system
>   and the inequalities it creates. When I speak of system,
>   I speak of the capitalist system. All these people on top,
>   and all those at the bottom, I just want to break all of this
>   and put everyone on the same level. I want to say, 'come
>   on guys, we all live on the same planet, we need to move
>   it, we need to do something!'
>   (FG2, YfC 2019)

> Grégory: Those who run the world, who know what will happen if
>   we carry on like this, don't want to slow down... I mean
>   the problem is growth, and if we try to de-growth and
>   limit our impact, it means letting others take power and
>   perhaps take our place. So, I think an enormous problem
>   in our world is that we don't think of the common good.
>   We think of our own country, our own people, and this
>   idea that 'one must do better than others'.
>   (FG2 YfC 2019)

Interestingly, feelings of unfairness tied to capitalism also hint at the normative background against which these are expressed; a system that should value 'humans', 'the planet' and 'the common good'; all under the pressure of the relentless pace of capitalist temporalities.

Lastly, feelings of unfairness vis-à-vis the primacy of our capitalist economy were also very explicit in the focus groups organized during the COVID-19 lockdown. They show themselves especially in respondents' critiques of the selectiveness of measures taken during the COVID-19 health pandemic, and the overall observation that the economy and profit seem to be privileged above everything else:

> Antoine: So. I wanted to follow up on what Lena said about the hairdressers and all that. At the beginning of the second lockdown, I had a major problem. Come on, I suddenly got very angry watching TV, because they (referring to the government) closed the hairdressers and closed the shops, but, for example, not the airports. They didn't close these places and that made me angry!
>
> Alicia: I agree. The choice is quickly made between restaurants and tourism (with a sarcastic tone). Airplane tickets and so on, travelling... All that generates more money than... than the pubs. It's all about making money, it's all about money, it's very serious!
>
> Antoine: That's what I consider revolting. We lose what makes us human. And the government' goal should be to put people first and money second. And unfortunately, we are losing all that.
>
> (FG 1, students, 2021)

Similarly, during the discussion with people from the cultural sector, most respondents denounced the arbitrariness of closing theatres while letting crowds flock to the main shopping streets (FG1 and FG2, cultural sector, 2020). The fact that the cultural sector was presented in the public debate as a 'non-essential' component of society fuelled resentment towards the politicians and governments who were responsible for making these decisions. While support and trust towards government originally improved during the first lockdown (Bol et al., 2020), the duration of measures and their perceived selectiveness and unfairness eventually created strong feelings of frustration, disgust, and weariness as well as being 'fed up'.

Unfit for our times: the a-synchronicities of politics

Across the focus groups, a second temporal theme emerged clearly in denunciations of the dysfunctions and inadequacy of contemporary representative politics. While some respondents problematise the myopia or short-sightedness of politics, others critique the style of politics and the figure of the 'career politician' to denounce an impression of politics as the activities of a self-serving elite. Both critiques express the feeling that politics can neither keep up with the growing discontent of our times, nor with the contemporary challenges of climate change, rising inequalities or the COVID-19 pandemic.

Confronted with what they describe as an immanent urgency, climate activists most explicitly denounce democratic myopia. As illustrated from the exchange below, there is an astute feeling that 'there is no time to waste' and that politicians fail to anticipate beyond their five-year electoral term.

> Loic: If a politician was forced to stop after one term, he could do whatever he wanted to; he is not gonna think of pleasing people or of the next term.... Politicians spend their lives thinking about the image they project to make sure they stay popular...
>
> Arthur: Yeah, and they keep saying 'it will be for the next government'...
>
> Loic: And meanwhile they waste time, they waste a lot of time...
>
> Arthur: [...] and a 5-year term is just not long enough, when you think of the climate... and what will happen in 2040... it's just not enough.
>
> (FG 1, YfC)

In other focus groups too, respondents expressed a range of feelings and reactions to the inadequate pace and temporalities of politics. In the discussions with Yellow Vests activists, respondents critiqued what they perceive as shallow and rushed decision-making. They contrasted politicians' perceived tendency to make decisions on a 'whim' without much consideration for citizens, with the long-term dismantling of the welfare state. As shown in the following extract, politicians are perceived as 'opportunistic liars', who take only 15 days to 'trigger a social tsunami':

Antoine: The opportunistic lies of politicians...With the N-VA: 'we won't touch the VAT on energy, pension, etc'. Whatever... it didn't take them 15 days to pff... trigger a social tsunami. That really disgusted me.

(FG1, YV 2019)

Julien: The people who we vote for... for example, nowhere was there a mention of the pension age at 67 years old, yet they shamelessly implement that from one day to the next. Only one party has that explicitly in its programme [Défi], the others didn't.

(FG1, YV 2019)

Students affected by the COVID-19 pandemic also denounced the short-sightedness of politics: they critiqued government's failure to account for the disproportionate impact that the COVID-19 health measures had on younger people and denounced the neglect of their generation, and the overall negation of their future, which they explicitly attributed to the government's irresponsibility.

Noor: To come back to the government and so on, I think they should... the government should pay much more attention to this, because students are the future, if they don't solve this problem. And the dropout rate, whether it's at university or even at school. I have little sisters, and I know what it's like, they're... when they had online classes, they were completely demotivated, and so on, and I believe that if the government doesn't do anything to solve this situation, to find solutions, because there are solutions to every problem, then I think that it would be a waste of the future and of young people in general.

Adel: Well, I also agree, it's the government that holds everyone's strings.

(FG1, students, 2021)

Elsewhere, respondents from the cultural sector identified as a problem the government's inability or unwillingness to provide adequate support and recognize the long-term impact of the pandemic on their sector. Overall, the distinctive temporalities of crisis management during the COVID-19 pandemic (the need for 'urgency' measures) was conceived as having disproportionate impacts on less privileged groups, leaving many people behind. For some, decisions during the pandemic were made too quickly and without consideration for their impacts on certain groups in society; others, especially in the cultural sector, denounced the lack of long-term vision and adequate anticipation of certain issues. Resentment can be seen here as an ensemble of affects grounded in the repetitive feeling of being unfairly treated by those who govern and by political practices that are framed by citizens in temporal terms (too fast, or too slow; with no long-term vision). In the excerpt below, Daniel expresses a sense of 'weariness' of being continuously 'fed up' (expressions that clearly belong to the category of resentful affectivity and echo the cumulative nature of resentment), while Pierre expresses anger towards politicians by describing the violence of their decisions and their effects. These are seen as disproportionate for the cultural sector, in the short and long term, in comparison to the benefits for society or in comparison to other groups.

Daniel: The, the weariness. We're all tired of it and so uh... yeah.

Pierre: But the violence of the images of the crowded Rue Neuve [a commercial street in Brussels], at the same time as the theatres were being closed, that's violent, that's... [...] Indeed, the fact that it's happening again, no matter how much we say about it [...] it's just that these are messages we don't want to see or hear, and the fact that it [referring to the shutdown of cultural places] happened once, twice, three times, in fact now it became a recurrent event [...] That's why, yes, clearly you can be, uh [Daniel agrees], in a state of anger and they [referring to the politicians] don't even realize the impact it has [...] I think it's going to have pretty terrible consequences.

                                                    (FG 1, cultural sector, 2020)

The distinctive nature of resentment as an incremental emotion that builds over repeated and cumulative experiences is clearly evident here. Respondents regularly denounce the self-referential character of politics and the fact that politicians don't want to hear what people have to say themselves. As Pierre puts it: 'these are messages we don't want to see or hear'.

In addition, across the focus groups, respondents' critiques of the dysfunctions of contemporary politics are laced with a clear resentment towards politicians specifically. Politicians are perceived as a self-serving elite that is out of touch with the daily realities and concerns of ordinary citizens. This is well expressed by Ismael, a Yellow Vests activist who denounces the family dynasties that characterize Belgian politics:

> Ismael: This is the problem that we have. We have been represented by people who have a personal interest in what they are doing. Being a politician today is just a thing that is passed down from father to son; they have turned it into a profession. That's my fear... it's to see people 'specialising' in this.
>
> Julien: I don't agree with this. I think everyone should do politics. We should have more workers, more women.
>
> (FG1 YV 2019)

Politicians, in general, are conceived as too caught up in the electoral race and as having lost sight of the common good; something which is well captured by Loic (FG1, YfC 2019) below, exasperated with what he sees as the 'personalisation' of politics.

> The problem is that all our politicians spend their time, preparing their term. I was listening to a political debate on the radio the other day [...] and all I heard was criticism and comments on the person, rather than about political ideas. I was horrified! It seems that politics is no longer about defending political ideas, but about specific individuals.
>
> (FG1, YfC 2019)

Overall, across the focus group discussions, resentment and feelings of unfairness are entangled within the broader diagnosis that politics, in its current shape, style and form, is not fit for our times. Across the discussions, this diagnosis is framed, in part, in temporal terms; with respondents referring to the short-term bias of politics, the abrupt and inconsiderate decision-making in crisis situations (the COVID-19 pandemic), the lack of consideration for future generations, and the obsessions with politicians' own life trajectories.

Lost futures and new horizons

This diagnosis is entangled with a final theme which cuts across all of the focus group discussions: the distinctive feeling of living through 'extraordinary times'. This is perceptible in the various ways each group engages with the 'now': as a moment of imminent change and collapse (YfC), a moment to rise up and bring the entire system to its knees (YV) or of irreversible change in people's lives (COVID-19 focus groups). There is also a diffuse and cross-cutting feeling that the future will be worse; that it has been stolen or is lost. Despite this gloomy vision of the future, participants also express—albeit to varying degrees—their remaining hopes in alternative democratic futures (cf. Celis et al., 2021); a finding that also emerges from other focus groups analyses carried out for this volume (see Chapter 5 and Chapter 10, in particular).

The complex mixture of hope and despair shows, for example, in the way climate activists give expression to their experiences of political empowerment and agency: they feel that the topic of climate change has, as the result of their weekly protests, gained salience and that politicians are increasingly held to account for their (lack of) actions. As Maxime (YfC 1 2019) puts it: 'For once, we are being heard. I don't think I am the only one who has thought about this. For a while, it was more like "Ok, until I am 18, I am just there to learn and then go to work".' Similar forms of empowerment and hope can be observed among the Yellow Vests who describe their movement as an 'oxygen bubble' they have been waiting for, for so long; a movement that is worth fighting for and that unites everyone at heart, 'even those who don't know it' (Knops and Petit, 2022).

This experience of empowerment stands in sharp contrast to the state of fatigue and desperation observed in the focus groups with students and cultural sector employees during the pandemic. Laurence (FG1, cultural sector, 2020), for instance, critiques the 'infantilisation of the population' and expresses how she first felt anger and then resignation (towards the health measures), and powerlessness.

Various levels of hope are also recognisable in some of the solutions articulated by the respondents. There is, for example, an explicit desire to reclaim society from the grip of capitalism and the economy coupled with, in the case of the Yellow Vests, an explicit demand to scrap the entire system of representative democracy to introduce new forms of direct democracy (based on citizens referenda). From a temporal lens, this can be seen as a demand to 'de-synchronise' politics and societies from the temporalities of capitalism and to 're-synchronise' them with other rhythms and times; those of the everyday struggle, the climate emergency, and the structural trends underpinning society.

In relation to the specific problem of democratic myopia, respondents, in the YfC movement for example, recognize that democratic decision-making takes time. At the same time, they demand that politicians look beyond the short-term temporality imposed by elections to situate politics against the horizon of geological and social tipping points. During the pandemic, some participants even empathized with politicians and recognized the burden of having to make decisions for the population at large. Meanwhile, they denounced the professionalization of politicians and the specific types of politicians elected to office, as well as the structures (e.g., the electoral cycle) that incentivize them to give priority to short term considerations. In other discussions, some participants (e.g., Julien FG1, YV 2019) argued that parliamentary mandates should be revocable. Whilst this may, paradoxically, add to the short-sightedness and personalisation of politics, this proposal does signal participants' wish to rethink the overall temporalities of the electoral system, the duration of electoral terms, the frequency and pace of electoral campaigns and the overall horizons along which representative democracy operates.

Lastly, and beyond specific proposals to improve democratic functioning and control, there is, across the focus groups, a demand for increased fairness. This is expressed in terms of fairness of treatment for those in need, but also a demand to be seen and recognized, which is voiced by those who feel trapped in a permanent cycle of struggle. It is also expressed in the demand for a 'fair' future, in the sense of being able to live on a habitable planet, and it is invoked in the insistence that some groups should not be disproportionally affected by certain political measures, even when they are taken in situations of societal emergency.

Discussion and conclusion

In this chapter, we aimed to study citizens' resentment by paying attention to time and temporalities. This approach allows us: 1) to situate citizens' resentment within a broader macro-political context by underlining the importance of capitalist temporalities, 2) to document different temporal facets of citizens' critique of politics and political institutions by unveiling three types of 'clashes of temporalities'.

Our interpretative reanalysis of focus groups with different groups of Belgian citizens (Yellow Vests and Youth for Climate activists, students and individuals employed in the cultural sector during the COVID-19 pandemic) highlight three types of clashing temporalities: 1) between the temporalities imposed by capitalism and the economisation of society, and the rhythm of human lives and societies; 2) between the temporality of politics and politicians and the temporality of one's everyday struggle, for example in the context of the COVID-19 pandemic and climate change where the inadequate temporalities of decision-making in representative democracy become particularly visible; 3) between the temporal dysfunctions of existing representative politics and imagined 'new futures', in which demands for fairness and a 're-synchronisation' of politics with the lives of ordinary citizens feature prominently.

Here, we also find that the unveiling of different temporalities reflects different intensities or types of resentment; between a long-lasting type of resentment that has been brewing for some time (e.g., among the Yellow Vests), and others that are specifically tied to the emergency-temporality of climate change, or forms of resentment that border with feelings of abandonment, weariness and resignation (e.g., employees in the cultural sector during the COVID-19 pandemic).

Our findings raise key normative questions for the future of representative democracy. Insights from the focus groups discussions elicit the tentative contours of institutional and democratic reform, within a strong desire to de-economise politics and society. This points to the important imbrication of democratic and economic reforms, together with a general reflection on the specific temporalities of electoral democracy (its short-term bias and the maintenance of the figure of the professional career politician, despite explicit critiques voiced by citizens).

There are however important limitations to our study. Clearly, the capacity to generalise our findings is limited by the temporal and context-specific nature of the focus groups and the type of respondents included in our study. Based on our data, we cannot discern whether broader segments of the population would agree with the need for a re-synchronisation of politics, everyday life, the economy and climate, and which trade-offs they would consider acceptable to attain these objectives. Nor can we determine whether the different types of feeling and resentment tied to the temporal narratives we observe may be generalised beyond our studied groups. For further illustrations of how citizens' resentment towards politics is expressed in group discussions, see Chapters 5 and 10 of this present volume.

This limitation notwithstanding, the temporal approach we adopt in this chapter opens interesting avenues for future research that better integrates affect and time when analysing citizens' relations to politics. Our findings confirm that attempts to restore trust in representative democracy must go beyond institutional engineering (e.g., participatory budgeting, improved transparency, and increased citizen participation) and must consider how the temporal qualities and rhythms of people's everyday lives inform their political judgment and, potentially, their resentment towards politics.

Citizens are not simply 'hateful' of politics but, as shown by our findings, they denounce the inability of politics to respond to the they ways in which global and systemic trends, such as capitalism, climate change and health pandemics, disrupt their everyday lives. Rather than overcoming some 'gap' or 'distance' between citizens and politics, our respondents denounce politics and political institutions as being 'out of sync' with everyday realities, and out of sync with the challenges of our times. Concretely, this means that democratic and institutional reform cannot be thought of separately from deeper political transformations that take place, not only at the level of practices and procedures, but also at the level of policies and political ideologies. This is particularly relevant in the context of mounting anti-capitalist sentiments and other feelings, ideologies and policies that will be needed to support transitions towards more sustainable societies—be it from an ecological, economic or a social perspective.

Lastly, our attention to resentment and temporalities also opens pathways for research on citizens' capacity for utopian thinking, where both time and affect play a crucial role, and where resentment may be surpassed by new forms of political and democratic engagement across the citizenry.

References

Alhadeff-Jones, M. (2019). 'Beyond space and time—conceiving the rhythmic configurations of adult education through Lefebvre's rhythmananalysis.' *ZfW*, 42, 165–181.

Adam, B. (1998). *Timescapes of Modernity: The Environment and Invisible Hazards.* London and New York: Routledge.

Ahmed, S. (2010). *The Promise of Happiness.* Durham: Duke University Press.

Aubert, N. (2010). *La Société Hypermoderne, Ruptures et Contradictions.* Paris: L'Harmattan, https://www.decitre.fr/livres/la-societe-hypermoderne-ruptures-et-contradictions-9782296116924.html

Bensaude-Vincent, B. (2021) *Pour une écologie des crises.* Paris: Le Pommier/ Humensis, 2021.

Blühdorn, I. (2013). 'The governance of unsustainability: Ecology and democracy after the post-democratic turn.' *Environmental Politics*, 22(1), 16–36.

Bol, D., Giani, M., Blais, A., and Loewen, P. J. (2020). 'The effect of COVID-19 lockdowns on political support: Some good news for democracy?' *European Journal of Political Research*, 60(2), 497–505, https://doi.org/10.1111/1475-6765.12401

Bottici, Ch. (2010). *A Philosophy of Political Myth.* Cambridge: Cambridge University Press.

Capelos, T. and Demertzis, N. (2018). 'Political action and resentful affectivity in critical times.' *Humanity and Society*, 42(4), 410–433, https://doi.org/10.1177/0160597618802517

Capelos, T. Chrona, S. Salmela, M. Bee, Ch. (2021). 'Reactionary politics and resentful affect in populist times.' *Politics and Governance.* Special Issue: Reactionary Politics and Resentful Affect in Populist Times, 9(3), 186–190.

Celis, K. Knops, L., Van Ingelgom, V. and Verhaegen, S. (2021). 'Resentment and coping with the democratic dilemma.' *Politics and Governance.* Special Issue: Reactionary Politics and Resentful Affect in Populist Times, 9(3), 237–247.

Chakrabarty, C. (2018). 'Anthropocene time.' *History and Theory*, 57(1), 5–32, https://doi.org/10.1111/hith.12044

Chesneaux, Jean (2000). 'Speed and democracy: An uneasy dialogue.' *Social Science Information*, 39(3), 407–420, https://doi.org/10.1177/053901800039003004

Clark, S. and Teachout, W. (2012). *Slow Democracy. Rediscovering Community, Bringing Decision-Making Back Home.* Vermont: Chelsea Green Publishing.

Cossarini, P. and Vallespin, F. (2019). *Populism and Passions: Democratic Legitimacy after Austerity, Routledge Advances in Democratic Theory*. New York and London: Routledge.

Cramer, K. 2016. *The Politics of Resentment: Rural Consciousness in Wisconsin and the Rise of Scott Walker*. Chicago: University of Chicago Press

Damasio, A. (2000). *The Feeling of What Happens. Body, Emotion and the Making of Consciousness*. London: Penguin.

De Moor, J. (2021). 'Postapocalyptic narratives in climate activism: their place and impact in five European cities.' *Environmental Politics*, https://doi.org/1 0.1080/09644016.2021.1959123

Delanty, G. (2021). 'Imagining the future: social struggles, the post-national domain and major contemporary social transformations.' *Journal of Sociology*, 57(1), 27–46, https://doi.org/10.1177%2F1440783320969860

Diehl, P. (2019). 'Temporality and the political imaginary in the dynamics of political representation.' *Social Epistemology*, 33(5), 410–421,https://doi.org/10.1080/02691728.2019.1652865

Fawcett, P. (2018). 'Doing democracy and governance in the fast lane? Towards a "politics of time" in an accelerated polity.' *Australian Journal of Political Science*, 53(4), 548–564, https://doi.org/10.1080/10361146.2018.1517862

Fleury, C. (2020). *Ci-gît l'Amer: guérir du ressentiment*. Paris: Editions Gallimard.

Gentile, J. (2020). 'Time may change us: The strange temporalities, novel paradoxes, and democratic imaginaries of a pandemic.' *Journal of the American Psychoanalytic Association*, https://doi.org/10.1177/0003065120955120

Gillan, K. (2020). 'Temporality in social movement theory: vectors and events in the neoliberal timescape.' *Social Movement Studies*, 19(5–6), 516–536, https://doi.org/10.1080/14742837.2018.1548965

Giroux, H (2004). 'The terror of neoliberalism: Rethinking the significance of cultural politics.' *College Literature*, 32(1), 1–19, https://www.jstor.org/stable/25115243

Hay, C. (2007). *Why We Hate Politics*. Cambridge: Polity Press.

Hickman, C., Marks, E., Pihkala, P., Clayton, S., Lewandowski, R. E., Mayall, E. E., van Susteren, L. (2021). 'Climate anxiety in children and young people and their beliefs about government responses to climate change: A global survey.' *The Lancet Planetary Health*, 5(12), e863–e873.

Hoggett, P. Beedell, H. and Wilkinson, Ph. (2013). 'Fairness and the Politics of Resentment.' *Journal of Social Policy*, 42(3), 567–585, https://doi.org/10.1017/s0047279413000056

Houdek, M. and Kendall R. (2020). 'Rhetoric and the temporal turn: Race, gender, temporalities.' *Women's Studies in Communication*, 43(4), 369–383, https://doi.org/10.1080/07491409.2020.1824501

Kenis, A. (2021). 'Clashing Tactics, Clashing Generations: The Politics of the School Strikes for Climate in Belgium.' *Politics and Governance*, 9(2), 135–145, https://doi.org/10.17645/pag.v9i2.3869

Knops, L. (2021). 'Stuck between the modern and the terrestrial: The indignation of the youth for climate movement.' *Political Research Exchange*, 3(1), 1–31, https://doi.org/10.1080/2474736X.2020.1868946

Knops, L., Petit, G. (2022). 'Indignation as affective transformation: An affect-theoretical approach to the Belgian Yellow Vests movement.' *Mobilization*. In press.

Knops, L. (2023). 'The Fear We Feel Everyday: Affective Temporalities in Fridays for Future.' Against the Day series, de Moor, J. (ed.). *South Atlantic Quarterly*. In press.

Lefebvre, H. (2004[1992]). *Rhythm-Analysis. Space, Time and Everyday Life*. London: Continuum.

Marcus, G. (2002). *The Sentimental Citizen: Emotion in Democratic Politics*. University Park, Pennsylvania: The Pennsylvania State University Press.

Mercenier, H. (2022). Politics and the Pandemic: Time, 'Timescapes', and the Shifting Ground of Political Dissatisfaction. Unpublished manuscript.

Merleau-Ponty, M. (2012(1945)). *Phenomenology and Perception*. Trans. by D. Landes. New York: Routledge.

Noordzij, K., W. De Koster, and J. Van der Waal (2021). '"They don't know what it's like to be at the bottom": Exploring the role of perceived cultural distance in less-educated citizens' discontent with politicians.' *The British Journal of Sociology*, 72(3), 566–579, https://doi.org/10.1111/1468-4446.12800

Norris, P. (2011). *Democratic Deficit. Critical Citizens Revisited*, New York: Cambridge University Press.

Petit, G. (2022). Tenir le rôle de Gilet jaune en Belgique: conditions d'un militantisme démocratique transnational. *Terrains travaux*, 41(2), 203–234.

Pettigrew, T. F. (2016). 'In Pursuit of Three Theories: Authoritarianism, Relative Deprivation, and Intergroup Contact.' *Annu Rev Psychol*, 67, 1–21, https://doi.org/10.1146/annurev-psych-122414-033327

Schmid, C. (2008). 'The production of space. Towards a three-dimensional dialectic.' In Goonewardena, K., R. Milgrom and C. Schmid (eds.). *Space, Difference, Everyday Life. Reading Henri Lefebvre* (pp. 27–45). London: Routledge.

Smith, B. G. (2015). 'Temporality.' In L. Disch and M. Hawkesworth (eds.). *The Oxford Handbook of Feminist Theory* (pp. 973–990). Oxford: Oxford University Press, https://doi.org/10.1093/oxfordhb/9780199328581.013.47

Severs, E. (2020). 'Legitimacy and hegemony: Two accounts of non-electoral representation.' In M. Cotta and F. Russo (eds.). *Research Handbook on Political Representation* (pp. 58–69). Cheltenham: Edward Elgar Publishing.

Tomba M. (2014). 'Clash of temporalities: Capital, democracy, and squares.' *The South Atlantic Quarterly*, 113(2), 353–366, https://doi.org/10.1215/00382876-2643666

Valgarðsson, V. O., Clarke, N., Jennings, W., & Stoker, G. (2021). The good politician and political trust: An authenticity gap in British politics?. *Political Studies*, *69*(4), 858-880.

Webster, S. and Albertson, W. (2022). 'Emotion and Politics: Noncognitive Psychological Biases in Public Opinion.' *Annual Review of Political Science*, 25(1), 401–418, https://doi.org/10.1146/annurev-polisci-051120-1053539

9. Is this really democracy? An analysis of citizens' resentment and conceptions of democracy

Louise Knops, Maria-Jimena Sanhueza,
Eline Severs & Kris Deschouwer

Abstract: Citizens' dissatisfaction with contemporary democracy has become somewhat of a commonplace. Yet scholars routinely struggle to make sense of citizens' critiques and expectations towards representative democracy: what exactly are citizens dissatisfied with? What is it, they expect from the central institutions of representative democracy? To answer these questions and account for the diverse and potentially contradictory beliefs citizens may hold towards representative democracy, this chapter advances a citizen-centred analysis of the concept of 'democracy'. It draws on 4366 responses to an open question 'what does democracy mean to you?' formulated in two Belgian national surveys (2009 and 2019). This dataset allows for identifying the institutions and practices citizens associate with democracy (e.g., parties, parliament, representation). Our findings demonstrate that citizens' accounts of democracy have changed over time. While representation was central to respondents' reflections in 2009, in 2019 they more frequently defined democracy in relation to elections and rules of decision-making. Our findings also shows that citizens' resentment correlates with these concerns and gives expression to unmet expectations. We identify three resentful tropes of democracy: democracy is unfair, democracy is a fake, and democracy is cold-hearted.

https://doi.org/10.11647/OBP.0401.09

Introduction

Over the last couple of decades, the belief that representative democracy is dysfunctional has gained traction. Decreasing levels of citizen trust in political authorities, high levels of citizen disengagement (e.g., declining voter turnout and party membership) and heightened support for populist and authoritarian movements are routinely perceived as signs of growing dissatisfaction with representative democracy and of a fundamental disconnect between citizens and traditional political institutions. The term democratic deficit, originally invoked in the 1990s, has today become somewhat of a commonplace in political analyses.

Despite this commonplace, much debate exists on how to correctly interpret these patterns. Pippa Norris (1997; 2011) originally argued that decreasing levels of political trust indicate the emergence of a 'critical citizenry', or of 'dissatisfied democrats' who adhere strongly to democratic values but find the existing structures of representative government, developed in the 18th and 19th centuries, unsuitable or unsatisfactory to meet their 'rising expectations' (2011, p. 134). The solutions advocated in this context mainly consist of changes to the design and functioning of central political institutions to boost political participation and enhance the transparency and responsiveness of decision-making (Dalton et al., 2001; Carman, 2010).

More recently, accounts of this nature have been considered flawed for several reasons. Amongst others, scholars argue that such accounts fail to adequately grasp the high emotional load of contemporary politics and political language (Wahl-Jorgensen, 2019; Webster and Albertson, 2022). In the time of the 'anger' of the Yellow Vests, the 'love and rage' of climate movements (e.g., Extinction Rebellion) and a widespread 'hate and disdain' for politics and political institutions (Hay, 2007; Crouch, 2004), the conceptual language of the critical citizenry and 'democratic deficit' seems to minimise or diffuse citizens' critiques of the central actors and institutions of representative democracy. Against this backdrop, a growing number of studies suggest that citizens have not only become critical, but also disillusioned, bitter and angry, resentful and indignant towards the model of representative democracy and its central institutions (Capelos and Demertzis, 2018; Celis et al., 2021;).Yet, despite an increasing recognition of the important role played by these emotions, insufficient attention has been paid to identifying what are the objects or causes of citizens' grievances.

Our chapter aims to fill this gap by focusing on citizens' conceptions of democracy. We investigate the key themes and ideas that citizens regularly associate with democracy, and seek to identify when and how resentment is expressed in this context. To do this, we draw on the results of two surveys carried out in Belgium (PartiRep survey 2009 and EoS RepResent survey 2019) and conduct a qualitative thematic analysis of respondents' answers to the open question: 'what does democracy mean to you?'.

This open question allows us to research how citizens themselves define democracy, while accounting for the affective connotations that accompany these definitions. In addition, the comparative analysis we carry out (between 2009 and 2019) allows us to examine whether these affective patterns and definitions change over time, and in which regards.

In the first part of our chapter, we outline our theoretical framework: we elaborate on the links between citizens' accounts of democracy and resentment, and the importance of citizens' own words and perspectives in this context. In the second part, we present our data and methodology before discussing our findings, structured in two parts: the main themes that respondents associate with democracy (in both 2009 and 2019) and the resentful tropes that we identify across these responses: democracy is unfair, democracy is a fake, democracy is cold-hearted. In the conclusion, we reflect on the limitations of our analysis and identify potential paths for future research.

Democracy and resentment: the importance of citizens' wordings

Citizens' criticism of and dissatisfaction with representative democracy has often been measured through indicators of trust, distrust, and satisfaction (Armingeon and Guthmann, 2014). Scholars have analysed the correlation between citizens' trust levels and macro-level variables of economic performance (countries' welfare levels) and political performance (the effectiveness and efficiency of decision-making) (Mauk, 2021; Nye et al., 1997; Seyd, 2015; Hetherington and Rudolph, 2008). These studies, however, remain inconclusive about the precise relationship between political (dis)trust and economic and political performance. Similarly, Holzer and Callahan (1998) show that many governments perform better than people think but fail to demonstrate their success.

Some scholars (e.g., Bertsou, 2019) suggest that political distrust is rooted in citizens' perceptions of failing mechanisms of representation such as elections and political parties. Opinion surveys from advanced democracies do indeed repeatedly find widespread support for forms of direct democracy, such as citizen initiatives, participatory budgeting, and referendums (Dalton et al., 2001; Budge, 1996). Yet, as Bowler et al. (2007, p. 351) state, it is not clear whether these patterns invariably signal citizens' desire for a more active role in decision-making. Some conceive of the popular approval of direct democracy as evidencing citizens' faith in the ideal of democratic self-government; whereby citizens seek to govern themselves by taking on a more direct and active role in decision-making (Carman, 2010; Morrell, 1999). Other scholars, in contrast, interpret citizens' endorsement for direct democracy as primarily showcasing their rejection of the current model of representative democracy, without entailing a clear preference for any concrete alternative political model (Hibbing and Theiss-Morse, 2002; Webb, 2013; Parvin, 2018).

Much of the research that seeks to unpack citizens' dissatisfaction or distrust is rooted in the assumption that citizens' evaluations of political actors and institutions depend on rational cost-benefit analyses. The tendency to approach citizens first and foremost as 'rationally thinking' individuals can be seen clearly in Pippa Norris' (2011) notion of 'critical citizens'. Citizens are believed to hold rising public expectations from democracy that representative systems—with institutions designed in the 18th and 19th centuries—increasingly fail to meet. Some level of distrust is, in this regard, conceived as being 'productive' to democracy. According to this line of thought, distrust fuels democratic oversight and has the capacity to offset the power of political elites who claim to speak on behalf of the citizenry (Rosanvallon, 2008).

In contrast to this line of reasoning, a growing body of scholars calls into question whether citizens' evaluations of political actors and institutions are primarily, or only, based on rational judgment (e.g., Wodak, 2015). Font et al. (2015, p. 14), for instance, critique scholarly attempts to categorise citizens according to their preferences for different models of government (participatory, deliberative, representative, or expert-based). Such attempts miss the point that citizens may prefer a combination of all of these aspects, or that, to them, democracy simply means something else entirely. Scholars have also become more critical of traditional survey techniques that largely rely on a deductive logic and, as such, rely on researchers' prior or assumed understanding of democracy. While a deductive logic is well suited to measure whether people share these scholarly ideas, it is less suited to examine what people themselves mean by democracy, what they expect from it and how they feel towards it (Schaffer, 2014).

Recently, more inductive approaches seem better attuned to the great diversity of views on democracy as well as the complexities, contradictions and unequal experiences that may underpin citizens' dissatisfaction with contemporary institutions of representative democracy (Ottemoeller et al., 2001). Schedler and Sarsfield (2005), for instance, find that citizens' attachment to democratic values and principles of equality are sometimes accompanied by exactly the opposite, through the expression of homophobia, racism and other forms of political intolerance. This debunks the notion that support for democracy is unequivocally embedded in a humanist or progressive ethos.

Inductive studies also signal that attachments to democracy and concrete democratic values vary across social groups. Studies document global support for democracy as the preferred political system ('or least bad system'), and signal that liberal democracy is considered the best system to support basic human rights, individual freedoms, and equality (Ceka and Magalhaes, 2016). Yet, citizens seem to differ on the type of goods and services that democracies are supposed to safeguard. Ferrin and Kriesi (2012, p. 321), for instance, find that groups with the highest socio-economic status tend to favour a 'minimalist' vision of democracy that is only based on democratic rights and processes. Citizens with lower socio-economic status, in contrast, favour 'maximalist' conceptions of democracy that include provisions for social justice and citizen participation.

Finally, scholars also increasingly approach citizens' distrust and dissatisfaction through the lens of an 'affective disconnect' (Coleman, 2013; Lordon, 2016) and suggest further studying how citizens' emotions underpin political judgment, attitudes and behaviour. Within this field, cognition and emotion are not conceived as opposites but as mutually constitutive. This insight is rooted in a broader epistemological turn in social sciences—the affective turn—which suggests that precisely the interaction between 'cognition' and 'emotion' helps us make sense of the ambivalence, paradoxes and unpredictability of citizens' judgements overall (Marcus, 2002; Clough and Halley, 2007).

A series of recent publications have extended this idea to the study of the crisis of representative democracy. Martha Nussbaum (2018), for example, speaks of a particular politics of fear, interlaced with emotions of anger and disgust, to explain current political crises. Similarly, scholars have researched feelings of hate and disdain towards politics (Hay, 2007), or the indignation directed at political and economic elites as a whole (Gerbaudo, 2017). In this field, scholars have also attributed closer attention to resentment, an affect that is routinely associated with populist preferences and electoral abstention. Resentment, along with political alienation and apathy (Dahl et al., 2017), is seen as a symptom and feature of the contemporary crisis of representative democracy and forms of political 'malaise' (Fukuyama, 2018; Hochschild, 2016). Similarly, resentment is tied to the decline of trust in representative institutions and democracy (e.g., Ure, 2015; Fleury, 2020). Additionally, concrete political events—such as Brexit or the election of US President Donald Trump—have been attributed, in part, to citizens' resentment (Bachman and Sideway, 2016; Cramer, 2016; Hochschild, 2016).

In this chapter, we investigate citizens' resentment towards democracy by examining what kinds of feelings are evoked when citizens define democracy in their own words, and what this, in turn, tells us about citizens' relationships to democracy and democratic institutions. We define resentment as a 'resentful affectivity' (Capelos and Demertzis, 2018; Celis et al., 2021) which covers a set of feelings and moral judgments, including feelings of injustice and unfairness, long-lasting anger, frustrations, fear, and hope. We draw on the key conceptual dimensions identified in Chapter 1 and Chapter 2 of this book and provide further details about how we unpacked resentment in the description of the coding and operationalisation in the following section and in the Appendix.

Data and methodology

We draw on two electoral surveys carried out in Belgium in the context of the PartiRep project of 2009 (N=2331) and the EoS RepResent survey of 2019 (N=2025). Both surveys included the following open question: 'Can you describe, in your own words, what democracy means to you'. The open question is ideally suited to our type of inquiry into citizens' conceptions of democracy. It allows us to combine the advantages of survey research whilst limiting its disadvantages: the large N provides opportunities for comparison while the open wording helps mitigate our scholarly biases of how citizens (should) conceive of democracy.

The settings of both surveys contain similarities but also some noteworthy differences, which we elaborate on in the Appendix. Despite these differences in how the surveys were conducted, both datasets provide a representative survey of voters based on a sample from the national register of the citizens in Belgium and are largely comparable in terms of the number of units of data collected. Reflecting the national scope of the surveys, answers to the question on the meaning of democracy were given in Dutch or in French. To carry out the analysis and ensure inter-coder reliability across two separate teams of multi-lingual coders (in 2009 and 2019), all answers were translated into English using automatic translation. Translations were verified by French- and Dutch-speaking researchers prior to the coding phase.

In 2009, the European and regional elections coincided. These elections followed two years after the federal elections in 2007. After an already difficult government formation period, the federal government remained greatly divided on communitarian issues and responses to the financial and economic crisis of 2008. Early elections were held in June 2010 and after an unprecedented 541-day formation period, a government coalition, under Prime Minister Elio Di Rupo of the Social Democratic party was formed.

We might expect that this long-lasting government crisis affected respondents' answers in the 2009 and 2019 surveys, and their evaluation and feelings towards political institutions in Belgium. Yet, we should be cautious in assuming too strong an effect. Earlier studies document that trust at the federal level remained fairly stable between 2009 and 2014 (Henry et al., 2015). Political trust levels, in contrast, showed a sharp decline at the regional level; suggesting that particularly the trustworthiness of the regional governments—who stayed in power during this turbulent period—was negatively affected (Henry et al., 2015). Other studies also signal that electoral turnout remained high and relatively stable (Reuchamps et al., 2015), partly due to compulsory voting in Belgium. Also, the proportion of invalid or blank votes remained stable over time. However, the 2019 electoral results, in contrast, signal the rise of protest voting; understood as voting behaviour that primarily seeks to reject the existing political elite and express dissatisfaction towards traditional political parties. In Flanders, the radical-right party Vlaams Belang ('Flemish Interest') gained 15 seats; making it the third largest party in the federal parliament. In Wallonia, the radical left-wing party PTB*PVDA similarly increased its electoral share; currently occupying 10 seats in the federal parliament. Earlier research (Hooghe and Dassonneville, 2018) found that low levels of political trust are strongly associated with a preference for protest parties like Vlaams Belang and PTB*PVDA; suggesting that—even with relatively stable levels of political trust—the Belgian electorate is characterised by an important and growing group of dissatisfied citizens.

To analyse the data, we conducted a two-step analysis. First, we coded respondents' answers to the question 'what does democracy mean for you?' according to thematic categories, classifying the answers into abductively generated categories of democracy (Vila-Henninger et al., 2022). Second, we coded respondents' answers for the affective connotations they carry. Here, we focused mostly on the emotions that belong to resentful affectivities (anger, frustration, fear, etc, see Chapter 1) and that are related to negative evaluations of democracy, or the overall observation that democracy is not functioning well.

Our thematic coding combines a deductive and inductive logic, and thus follows the general principles of abductive qualitative research (Vila-Henninger et al., 2022). We based our work on an earlier study (Deschouwer, Ferrin and Tanasescu, 2011) of the 2009 dataset in which the authors developed a set of categories that drew from general theoretical assumptions about what democracy is (Diamond and Morlino, 2005). These categories refer both to the practical organisation of democracy (e.g., the actors, institutions, mechanisms, and decision-making processes associated with it) and to the norms and ideals associated with democracy (e.g., freedom, equality, tolerance).

In our analysis of the 2019 dataset, we adopted a similar approach. Table 9A.2 (in the Appendix) provides an overview of all categories identified and how each individual category was operationalized. For both the 2009 and 2019 data, each answer was coded in a non-exclusive way, meaning that one answer could be coded across multiple categories. This allowed us to account for the multiple and sometimes paradoxical or contrary meanings citizens attribute to the concept of democracy. For the 2009 data, 4149 codes were attributed across all thematic categories; compared to 3475 for 2019. To guarantee inter-coder reliability, we took several measures: regular coding tests across the dataset, team meetings to exchange feedback and preliminary results, and the writing of joint coding memos and operationalisations of each category.

The thematic coding was complemented by a coding for resentment. When answering the open question, several respondents took the opportunity to spontaneously express a range of negative feelings and moral judgments towards democracy. Resentment precisely covers these dimensions. It is a complex emotion which covers a broad affectivity (Capelos and Demertzis, 2018) fuelled by fear and anger, but also frustrated hopes, feelings of unfairness and injustice (Scheler, 1913; 1994). As we unpack in Chapter 1 of this book, it is a multi-layered emotion made of 'disappointment, anger and fear' (Tenhouten, 2007), and is situated on the same affective continuum as anger and contempt (Solomon, 1993). Resentment is thus better understood as a 'resentful affectivity' (Capelos and Demertzis, 2018) that covers several emotions which may be expressed in relation to democracy. Resentment is also commonly defined as a moral judgment, which implies a normative evaluation of democracy, a denunciation of unfairness and injustice (Ure, 2015; Fleury, 2020).

For both the 2009 and 2019 datasets, answers were coded as resentment only once, even if, as we will see, multiple emotions were expressed, and multiple features of democracy were invoked. We decided not to multiply the sub-categories of resentment (and hence coded 'resentful' answers only once) given the difficulties of identifying precise affective connotations based on survey responses only. However, in coding the answers, we developed an operationalisation of the resentful answers around the following types of feelings: feeling ignored, disconnected, misunderstood; feeling betrayed, deceived, disillusioned; feeling discriminated, feelings of injustice; feeling hopeless, powerless, resigned; feeling exasperated; feeling hopeful. These were identified at the more interpretative stage of our qualitative analysis and included in the presentation of our findings below.

We coded responses as resentment when respondents expressed one or several of these negative feelings and emotions as well as a negative moral judgment about democracy. In addition, given that resentful affectivities also include the more positive emotion of 'hope', we also included hope and related emotions in our coding. Respondents expressed their resentment in various styles and linguistic registers (more or less formal, sometimes sarcastic, sometimes vulgar) and with varying forms of affective connotations. Table 9A.3 (in the Appendix) shows our interpretation of the different sets of feelings that emerged from the responses and how each of them was operationalized.

Results

Our findings are structured in two sections, which mirror our two-level analysis. First, we present the comparative analysis based on the thematic coding which unpacks the objects of citizens' resentment towards democracy in 2009 and 2019. Second, we identify the affective connotations that are associated with these themes and identify three resentful tropes across the responses: democracy is unfair, democracy is a fake, democracy is cold-hearted.

Respondents' conceptions of democracy

The analysis reveals that, in both 2009 and 2019, citizens attach a wide range of meanings to democracy. Democracy is clearly associated with—sometimes even equated to or reduced to—elections, voting, participation, or being politically represented. Explicit references to political parties, as central intermediary bodies, feature only marginally in respondents' conceptions of democracy (2.3%, respectively, 2.8% of the total number of codes attributed). Political parties are, however, referred to or targeted in implicit ways when democracy is associated with existing institutions or electoral procedures.

We also find that citizens relate democracy to a distinct set of norms and values, such as equality, freedom (of speech), tolerance and (respect for) the rule of law. As shown in Table 9.1, citizens associate democracy most clearly with the values of equality and freedom. Here, respondents referred to equal (social and political) rights, equal treatment, equality between groups in society, and also the general principle of 'equality'. Values such as tolerance and respect for the rule of law feature less strongly in respondents' answers. Only a small share of respondents associate democracy with a certain notion of 'quality of life'.

Table 9.1 Frequency of responses per category of democracy (percentages).

	2009	2019
Elections	14.3	18.7
Parties	2.3	2.8
Representation	13.3	25.7
Participation	14.4	16.3
Direct democracy	3.9	6.3
Decision rules	7.7	15.8
Equality	22.4	16.3
Freedom of speech	31.7	8.0
Freedom	23.5	18.3
Tolerance (values)	8.7	5.4
Rules of law	8.2	3.8
Quality of life	5.0	4.0
No answer	10.5	11.0

When we compared across 2009 and 2019, a few striking differences emerge. We first noticed that, in 2019, respondents were less likely to include reflections on democratic norms and values in their answers. Most striking here is that, in 2009, respondents showcased a more principled attachment to values of freedom and, especially, freedom of speech. In 2009, the categories 'freedom' and 'freedom of speech' together make up 55.2% of the total number of codes attributed to respondents' answers. Responses coded in these categories referred to the overall idea that in a democracy, people should have the right to an opinion (any opinion); to be able to express it; and that everyone's opinion should be respected. Respondents stated, among other things: 'Democracy is when one can speak out [...]', '[Democracy means] that everybody can speak out' and '[Democracy means that] you can say what you think'.

By 2019, the aggregate share of the categories 'freedom' and 'freedom of speech' drops to 26.3%. The starkest drop is for the category 'freedom of speech'. This is somewhat surprising given the salience of the issue especially among right-wing and radical-right parties that have gained popularity during that time. We also find that the decreasing attention to norms and values is compensated by greater scrutiny over the institutions and mechanisms of democracy. Compared to 2009, respondents in 2019 more frequently refer to 'elections' (from 14.3% to 18.7% in 2019), 'representation' (from 13.3% to 25.7% in 2019) and to 'direct democracy' (3.9% to 6.3% in 2019). In 2019, 'elections' feature as the dominant category across respondents' answers. The latter may reveal an explicit call for improved political representation and better representatives, as shown in this extract:

> In my opinion, democracy is [about] giving the opportunity to every citizen member of a nation to give their opinion on the political direction of the country. Give the opportunity to select the conductors who represent them and have the same ideas as them.

Mirroring to a certain extent the progression of radical-right ideas within Belgian society, respondents also sometimes deplore, for instance, the lack of political representation of radical right-wing voters and criticize the introduction of a 'cordon sanitaire' perceived as an undemocratic measure (more so in 2019 than in 2009).

Despite these noteworthy changes in respondents' answers, the number of 'no answers' remains relatively stable (from 10.5% in 2009 to 11% in 2019). Respondents' answers were coded as 'no answer' when the response box was left blank, when they answered 'nothing', 'no idea', 'don't know' or when incomprehensible statements were made.

The fact that approximately 11% of respondents failed to provide an answer to the question 'what does democracy mean according to you?' opens up a number of interpretations. It may simply signal the difficulty of answering open questions and survey questions in general. Alternatively, 'no answers' may be attributed to a dissonance experienced by some respondents, between their ideal-typical conceptions of democracy and their everyday experiences with existing democracies. Respondents of this type may have felt uncertain about how to answer the question. Or it could signal citizens' indifference to the question, and towards the signifier 'democracy' at large. However, our data does not allow us to go further in either of these interpretations.

Respondents' resentment towards democracy

Unpacking resentment

When answering the open-ended question on democracy, several respondents also took the opportunity to express a negative evaluation or a moral judgement on democracy or Belgian politics specifically. We coded these responses under the transversal category 'resentment'. In 2019, 13.8% of the total number of responses expressed political resentment (N = 280/2035); compared to 8.9% in 2009 (N = 208/2331). The increase in the affective load of respondents' answers may be interpreted in different ways. On the one hand, an increase of affectively loaded answers is consistent with the scholarly literature which mentions an increasing affective explicitness and overall affective polarisation across politics and society (Wahl-Jorgensen, 2019; Webster and Albertson, 2022). On the other hand, it could point to the heightened anonymity of the online survey setting (in 2019, compared to face-to-face in 2009): in face-to-face settings, citizens may experience a greater hesitancy to express their grievances in an affective manner. However, we should be cautious not to over-estimate the relative increase in affectivity given the marginal share of affectively loaded answers in the total dataset, and the fact that the differences in the teams of coders in 2009 and 2019 may have also led to small variations in the interpretation of the 'resentful' answers. Either way, the aim of our analysis is rather to unpack the way in which resentment is being voiced by those who, while defining democracy, also voice their discontent in an affective manner.

To clarify what the objects of respondents' resentment may be, we cross-tabulated the results of the resentment coding with the results of our thematic categorisation (see Table 9.2). For 2009, the categories with the highest resentment load are 'freedom of speech' (20.3%), 'representation' (19.7%), 'freedom' (16.4%), and 'elections' (15.5%). The distribution of the resentful responses greatly mirrors the overall distribution of thematic categories in the broader dataset (see Table 9.1). Some exceptions, however, can be observed. While the categories 'parties' and 'quality of life' feature only marginally in the 2009 answers, these themes do attract significant resentment.

Table 9.2 Thematic categorisation of resentment.

Resentment answers 2009		Resentment answers 2019	
Total resentment	N=208	Total resentment	N=280
Expressed in %		*Expressed in %*	
Elections	15.8	Elections	33.9
Parties	10.1	Parties	11.4
Representation	19.7	Representation	40.4
Participation	13.5	Participation	19.3
Direct democracy	5.3	Direct democracy	11.4
Decision rules	10.6	Decision rules	22.5
Equality	16.3	Equality	18.9
Freedom of speech	20.3	Freedom of speech	13.6
Freedom	16.4	Freedom	13.6
Tolerance	7.7	Tolerance	9.3
Rule of law	5.8	Rule of law	6.4
Quality of life	7.2	Quality of life	12.1

For the 2019 dataset, the categories that capture most resentment are 'representation' (40.4%), 'elections' (33.9%), 'decision rules' (22.5%) and 'participation' (19.3%). Across the years, the most striking increase in resentful load is for 'elections' (from 15.8% to 33.9%), 'representation' (from 19.7% to 40.4%), and 'decision rules' (from 10.6% to 22.5%). As we discussed earlier (see above), these categories also gained salience in respondents' 2019 answers, suggesting that the themes that citizens associate with democracy do not only change over time but that their priorities change in relation to the frustrations they experience with existing democracies.

Overall, 'resentful' responses showcase a high level of discontent with the overall organisation of elections; more specifically, the act of voting itself, the electoral cycle that promotes democratic myopia, the compulsory nature of voting and the preferential voting system. Respondents' answers, however, do not simply contain criticism; they also carry a more diffuse sense of betrayal and disillusion. Based on our inductive coding, we identified three resentful tropes that emerge from the answers: (1) the idea that democracy is simply unfair and fails to promote justice, (2) the idea that democracy is a hoax, and (3) the idea that democracy is cold-hearted.

Democracy is unfair: feelings of injustice, inequalities and imbalance

The first, and most significant, resentful trope challenges the idea that democracy brings equality and freedom. Instead, democracy is associated with the exact opposite: it is conceived as a highly unequal political system that favours only the interests of the most powerful. While it should be guaranteeing individual freedoms, it is conceived as restraining them: respondents express a feeling of being limited in the exercise of their individual freedoms by the very practice of democracy, its laws and institutions. Under this trope, democracy is turned upside down; the rule of law becomes the enemy, not the safeguard, of democracy:

> Democracy, it's a word that doesn't serve for anything. Democracy means in principle doing what we want whereas in fact this is not true. (2009)

> Being free. But one must respect the law and one is therefore actually never free. (2009)

Resentful respondents expressed feelings of being 'oppressed', rather than empowered by democracy; of being constrained in one's everyday life by democracy, of not being able to live one's life as one wishes to. Democracy, to them, is related to experiences of oppression, discrimination and sometimes victimisation: 'democracy suppresses the will of the honest men. It is the worst example' (2009); 'a way to keep the people enslaved to the few' (2009).

The aspect of oppression gains traction in 2019: responses start to point explicitly to the right to speak one's mind, without fearing repression. Democracy became associated with 'the right to express oneself without risk of reprisals'; 'freedom to do and say things as you want !!!; Living freely? Expressing yourself without any risk'.

Respondents' denunciations sometimes pointed to specific forms of oppression related to socio-economic inequalities and open-border policies. Respondents, for instance, denounced income inequalities and the difficulties of getting by while the political system does nothing to redistribute wealth and continues to privilege the 'happy few':

> Democracy of the powerful: golden parachutes. Democracy of the weak: workers who do not have the means to live decently. People with a high status are taken too many liberties compared to the others. For me, in a democracy some people are being listened to and others are not. (2009)

Respondents clearly signal a feeling of being subordinated, of being 'below', compared to those 'on top'. These feelings were more recurrent and explicit in the responses of 2019, compared to 2009. In 2019, some of the respondents explicitly pointed to a right to dignity, a decent life, sometimes invoking their own personal struggles in the responses.

Some of these feelings of injustice and oppression were also tied to nationalist narratives, sometimes presenting features of radical-right, xenophobic and supremacist narratives. Some respondents grasped the opportunity to reclaim their own status and supremacy in society, emphasising the need to respect the 'real Belgians', allegedly under the oppression of 'foreigners'. This could be conceived as an ethno-nationalistic expression of resentment, and responses here denoted feelings of fear and of being under threat:

> Some [level of] respect of people for each other. The foreigners should respect us, not only the other way round. One needs to do something about the foreigners. In a democracy there is respect. (2009)

Sometimes, answers mixed both a nationalist narrative and a denunciation of socio-economic unfairness; targeting not 'the rich', but the figure of 'the foreigner'. Respondents challenged the social security benefits that foreigners have access to, stating 'We are the black sheep. We, the ordinary people have to pay for them (2009)'–echoing here the growing salience of populist, racist and anti-immigration narratives in Belgium.

Finally, these feelings of victimhood and injustice also came through in the explicit context of representative democracy, where respondents expressed feeling ignored, unheard, and being looked down upon by the people elected to speak on their behalf. These statements add another layer of affective connotation: feelings of powerlessness, fatalism, and resignation. Respondents describe the feeling that even when they speak up or signal problems, little to nothing is done in response to their voice: 'They always decide above my head. Everybody's opinion should be respected (2009)', 'Democracy is the voice of the people. Yet one does not hear that voice (2009)', and 'We should have our say, but we suffer... the vote is useless... (2019)'.

Democracy is a fake: feelings of betrayal and disillusion

Another trope of resentment, recurrent in both datasets, expresses betrayal, manipulation, and deception. In some of their answers, respondents clearly denounce the deceitful, unfaithful and dishonest character of democracy. This seems to have gained traction between 2009 and 2019.

Some respondents point directly to the deceitful character of democracy, by denouncing corruption and vested interests; that democracy is about politicians 'distributing posts and filling their own pockets!' (2019); or that 'in fact, we know that democracy is controlled by finance' (2009). In most cases however, respondents rely on broader terms, expressing a more diffuse feeling of betrayal and disillusion; that it 'does not exist'; it is 'nothing', or 'presently not so much, it is disguised' (2009); that its practice goes against democratic ideals.

> They say we are in a democracy but it is not true. One cannot say what one wants and one cannot do what one wants. (2009)

> We vote for nothing, it is fucked up whatever happens :-) (2019)

Respondents sometimes express this in a moderate way, stating that 'it is not perfect' (2009) or 'in theory very beautiful but in practice hot air'

(2019). Others deploy more derogatory language to express themselves, equating the Belgian political system to 'rubbish' (2009), nothing but 'wind and blabla' (2019), 'empty promises' (2019). In these types of responses, democracy becomes defined through other types of political systems; in particular dictatorship, or (more rarely) anarchism—here perceived in a negative light, not as a political ideal to attain. This is sometimes used to denounce a feeling of restricted freedoms of expression and a sense of victimisation in the face of alleged racist or xenophobic accusations, or the broader idea of being 'muzzled' or repressed for expressing one's opinions.

> A masked dictatorship. (2009)

> Democracy means constant chatting. There is a proverb which says that communism is [to] shut up and democracy [means that we] keep on talking. Democracy makes us falsely believe that we have rights like voting rights. And at the end of the day there are coalitions, and democracy has become anarchy. (2009)

> Democracy, for me, is to give the floor to citizens who have the right to defend their opinions, to decide what is best for their country, not to be muzzled or punished for giving their opinion. (2019)

Sometimes the trope that democracy is a 'fake' is marked by a form of resignation, a moderate form of resentment, tinted with hope and nostalgia for 'the good years'. Here respondents say that democracy is not the best system, but it is 'the 'best bad' one that we have come [up] with' (2009); 'it is [...] a nice dream that one should stick to, because there is nothing better.' (2009); and it is something that belongs to the past. Democracy is 'like 30 years ago' (2019); 'I no longer believe that every vote counts' (2019).

Democracy is cold-hearted: compassion, hope and togetherness

A third trope of resentment, which is more prevailing in the 2019 dataset, depicts democracy as cold-hearted. This trope is underpinned by an explicit demand for more togetherness, more solidarity, and more attention to citizens struggles and socio-economic difficulties. Across the responses here, there is a denunciation of 'too much carelessness' and 'indifference' (2009), anchored in what could be seen as a critique of individualism and the neoliberal society where 'everybody just takes care of himself' (2009). This is close to the trope that democracy is unjust or unfair, but it goes further; it is associated with feeling left behind—either ourselves or similar others with whom we identify and for whom we feel compassion. These answers often display a more prognostic and normative style, describing what democracy *should* deliver for human societies, and are tinted with an affective connotation of a different kind: hope, care, love and compassion.

Democracy here becomes entangled with a demand for more social cohesion and solidarity. 'The country should stick more together' (2009); 'Flemings and Walloons should understand each other better to form unity again' (2009). These appeared in both 2009 and 2019, albeit in a slightly different form: 'Togetherness and being heard, respecting each other and standing up for the working person'; 'At present, the Union is no longer strong; there is no more Union! Sad' (2019).

> Democracy represents mutual aid. Before everybody helped each other out and now everybody is indifferent. (2009)

> Democracy is about helping others in need, but we are really far from it. (2019)

> We should have our say but we suffer... the vote is completely useless.... (2019)

These feelings are indicative of the normative expectations of resentful citizens; that democracy should be a political system that cares for its differently situated citizens, by prioritising their needs and recognising the challenges they experience daily ; a system that strives towards inclusion and pays particular attention to discriminated minorities and the most vulnerable. Democracy is here conceived in terms of recognising the dignity of individuals, and the open question is grasped as an opportunity for describing how 'democracy' does not ensure that (anymore).

> To be free to do what you want while respecting others. And be able to do what we feel with our goods and money, especially middle-class people who are struggling to make ends meet and are working! (2019)

> I have worked 45 years (married) and have to live with a pension of € 1400 and I still pay taxes on that. (2019)

Elsewhere, this trope can also be found entangled with the two others, for example between the idea of cold-hearted and unfair democracy (in the first quote), or between cold-hearted and 'fake' democracy (in the second quote):

> Democracy of the powerful: golden parachutes. Democracy of the weak: workers who do not have the means to live decently. People with a high status have more possibilities than the others. For me in a democracy some people are being listened to and others are not. (2009)

> Democracy has no meaning any more now. Everybody defends himself. Frankly there is not much more that I can say. (2009)

Conclusion

Our chapter aimed to uncover the meanings and feelings that citizens express and experience in relation to the concept of 'democracy'. Our findings shed light on the multiplicity of meanings and ideas that citizens associate with the signifier democracy, but also on the feelings of resentment that 'democracy' triggers. It thus contributes both to ongoing scholarly debates on the crisis of representative democracy and on the affects and emotions that revolve in and around this crisis.

Our comparative findings—of the survey responses in 2009 and 2019—revealed interesting variations in the specific objects and dimensions that come to citizens' mind when asked to define democracy. In 2019, citizens mention more often the 'procedural' aspects of democracy in their definitions: political parties, decision-making, participation. They also refer more frequently to representation. In contrast, between 2009 and 2019 there is a relative decrease of responses emphasising normative values (freedom, equality, etc.) with a particularly sharp decrease regarding 'freedom of speech'.

In our comparative analysis of the affective connotations of responses between 2009 and 2019, we focused our attention on affective connotations that belong to resentment, which we unpacked and operationalized through the notion of resentful affectivity (Capelos and Demertzis, 2018). We distinguished a set of specific feelings: feelings of oppression and injustice, feelings of betrayal and disillusion, feelings of powerlessness, of fear and resignation. In both 2009 and 2019, these responses amounted to a relatively small amount of the total responses

(8.9% in 2009 and 13.8% in 2019). To be sure, and although we coded these responses as 'resentful', we should not take this as evidence that all these respondents are only and necessarily 'resentful'. Rather, what we find highlights different types and tropes of resentment in the way some citizens conceive of democracy today.

We observed a difference in the objects of this resentment between 2009 and 2019. More concretely, in 2009, 15.8% of the resentful respondents referred to elections, against 33.9% in 2019. A similar pattern of change is observed in the category of representation, where the share of resentful answers that referred to representation doubled (from 19.7% in 2009 to 40.4% in 2019). However, a major limitation of our analysis lies in its relative sociological blindness. We do not specify who (in which social position) expresses more resentment in relation to what specific aspect of democracy (although some socio-demographic profiles can be drawn from Table 9A.4). This would allow us to further examine the differences of resentment across society.

Our affective coding allowed us to bring these results together and identify three recurring tropes in the answers given by respondents who used the open question to voice their criticism and discontent: democracy is unfair, democracy is a fake, and democracy is cold-hearted.

These tropes are interesting in and of themselves, but also when situated against broader normative debates and a general context of democratic backsliding. These include, for example, the democratic implications of rising inequalities and the persistence of multiple forms of injustice in systems that claim to be 'democratic'. They also link back to debates on the distant, cold nature of political institutions and their responsibility in the gradual dismantling of the welfare state over recent decades, which has resulted in increasing feelings of abandonment across society. Our findings also speak to debates on the rise of anti-democratic sentiments; those that express a form of disillusion with the way democracy currently works, and those that express anti-democratic preferences, especially in relation to equality and tolerance. Similarly, the resentful tropes centred on the notion of 'freedom' connect to contemporary debates on the perceived threat that some citizens experience in relation to their individual rights and freedoms, and to the different democratic meanings and beliefs that may be attached to the notion of 'individual freedoms'—at a time when the reign of the modern, liberal individual is increasingly called into question. But they also connect to the weaponization of the freedom of speech discourse by the radical-right which has fundamentally different democratic implications. Relatedly, the idea that democracy is 'a fake' links to ongoing discussions about the resurgence of authoritarianism in certain modern democracies, to the resurgence of a citizenry that may lean towards anti-democratic ideals and belief systems and to the inability of current democratic systems to respond to broad societal challenges such as social cohesion, inequalities or climate change. Finally, it brings attention to the necessary inclusion of affects and emotions not just in political theory, but also in the development of a more 'affective' type of democratic politics centred on care, solidarity and compassion.

References

Armingeon, K. and Guthmann, K. (2014). 'Democracy in crisis? The declining support for national democracy in European countries, 2007–2011.' *European Journal of Political Research*, 53(3), 423–442, https://doi.org/10.1111/1475-6765.12046

Bachman, V. and Sidaway, J. (2016). 'Brexit Geopolitics.' *Geoforum, 77*, 47–50, https://doi.org/10.1016/j.geoforum.2016.10.001

Benski, T. and Langman, L. (2013). 'The effects of affects: the place of emotions in the mobilisations of 2011.' *Current Sociology*, 61(4), 525–540, https://doi.org/10.1177/0011392113479751

Bertsou, E. (2019). 'Political Distrust and its Discontents: Exploring the Meaning, Expression and Significance of Political Distrust.' *Societies*, https://doi.org/10.3390/soc9040072

Bornand, T., Biard, B., Baudewyns, P., and Reuchamps, M. (2017). 'Satisfaits de la démocratie? Une analyse du soutien démocratique à partir de la comparaison de deux méthodes de classification des citoyens.' *Canadian Journal of Political Science/Revue canadienne de science politique* 50(3), 795–822, https://doi.org/10.1017/s0008423917000671

Bowler, S., Donovan, T., Karp, J. A. (2007). 'Enraged or engaged? Preferences for direct citizen participation in affluent democracies.' *Political Research Quarterly*, 60(3), 351–62.

Capelos, T. and Demertzis, N. (2018). 'Political Action and Resentful Affectivity in Critical Times'. *Humanity and Society*, 42(4), 410–433, https://doi.org/10.1177/0160597618802517

Cattenberg, G. and Moreno, A. (2006). 'The individual bases of political trust: Trends in new and established democracies.' *International Journal of Public Opinion Research*, 18(1), 31–48, https://doi.org/10.1093/ijpor/edh081

Ceka, B. and Magalhaes, P. (2016). 'How People Understand Democracy: a Social Dominance Approach.' In Monica Ferrin and Hanspeter Kriesi (eds.). *How Europeans View and Evaluate Democracy* (pp. 80–110). Oxford: Oxford University Press, https://doi.org/10.1093/acprof: oso/9780198766902.003.0005

Celis, K., Knops, L., Van Ingelgom, V. and Verhaegen, S. (2021). 'Resentment and coping with the democratic dilemma.' *Politics and Governance*, 9(3), 237–247.

Coleman, S. (2013). *How Voters Feel.* Cambridge: Cambridge University Press.

Clough, P. and Halley, J. (2007). *The Affective Turn: Theorising the Social.* Durham, NC: Duke University Press.

Cramer, K. (2016). *The Politics of Resentment: Rural Consciousness in Wisconsin and the Rise of Scott Walker.* Chicago: The University of Chicago Press.

Crouch, C. (2004). *Post-Democracy.* Cambridge: Polity Press.

Deschouwer, K., Ferrin, M., and Tanasescu, M. (2011). *Your Democracy or Mine? Citizen Definitions of Democracy.* Working Paper, PartiRep Project.

Diamond, M. and Morlino, L. (eds.). (2005). *Assessing the Quality of Democracy.* Baltimore: Johns Hopkins University Press.

Dalton, R. (2004). *Democratic Challenges, Democratic Choices: The Erosion of Political Support in the Advanced Industrial Democracies.* New York: Oxford University Press.

Duffy, B., Smith, K., Terhenian, G., and Bremer, J. (2005). 'Comparing Data from Online and Face-to-face Surveys.' *International Journal of Market Research*, 47, 615–639, https://doi.org/10.1177/147078530504700602

Edwards, D. (1999). 'Emotion Discourse.' *Culture and Psychology*, 5(3), 271–291, https://doi.org/10.1177/1354067x9953001

Ferrin, M. and Kriesi, H. (2016). *How Europeans View and Evaluate Democracy.* Oxford: Oxford University Press, https://doi.org/10.1093/acprof: oso/9780198766902.001.0001

Fleury, C. (2020). *Ci-gît l'Amer: guérir du ressentiment.* Paris: Editions Gallimard.

Font, J. Wojcieszak, M. and Clemente J. Navarro. (2015). 'Participation, representation and expertise: citizen preferences for political decision-making processes.' *Political Studies*, 63(1), 152–72, https://doi.org/10.1111/1467-9248.12191

Fukuyama, F. (2018). *Identity: The Demand for Dignity and the Politics of Resentment.* New York: Farrar, Stras and Giroux.

Gerbaudo, P. (2017). 'The Indignant Citizen: Anti-Austerity Movements in Southern Europe and the Anti-Oligarchic Reclaiming of Citizenship.' *Social Movement Studies*, 16(1), 36–50, https://doi.org/10.4324/9781315122564-3

Goodwin, J., Jasper, J. M. and Poletta, F. (2001). *Passionate Politics: Emotions and Social Movements*. Chicago and London: University of Chicago Press.

Grimes, M. (2006). 'Organizing consent: The role of procedural fairness in political trust and compliance.' *European Journal of Political Research*, 45(2), 285–315.

Groenendyck, E. (2011). 'Current Emotion Research in Political Science: How Emotions Help Democracy Overcome its Collective Action Problem.' *Emotion Review*, 3(4), 455–463, https://doi.org/10.1177/1754073911410746

Hay, C. (2007). *Why We Hate Politics*. Cambridge: Polity Press.

Henry, L., van Haute, E., and Hooghe, M. (2015). 'Politiek vertrouwen en partijvoorkeur.' In K. Deschouwer, P. Delwit, M. Hooghe, P. Baudewyns, and S. Walgrave (eds.). *De Kiezer Ontcijferd. Over Stemgedrag en Stemmotivaties*. Tielt: Lannoo Campus, pp. 203–217.

Hetherington, M. J. and Rudolph, T. J. (2008). 'Priming, performance, and the dynamics of political trust.' *The Journal of Politics*, 70(2), 498–512, https://doi.org/10.1017/S0022381608080468

Hibbing, J. and Theiss-Morse, E. *Stealth Democracy: Americans' Beliefs about how Government Should Work*. New York: Cambridge University Press.

Hill, L. (2016). 'Voting turnout, equality, liberty and representation: epistemic versus procedural democracy.' *Critical Review of International Social and Political Philosophy*, 19(3), 283–300, https://doi.org/10.1080/13698230.2016.1144855

Hochschild, A. R. (2016). *Strangers in Their Own Land: Anger and Mourning on the American Right*. New York: The New Press.

Hooghe, M., and Dassonneville, R. (2018). 'A Spiral of Distrust: A Panel Study on the Relation Between Political Distrust and Protest Voting in Belgium.' *Government and Opposition*, 53(1), 104–130, https://dx.doi.org/10.4135/9781446270073

Hoggett, P., Beedell, H. and Wilkinson, P. (2013). 'Fairness and the Politics of Resentment.' *Journal of Social Policy*, 42(3), pp. 567–585, https://doi.org/10.1017/s0047279413000056

Marc, H. and Callahan, K. (1998). *Government at Work*. Thousand Oaks: Sage Publications.

Inglehart, R. (2003). 'How solid is mass support for democracy—and how can we measure it?' *PS: Political Science and Politics*, 36(1), 51–57, https://doi.org/10.1017/s1049096503001689

Jasper, J. M. (2014). 'Constructing indignation: anger dynamics in protest movements.' *Emotion Review*, 6(3), 208–2013.

Johnson-Laird, P. and Oatley, K. (1989). 'The language of emotions: An analysis of a semantic field.' *Cognition and Emotion*, 3(2), 81–123, https://doi.org/10.1080/02699938908408075

Knops, L. (2021). Political Indignation: A Conceptual and Empirical Investigation of Indignant Citizens (Belgium 2017-2020). Unpublished doctoral dissertation.

Knops, L. and Petit, G. (2022). 'Indignation as affective transformation: an affect-theoretical approach to the Belgian Yellow Vest movement.' *Mobilization: An International Quarterly*, 27(2), 169–192.

Linde, J. and Ekman, J. (2003). 'Satisfaction with democracy: A note on a frequently used indicator in comparative politics.' *European Journal of Political Research*, 42(3), 391–408.

Marcus, G.E. (2002). *The Sentimental Citizen: Emotion in Democratic Politics*. The Pennsylvania State University Press.

Mauk, M. (2021). 'Quality of democracy makes a difference, but not for everyone: how political interest, education, and conceptions of democracy condition the relationship between democratic quality and political trust.' *Frontiers in Political Science*, 3, https://doi.org/10.3389/fpos.2021.637344

Morrell, M. (1999). 'Citizens' evaluations of participatory democratic procedures.' *Political Research Quarterly*, 52(2), 293–322, https://doi.org/10.2307/449220

Mounk, Y. (2018). *The People vs. Democracy: Why Our Freedom Is In Danger and How to Save It*. Cambridge, MA: Harvard University Press.

Newton, K. (2006). 'Political support: Social capital, civil society and political and economic performance.' *Political Studies*, 54(4), 846–64, https://doi.org/10.1111/j.1467-9248.2006.00634.x

Norris, P. (1997). 'Representation and the democratic deficit.' *European Journal of Political Research*, 32(2), 273–282.

Norris, P. (2011). *Democratic Deficit. Critical Citizens Revisited*. New York: Cambridge University Press.

Nussbaum, M. (2019). *The Monarchy of Fear: A Philosopher Looks at Our Political Crisis*. New York: Simon and Schuster.

Nye, J., Zelikow, P. and King, D. C. (1997). *Why People don't Trust Government*. Massachusetts; London: Harvard University Press.

Ottemoeller, D., Marcus, R. and Mease, K. (2001). 'Popular definitions of democracy from Uganda, Madagascar, and Florida, USA.' *Journal of Asian and African Studies*, 36(1), 113–132.

Parvin, P. (2018). 'Democracy without participation: A new politics for a disengaged era.' *Res Publica*, 24, 31–52.

Reuchamps, M., Caluwaerts, D., De Winter, L., Jacquet, V., and Meulewaeter, C. (2015). 'Stemplicht en absenteïsme in een multilevel perspectief.' In K. Deschouwer, P. Delwit, M. Hooghe, P. Baudewyns, and S. Walgrave (eds.). *De Kiezer Ontcijferd. Over Stemgedrag en Stemmotivaties*. Tielt: Lannoo Campus, pp. 168–184.

Rosanvallon, P. (2008). *Counter-Democracy. Politics in an Age of Distrust.* Cambridge: Cambridge University Press.

Runciman, D. (2018). *How Democracy Ends.* London: Basic Books.

Schaffer, F. (2014). 'Thin descriptions: the limits of survey research on the meaning of democracy.' *Polity*, 46(3), 303–330, https://doi.org/10.1057/pol.2014.14

Schedler, A. and Sarsfield, R. (2007). 'Democrats with Adjectives: Linking Direct and Indirect Measures of Democratic Support.' *Political Concepts Committee on Concepts and Methods Working Paper Series*, 46(5), 637–659, https://doi.org/10.1111/j.1475-6765.2007.00708.x

Scheler, M. (1994). *Ressentiment* Ashland: Marquette University Press.

Shin, D., Dalton, R. and Jou, W. (2007). 'Popular Conceptions of Democracy.' *Political Concepts Committee on Concepts and Methods Working Paper Series*, 15.

Seyd, B. (2014). 'How do citizens evaluate public officials? The role of performance and expectations on political trust.' *Political Studies*, 63(1), 73–90, https://www.doi.org/10.1111/1467-9248.12163

Solomon, R. C. (1993). *The Passions: Emotions and the Meaning of Life.* Indianapolis/Cambridge: Hackett Publishing.

Tenhouten, W. D. (2007). *General Theory of Emotions and Social Life.* Abingdon; New York: Routledge.

Thompson, S., and Hoggett, P. (2012). *Politics and the Emotions.* London: Continuum.

Ure, M. (2015). Resentment/Ressentiment. *Constellations*, 22(4), 599–613, https://www.doi.org/10.1111/1467-8675.12098.

Valentino, N., Brader, T., Groenendyck, E. W., Gregorowics, K., and Hutchings, V. (2011). 'Election Night's Alright for Fighting: The Role of Emotions in Political Participation.' *The Journal of Politics*, 73(1), 156–170.

Vila-Henninger, L., Dupuy, C., Van Ingelgom, V., Caprioli, M., Teuber, F., Pennetreau, D., Bussi, M. and Le Gall, C. (2022). 'Abductive Coding: Theory Building and Qualitative (Re) Analysis.' *Sociological Methods and Research*, 1–34.

Wahl-Jorgensen, K. (2019). *Emotions, Media and Politics.* Cambridge, UK: Polity Press.

Webb, P. (2013). 'Who is willing to participate? Dissatisfied democrats, stealth democrats and populists in the United Kingdom.' *European Journal of Political Research*, 52(6), 747–772.

Webster, S. and Albertson, W. (2022). 'Emotion and Politics: Noncognitive Psychological Biases in Public Opinion.' *Annual Review of Political Science*, 25(1).

Wodak, R. (2015). *The Politics of Fear. What Right-Wing Populist Discourses Mean.* London: Sage, https://dx.doi.org/10.4135/9781446270073

Appendix

Table 9A.1 Key socio-demographic variables for respondents in 2009 and 2019.

	2009 (in %)	2019 (in %)
Total number of respondents	N = 2331	N = 2035
Male	49.2	51.5
Female	50.8	48.3
Age (mean)	48.2	48.3
Region Wallonia	47.3	50.3
Region Flanders	52.7	49.7
Language French	49.7	51.9
Language Dutch	50.3	48.1
Education (Secondary Level)	68.9	66
Education (University/Post-Secondary)	31.1	34

Different survey techniques

In 2009, the question was asked in a pre-electoral survey conducted before the 2009 regional and European elections in Belgium (May and June 2009). The survey was conducted as part of the *PARTIREP Election Study–Regional 2009*. The survey was conducted face-to-face and lasted approximately 45 minutes. The respondents were recruited based on a geographically stratified sample of eligible voters in Flanders and Wallonia drawn from the national registry. Halfway into the survey interview, the following question was asked: 'The next question might be a bit more difficult, but could you please describe what the word democracy means for you'. Interviewers were asked not to suggest anything but to insist on receiving an answer. The interviewers took note of respondents' answers exactly as they were given. This resulted in 2331 units of data, going from 'no answer' responses to relatively long and elaborate answers. In 2019, the question was asked in a national survey carried out online and sent to a representative sample of respondents after the national elections in Belgium (end of May to June 2019), as part of the RepResent project. As in 2009, the 2019 online survey was conducted in both Dutch and French. Respondents could choose the language of their preference at the beginning of the survey, which lasted on average 46 minutes. We collected 2035 units of data, again including 'no answer' responses.

The difference in techniques to conduct the surveys is an important aspect to consider. The literature on survey methods suggests that there may indeed be meaningful differences in the data gathered face-to-face vs data gathered online (Duffy et al., 2005). In an online scenario, the means at the disposal of the respondents are different than those available to them in an offline setting. Consider, for instance, respondents' access to punctuation or capital letters that help bring an affective connotation to the answer. The physical interaction with a professional interviewer may also play role: as a facilitating agent (e.g., the interviewer may probe the interviewee to answer the question), or rather as a detractor (e.g., the interviewer's presence might be intimidating and therefore less conducive to open, honest or controversial answers).

Table 9A.2 Categories and definitions of democracy codebook.

Thematic category	Operationalisation
Parties	Explicit references to political parties, lists, programs, coalition forming. Implicit references to the role or power of political parties within institutional functioning.
Elections	Explicit references to elections, voting, voting rights, regular or free and fair elections and implicit references to the electoral process.
Representation	Defined as the link between citizens and those who they elect to represent them; in particular to the general idea of good representation and being represented. Explicit references to politicians, government, representatives, or implicit comments that mention those who represent people's interests. This category relates to the principle of representative governments.
Participation	The idea that people have a say in the way political decision are made, or rights to influence decision-making. This category is constructed as a middle point between representation and direct democracy, where people neither support the representative principle nor wish to make decisions themselves.

Direct Democracy	Comments that defend the idea that democracy means decision-making by the people, via means such as referendums or consultation. It also includes comments in which respondents wish for direct control of decision and policymaking.
Decision Rules	References to how decisions are made or who decides. These comprise the process, laws, and procedures of decision-making (consultative, delegation); the actors involved and how decisions are taken (by majority, consensus, majorities, agreements); as well as general references to policies (what is being decided).
Equality	General reference to equality between people, between groups in society at economic, political, societal level.
Freedom	All references to freedom in democracy.
Rule of Law	Definitions where democracy means that public authorities respect the law; protection against power abuse. The category includes comments where people define democracy as opposed to dictator or totalitarian regimes.
Tolerance	The idea of living together and respecting certain values (e.g., the need to live together).
Quality of Life	All references to the ultimate objective of democracy and what democracy should deliver, as being e.g., peace, decent life, economic security, welfare.

Table 9A.3 Resentment codebook

Affective connotation linked to resentment	Operationalisation
Feeling ignored, disconnected, misunderstood	Answers that make an explicit reference to the ideas of 'not being heard', 'not having a say' accompanied by a negative evaluation of the current situation; feeling 'small' in comparison to 'those above', feeling neglected.

Feeling betrayed, deceived, disillusioned	Answers that make an explicit reference to the 'deceiving' nature of democracy, 'fake' democracy, the increasing lies, the scandals, the corruption. Feelings of being misled, misrepresented, misgoverned, fooled, expressed with more or less anger or longing for an ideal. The idea of broken dreams, broken promises.
Feeling discriminated against, feelings of injustice	Answers that make an explicit reference to unjust treatment, unfair privileges or benefits granted to 'others', compared to 'us'; feelings of jealousy and resentment towards others. Involves an explicit comparative element, between 'us' and 'others like us' who are enjoying unmerited benefits.
Feeling hopeless, powerless, resigned	Answers that make an explicit reference to the idea that 'nothing will change anyway'; 'I vote but it changes nothing', a feeling of resignation, powerlessness, fatalism. It is associated to cynicism, disillusion, and nostalgia (words and narratives denoting time going by and the feeling that 'it was better before', explicit references to 'the good old times')
Feeling exasperated	Answers that denote the idea that 'this has lasted for too long!'; 'I am fed up', 'things need to change'!
Feeling hopeful	Answers that make an explicit reference to an ideal of democracy that is out there, defined in detail, mentioning the 'good' about democracy, what it should deliver for all people, whilst remembering that 'it is not happening right now'. The feeling that democracy has become an unattainable utopia, hence creating new feelings of frustration (and resentment)

In our affective coding, we drew inspiration from linguistic studies (Laird and Oatley, 1987) and discursive psychology (Edwards, 1999); we paid attention to emotion-words, metaphors and analogies, linguistic tropes, and punctuation. Indeed, many respondents denounced, blamed, or regretted the current state of democracy, by using words denoting emotions explicitly ('it's unfair', 'I am sad' etc.). Respondents also relied on other linguistic indicators to convey their feelings, such as intonation (the presence of exclamation marks (!!!), the use of ellipsis (...) at the end of a sentence), the use of figures of speech such as metaphors, repetitions, or the use of capital letters to emphasize an idea strongly (e.g., 'we do NOT live in a democracy!'). Some respondents also situated their responses within broader narratives of oppression and victimisation, by using words denoting unfair power relations, discrimination, injustice, etc.

Socio-demographic variables and socio-demographic traits of respondents per category

Table 9A.4 may be viewed online at https://doi.org/10.11647/OBP.0401#resources

10. What do resentful citizens want from democracy?

Soetkin Verhaegen, Virginie Van Ingelgom,
Louise Knops, Karen Celis &
Kenza Amara-Hammou

Abstract: Political resentment is increasingly discussed, especially in the context of citizens' dissatisfaction with the current political system as expressed on social media, in the streets, and through support for populist parties. Political resentment is posited as the reflection of a deep discontent with representative democracy, leading to a longing for change. While it is often assumed that the change that the politically resentful look for lies outside the realm of democratic institutional arrangements, there are many alternatives to the current institutional design of democracies that may offer alternatives. This chapter asks two sets of questions. First, the chapter inquires what resentful citizens identify as problematic in the current functioning of democracy, and what they are resentful about. Second, the chapter asks what resentful citizens' (anti-)democratic preferences are, and what alternative (democratic) institutional designs they prefer. These questions are answered using a mixed-methods design integrating survey data of representative samples of Flemish and Walloon citizens, focus groups with Belgian citizens, and democratic theory. Drawing on survey data and qualitative insights from focus groups discussions, the analyses show that citizens with higher levels of political resentment show lower satisfaction with the way in which democracy works, hold more populist attitudes, are more likely to vote blank or abstain, and are more supportive of referenda and citizen fora. The latter democratic innovations may attract the support of resentful citizens because of their perceived novelty and shift away from the 'distrusted representatives'. Remaining hope and expectations vis-à-vis representatives, however, also calls for reflections on how to improve representative relationships in a way that responds to the resentful citizens' concerns. Recursive and reflexive representative relationships are discussed as a way forward in that respect.

Introduction

Across the literature, there is an increasing acknowledgement of the rise of critical citizens (Norris, 1999), dissatisfied democrats (Klingemann, 2014; Kumlin 2011), assertive citizens (Dalton and Welzel, 2014), counter-democrats (Rosanvallon, 2006), and indifferent citizens (Van Ingelgom, 2014). Through their investigations of how Western democracies have become *Disaffected Democracies* (Pharr and Putman, 2000) or of *Why We Hate Politics* (Hay, 2007), scholars share the conviction that there is a 'crisis of representative democracy' and that feelings of disaffection, anger and disengagement have become important political features of Western democracies.

Among other things, citizens have grown increasingly resentful towards the institutions of representative democracy. This shows itself, for example, in explicit expressions of moral anger directed at formal institutions of representative democracy and (local) representatives of the political elite. For example, this was the case during the Yellow Vest mobilizations and other protests of recent years, including the protests against COVID-19 related measures (Vieten, 2020). These are expressions of hatred and disdain towards representative democracy as it is organized today (Hay, 2007), and resentment—consisting of feelings of anger, fear, disappointment, and a moral judgement resulting from the persistent and cumulative experience of unfairness—is a central part of the story (see Chapter 1; Capelos and Demertzis, 2018; Celis et al., 2021; Fleury, 2020). Political resentment—and the politics of resentment—have also played an important role in typically 'populist' moments or trends such as Brexit or the Trump election in 2016 (Bachmann and Sideway, 2016). Here, feelings of unfair treatment of 'the people' as opposed to 'the elite' and scepticism about political institutions are mobilized (Cramer, 2016; Bonikowski, 2017; Bonikowski and Gidron, 2016).

These examples indicate that political resentment is an important factor for understanding contemporary politics and the many facets of the contestation that may be expressed against representative institutions. They also show that political resentment is linked to a longing for change; the Yellow Vests protestors, for instance, had very clear demands about democratic reforms, in the same way that the fiercest Brexit defenders also had very clear demands to 'take back control'. These demands for change may be located within or outside the realm of democratic politics; there are different ways in which political systems could be steered in anti-democratic directions, but there are also many democratic alternatives to the current institutional design of Western representative democracies (often bundled together under so-called 'democratic innovations'). Indeed, recent research has shown that neither resentment, nor populism, by essence or by definition, lead citizens to reject democratic ideals, actors and practices (Kaltwasser and Van Hauwaert, 2020). Resentful individuals often have complex expectations towards the institutions of representative democracy, beyond a mere antagonism toward 'the establishment', or the complete rejection of representative democracy (Celis et al., 2021). This contradicts the often-assumed relationship between resentment, anti-democratic attitudes such as populist preferences, and calls for a more nuanced understanding of how resentment shapes and steers democracies in different and sometimes competing directions.

Given the importance of resentment in contemporary politics and the gaps in our understanding of how political resentment relates to attitudes about the political system, this chapter investigates what resentful citizens are resentful about, their attitudes towards democracy, and what, if at all possible, political institutions can do to (re)connect with resentful citizens. What kind of democratic innovations could meet their desire for political and institutional change? By answering these questions, we seek to contribute to the identification of pathways towards democratic reforms that speak to the current dissatisfaction and resentment towards representative democracy. In exploring future directions for democratic reform and the improvement of democratic functioning overall, our contribution hence seeks to 'democratize democracies' (Saward, 2020).

Relying on survey data, focus group data and on democratic theory, this chapter further disentangles the relationship between political resentment, populist attitudes and democracy. We study this in Belgium, a representative system rooted in 'consociational democracy' (Lijphart, 1969) and mirroring a deeply divided society. Different types of resentful citizens can be observed in this context, such as populist and far-right voters (in particular in the north of the country), and protesters and activists such as those belonging to climate movements, the Yellow Vests, or protests against measures to combat COVID-19. More generally, the Belgian population is also characterized by important socio-economic and socio-cultural inequalities, which lay the foundation for resentment to emerge. Through a 'conversation' between quantitative, qualitative and theoretical investigation, the chapter makes two main contributions.

First, the empirical analysis shows that political resentment is indeed associated with populist attitudes and with dissatisfaction with current democratic arrangements. An association is also observed between support for vote abstention and blank voting. Yet, withdrawal and protest voting are not the only behavioural preferences related to resentment. Resentful citizens also opt for democratic alternatives (referenda and citizen fora). It is both the shift away from the 'distrusted representatives' and the relative novelty of these democratic innovations that attract the support of resentful citizens. These democratic alternatives offer a response to the general, diffuse and long-lasting dissatisfaction with the traditional ways of 'doing politics', with classical channels of participation, and with today's actors and institutions of representative democracy. At the same time, they build on the remaining hope and expectations that representatives and representative institutions may still offer solutions.

Second, our discussion also tackles a series of normative questions, in particular pathways for democratic reform within representative democratic designs. Given the remaining hope and expectations that citizens still hold in existing institutions, we engage in a more speculative discussion on possible improvements to the quality of representative relationships, albeit without presuming that this would be the only way forward—be it within or outside the realm of representative institutions. Drawing on democratic theory, we argue that democratic systems could respond to resentment by establishing a recursive and reflexive representative relationship. This could complement other preferred democratic innovations such as citizen fora and referenda.

Overall, our chapter shows that resentment can provide an affective texture to studies that aim to better understand the current dysfunctions and gaps in existing representative systems. It also indicates what may be envisaged in terms of democratic solutions to the current representative systems.

Resentment and the crisis of representative democracy

Resentment, dissatisfaction with democracy, populism, and electoral behaviour

Various scholars have claimed that the relationship between citizens and representative institutions cannot be solely approached through the lens of rational interests and ideological views; it also relies on different forms of affective dynamics and identifications (e.g., Marcus, 2002; Mouffe, 2005; Mouffe, 2018; Slaby and von Scheve, 2019). Resentment, as a complex emotion, can therefore be expected to play an important role in explaining negative evaluations about the current democratic system. Specifically, dissatisfaction with democracy comes together with feelings of disaffection, anger and disengagement (Pharr and Putman, 2000; Hay, 2007). This can be seen in explicit expressions of moral anger directed at political representatives by social movements, amongst other examples. The Yellow Vests movement, for instance, became known by its explicit collective identifier as 'the *anger* of the people' (Knops and Petit, 2022; Béroud et al., 2022). Anger is a core emotion of political resentment, or 'resentful affectivities' that can be aimed at both the processes and the outcomes of a political system (Capelos and Demertzis, 2018; Celis et al., 2021), or at the very idea and principles of the representative logic that underpins existing representative systems (Van de Sande, 2020). Similarly, disappointment and experiences of unfairness may be invoked by the political system. As such, we expect that:

> H1: The higher one's political resentment, the lower one's satisfaction with the way in which democracy works.

A specific set of critical or resentful attitudes regarding representative democracy can also be found in the phenomenon of populism, and the expression of populist preferences across the citizenry. In the literature, populism is often defined and operationalized as 'a set of ideas that concerns the antagonistic relationship between the corrupt elite and virtuous people' (Rooduijn, 2018). From a populist point of view, established and traditional representative institutions are perceived as serving the interests of corrupt elites, and positioned against the interests of 'the people' (Mudde, 2004). Constitutive of this antagonism are underlying feelings of having been unfairly treated compared to other groups of citizens, and feelings of injustice regarding the privileges and power enjoyed by the elites compared to the 'ordinary citizen'. Given that moral judgements resulting from experiences of unfairness are central to political resentment (see Chapters 1 and 2 of the present volume), we expect an association between political resentment and populist attitudes:

> H2: The higher one's political resentment, the higher their populist attitudes.

Citizen participation in elections is a key aspect of representative democracy. Indeed, as Chapter 4 in this volume has convincingly demonstrated, intense feelings of hope and anger determine political behaviour, i.e., protest participation, a refusal to vote, or a vote for a mainstream party. In addition, previous research has shown that perceptions of the overall functioning of the political system are associated with the decision to vote blank or abstain. Dissatisfaction with democracy is usually regarded, at least implicitly, as an important cause of civic disengagement and thus of abstention (Norris, 2011; Kostelka and Blais, 2018). Since political resentment consists of disappointment with the political system and experiences of unfairness, we expect that this resentment will be reflected in how citizens view elections, and as a result how they behave in them. We expect that political resentment is associated with lower electoral participation. In other words, and quite logically: when citizens are disappointed with the way in which the current representative democratic system works and perceive the system to be unfair, we may expect that they would be less willing to make the effort to turn out and vote. In this context, an 'electoral' alternative to expressing resentment through abstention may be found in voting blank. This is a tool that citizens can use to express their opposition to the system, and to indicate that they do not perceive a viable partisan, institutional option in the choices they are offered, or that they have become entirely disillusioned with electoral politics altogether. We thus expect that:

> H3: The higher one's political resentment, the higher their probability of voting blank or abstaining.

Resentment and democratic alternatives

Above we explored the option of using the electoral system to express resentment by voting blank and/or by supporting populist alternatives. We also explained why resentful citizens might choose to abstain from electoral politics. Another likely consequence of feeling resentment towards the current political system is that people will favour alternative democratic arrangements. This expectation builds on literature that shows that citizens who are dissatisfied with representative democracy tend to favour deliberative, participatory forms of democracy (e.g., Christensen, 2020; Pilet, et al., 2023), and want to be more involved in democratic decision-making overall. Social movement research in recent years—ranging from the 2011 Occupy and Indignados movements to the Yellow Vests or the Youth for Climate movement—has also documented how some citizens involved in social movements may express explicit preference for alternative democratic designs in the form of Citizens Assemblies or Citizens' Referenda (Van de Sande, 2020; Gerbaudo, 2017; Knops and Petit, 2022; Della Porta and Felicetti, 2022).

In addition, recent research shows the tendency of 'populist' citizens to support direct democratic instruments—yet without always actively participating in these instruments when given the opportunity (Trüdinger and Bächtiger, 2022). Citizens sometimes combine support for various democratic designs, for instance a combination of expert and citizen assemblies, or the inclusion of consultative referenda into other democratic designs (Pilet et al., 2020). In sum, even when citizens feel anger, disappointment, and that the current system is unfair, they may search for alternatives within the democratic realm rather than turning their backs on democratic values and processes altogether. In fact, the disappointment with the system of representative democracy might stem precisely from placing a high value on democratic governance and citizen participation (Celis et al., 2021) and being aware that the current system does not reach those democratic expectations. We thus expect that:

> H4: The higher one's political resentment, the higher the probability that one will support democratic alternatives (referenda and citizen fora).

A mixed-methods approach to studying political resentment

To test these hypotheses about the relationship between political resentment, attitudes and behaviour regarding representative democracy and democratic alternatives, we draw on the survey data collected by the RepResent consortium in November 2021 (4th EOS RepResent Cross-Sectional survey, 2021; see the general methodological Appendix of the book, and Elie et al., 2023), and focus groups that took place in Brussels (see Chapter 2) with citizens who were expected to be politically resentful (and indeed often showed this sentiment). The analysis uses a mixed-methods design that integrates both data sources to draw conclusions about what resentful citizens are resentful about, and that discusses ways for democratic systems to respond to citizens' resentment. We use an explanatory sequential design where we first perform a quantitative analysis with the survey data and use the focus groups to further explain the results (Creswell, 2015, p. 23). Studies using both focus groups and opinion surveys, drawing on qualitative and quantitative data, are very common (Van Ingelgom, 2020).

The survey

Political resentment is measured in the survey with the newly developed measurement scale as described in Chapter 2. Respondents were asked to indicate their agreement with seven statements, on a scale that ranges from 0 to 10 (see Table 10.1). The statements tap into disappointment, anger, feeling infantilized (as a proxy for anger), experiences of unfairness, and the perception of a long-lasting bad experience. The factor analysis reported in Chapter 2 indicates that the seven survey items form an internally consistent scale. The factor score of each respondent on this scale is used in the analyses in this chapter. The scale allows us to distinguish between more and less resentful survey respondents.

Average agreement with these statements is 6.284 (Standard Deviation= 2.143, range 0-10), indicating that, overall, respondents lean towards showing political resentment. This is the main independent variable in this chapter.

Even if the survey question taps into different elements of resentment that combine in one scale, it is interesting to observe the variation in average agreement with each of the response statements. Taking a closer look at Table 10.1, we see which concerns and feelings are most vividly present among respondents. We observe the highest agreement with the statement about the length of time the Belgian political system has been malfunctioning (item 7), and with the statements that express a general disappointment in politics (items 1 and 2). The next most important problems, according to the respondents, are related to the actors and processes of formal, electoral politics (items 4 and 6). Feelings of anger and unfairness are least supported by the respondents (items 3 and 5), even if they are still widespread.

Table 10.1 Formulation survey question on political resentment.

How strongly do the following statements correspond to your opinion about politics?	Mean
1. What the government decides is often less good than what I hoped for.	6.618
2. I'm generally disappointed in politics in Belgium.	6.796
3. I get angry when I think about politics.	5.721
4. Most politicians don't take citizens seriously, they rather treat us as children.	6.526
5. Policy is usually better for others than for people like me.	5.279
6. Elections don't matter, everything has been decided on beforehand anyway.	6.204
7. The political system in Belgium has been malfunctioning for a long time.	6.825

Source: EOS RepResent Cross-Sectional survey, Fall 2021[1]. Notes: Response options range from 0= Doesn't correspond to my opinion at all; 10= Corresponds to my opinion very well. *Cronbach's Alpha*= 0.883 for these items combined.

---

1   For more details see the Appendix. The full dataset of the cross-sectional survey and its codebook can be found here: https://ssh.datastations.nl/dataset.

The analyses have four dependent variables. Satisfaction with democracy is measured on a scale from 1 (very dissatisfied) to 5 (very satisfied). Average satisfaction with democracy is 2.429, with a Standard Deviation of 1.008. Overall, respondents lean towards being dissatisfied. Populist attitudes are measured with a survey question consisting of five items, each rated on a scale from 1 to 5.[2] Average populist attitudes in the sample are 3.566 (Standard Deviation= 0.670), leaning towards populist sentiment. The analyses use the factor scores for this composed measure. We further observe that 4.57% of the sample indicated that they would have voted blank if there were elections at the time of the survey, and 8.40% of the respondents indicated that they would have abstained (even though there is compulsory turnout in Belgium). These groups of respondents are combined as the third dependent variable, comparing them to the 87.03% of respondents who said that they would have voted. Support for democratic alternatives is evaluated on the one hand by a variable that indicates respondents' support for referenda, and on the other hand for deliberative citizen fora. For each, respondents were asked to identify their opinion on a scale from 1 (strongly against) and 5 (strongly in favour). Overall, respondents are in favour of both alternatives. Mean support for referenda is 3.935 (Standard Deviation= 1.023) and mean support for citizen for a is 3.682 (Standard Deviation= 1.057). A paired *t*-test indicates that support for referenda is significantly higher than support for citifor afora ($p<0.001$), even if the averages are rather close.

The first model that is estimated for each dependent variable includes political resentment as explanatory variable and six control variables: age, gender, education level, satisfaction with the income of one's household, left-right self-placement, and interest in politics. These may mediate the relationship between political resentment and each of the dependent variables.[3] The second model estimated for each

---

        xhtml?persistentId=doi:10.17026/dans-zkg-rftw
2   Respondents were asked to indicate their agreement with each of the following
        statements: Politicians in parliament should follow the opinion of the people;
        Oppositions regarding politics are larger between elites and regular people than
        between the people themselves; I prefer being represented by a regular citizen
        than by a professional politician; What most people call a compromise is actually
        just to let go of your principles; Most politicians do not care about the people.
3   The survey question formulation for all variables used can be accessed
        here: https://ssh.datastations.nl/dataset.xhtml?persistentId=doi:10.17026/
        dans-zkg-rftw

dependent variable includes the above-mentioned variables, adding alternative explanations. We consider institutional trust, external efficacy, and political cynicism. As explained in Chapters 1 and 2, these concepts are closely related to political resentment and tap into similar types of sentiments towards the political system. Including these in the models allows us to better evaluate the explanatory value of political resentment. The analyses are run in two steps, since some caution is required as there is a high correlation between resentment and both cynicism and external efficacy (respectively $r=0.586$ and $r=0.566$), and between cynicism and institutional trust ($r=-0.639$). However, there is no multicollinearity, which would prevent us from estimating the models. The variance inflation factors (VIF) are not alarming, but the VIF is close to 2 for cynicism and trust in (nearly) all the models.

Focus groups

In addition to survey data, the analyses in this chapter draw on focus group data, gathered in the Brussels region between 2019 and 2021. Focus groups are composed of participants from diverse socio-economic backgrounds and where political resentment is expected to be observed. In these groups, political resentment is expected given participants' involvement in certain social movements or because of their social position. More details on the sampling and procedures of the focus groups are presented in Chapter 2. This chapter draws on quotes from focus groups with inhabitants of Molenbeek (one of Brussels' least advantaged areas adjacent to one of the city's most advantaged areas—Dansaert), a focus group in Dansaert, involving participants in the Yellow Vests protests, blue-collar workers in the European Parliament, participants in the Youth for Climate movement, individuals who are working in Brussels as lived-experience poverty experts, and participants in socio-economically difficult situations who were members of the Syndicat des Immenses (SDI), an action group that fights against homelessness, precarity and social exclusion.

Findings

Tables 10.2 and 10.3 present the results of the regression analyses that test the hypotheses about the relationship between political resentment on the one hand, and attitudes towards the representative democratic system and support for democratic alternatives on the other. We observe support for each of the four hypotheses.[4] Yet, we observe large differences between the models in terms of the explanatory value ($(pseudo\text{-})R^2$). The models explain a substantial proportion of variation in satisfaction with democracy and populist attitudes, but the explanatory value of the models is modest for support for democratic alternatives, and voting blank or abstaining in elections. Hence, while political resentment is significantly associated with support for these types of political engagement and behaviour, additional explanatory factors must be explored in future research. Below, we discuss the results in dialogue with the findings of the focus groups, as these help us to interpret the general associations observed in the quantitative analysis and to situate some of our findings within the broader political and socio-economic context in Belgium (and Brussels in particular).

Table 10.2 may be viewed online at https://doi.org/10.11647/OBP.0401#resources

Table 10.3 Explaining voting blank and abstaining.

	Vote blank or abstain	Vote blank or abstain
Resentment	1.160*	0.988
Age	0.992	0.993
Gender (ref. is female/other)	1.517**	1.503**
Education	0.845*	0.853*
Satisfaction household income	0.922**	0.973
Left-right self-placement	0.973	0.960
Interest in politics	0.798***	0.835***
Trust in political institutions		0.663***
Political cynicism		1.208
External efficacy		0.899
Intercept	1.601	1.207
N	2009	1999
Pseudo-R^2	0.092	0.115

---

4   The coefficient for resentment in relation to voting blank or abstaining only becomes insignificant when controlling for alternative explanations. This suggests that the relationship between resentment and these expressions of discontent with the current (party) political system is mediated by these other attitudes.

Source: 4th EOS RepResent Cross-Sectional survey, 2021. Notes: Logistic regression, entries are odds ratios (OR); * p<.05, ** p<.01, *** p<.001.

Regarding H1, we find that resentment is a political attitude that is associated with specific attitudes towards the current functioning of democracy such as (dis)satisfaction with the way in which democracy works. In the focus groups, participants explained that they are dissatisfied with the quality of democracy, as provided by the current political system. The comments made by Naïm and Sophie, two participants in socio-economically difficult situations who are also members of the SDI action group, and Cathie, who participated in the focus group with EU blue collar workers, are illustrative; politicians are said here to 'crush' or 'squeeze' people, particularly those living in poverty. Cathie also voices the concern that the current system of representative democracy encourages politicians to care about re-election, but not to consider citizens' views at other times. This assessment recurs in various other focus groups too.

Naïm:	But politicians uh… They all say 'we care about democracy' but in reality…
Sophie:	Yeah, there is no democracy. We are not living in a democracy at all.
Naïm:	[continues] But it isn't a democracy. You know, I call it a 'démocraser'.[5] [...]. For the reason that politicians take the poor uh, hostage.
Sophie:	And when you see what the money for so called social affairs is really spent on.
Naïm:	So everyone says 'democracy, democracy', but as I see it, it's a, it's a 'démocraser'. [...]. That's what they [politicians] have learned to do: 'démocraser'. It is not democracy.

(Syndicat des Immenses focus group,
conducted in Ixelles, in December 2019)

Cathie:	[...] politicians promise people that good days lie ahead. At election time, they promise us [people] everything but once we've voted for them and the elections are over, we receive nothing at all. Yes, additional taxes uh, everything

---

5   This is a play on words: the participant connects the word democracy to 'écraser', which means 'to crush' in French.

is done to make things more difficult for people instead
of helping them.

(Blue-collar-worker focus group, conducted in
EU district, in February 2020)

These quotes illustrate that participants value democracy as a system,
but do not find the current system really 'democratic' in its functioning
and its ability to meet important democratic values and goals such as
equality. Instead, they feel like politicians do not properly represent
people with their policies, but rather 'crush' them; and in particular
those who are already excluded from society or at risk of social exclusion.
These quotes also hint at a perceived feeling of distance between
'politicians' and 'the people (in poverty)', which corresponds to the
observed significant association between feelings of political resentment
and populist attitudes in the survey data (H2). Various other quotes in
the focus groups express similar sentiments. For instance, in the focus
group organized with individuals active in the Yellow Vests movement,
participants expressed a real sense of disconnection, outrage, and
disgust, even, with 'them above', who were viewed as opposed to 'the
people'.

Thomas: People are simply not taken into account... they [politicians]
            are not aware of people's demands. [...]. Those are
            the things that really make me outrageous.[6] [...]. Each
            time I talked to people, I heard the same complaint: the
            purchasing power, the problem of ... [is looking for the
            word] political trust, yes, that was repeated quite often.
            [...]. People don't believe in anything anymore [...]. And
            well, politics...well, you vote for one thing and then they
            do whatever they want with it.

Frank: I think this is really important; this disdain expressed by the
            system, politicians, those above. In France, how can
            Macron dare to say 'people who are nothing' ['une gare
            où les gens qui sont rien'] [...].

Antoine: The opportunistic lies of politicians... With the N-VA: 'we
            won't touch the VAT on energy, pension, etc'. Whatever...
            it didn't take them 15 days to pff [makes an abrupt

---

6   In French: « ça m'a révolté ».

move with his arm] trigger a social tsunami. That really
disgusted me.

(Yellow Vests focus group, Brussels, January 2019)

In the focus group with EU blue-collar workers, Cathie related the
distance between politicians and people like herself to the lack of a
shared experience. She feels that politicians live in a different world,
which has to do, in particular, with social inequality and the wealth
disparities between 'politicians' and 'us'. She argues that politicians
should experience life as people like her do—on a lower budget—in
order to truly be able to understand them.

> Cathie: I think that if they [politicians] would lower their salaries and
> would learn to live with the wages that we are paid every
> month, I believe that they wouldn't manage. It would
> also be good that, instead of always coming up with their
> blabla and all, if they would learn to live like us, with the
> same monthly budget, we would see whether they still
> come up with the same proposals.
>
> (Blue-collar-worker focus group, conducted in
> EU district, in February 2020)

Yet interestingly, and somewhat counter-intuitively, focus group
participants who express strong disappointment, frustration and
sometimes outrage at representatives (or elites in general), also discuss
and express how they keep on trying to be heard by politicians and by
representative institutions. Here, some participants explained that they
voted for political actors who provide an alternative to the mainstream
politicians such as populist parties, or 'extreme' parties more generally.

> Jordy: I think that I'll vote for a small party, you know, just because
> that's the only way to boycott.
>
> Lara: For an extreme party, you mean.
>
> Jordy: To vote against [all other parties] because if I give my vote to a
> small party, I know that they will never win enough seats
> to make a change. They won't have that anyway. But then
> I would also not lose my vote by abstaining.
>
> (Yellow Vests focus group, conducted
> in St-Gilles, in April 2019)

In the analysis of the survey responses, we further observe that resentment is expressed through political behaviour such as voting blank or abstaining in elections (H3). Participants explained that they voted blank because of their distrust in politicians and their perceived distance from themselves, or to invite politicians to query why people vote blank. The exchange between Abbou and Mehmet, inhabitants of Molenbeek, clearly illustrates this. Others, as illustrated by Lara (Yellow Vests), experience the lack of a party that they want to support as a violation of their right to vote. She questions voting blank as a viable option because it implies supporting the largest party.

Abbou: There is no longer any contact between the inhabitants and the politicians. It's rather normal that we [people] vote blank.

Mehmet: [interrupting him] There are a lot of blank votes, yes, yes.

Abbou: Well, it's normal [to vote blank] because we no longer believe what politicians say. I don't believe them anymore. I have been voting blank for several years. [Agitated] There must be blank votes because I want politicians to ask themselves the question '*why* are there so many blank votes?'! I want them to ask themselves the question whether it is due to anything they said or did not say, on TV for instance, I want them to think about why there is a change. You see?

Mehmed: Yeah, in fact, in fact, in fact they have to ask themselves this question; why do people vote blank? That's all. Politicians need to think about it.

Walid: They have to become aware, yeah.

Abbou: So, the solution is that politicians have to react, that's all. It's so simple.

Adil: [interrupting him] Yes, it's true, but a blank vote is, is that really the solution?

Abbou: Of course it might not be the solution, but I can't give my vote to these politicians who do not... Who do not keep their word. So I can't, I can't conceive...

Mehmet: [interrupting him] In fact, they have to ask the question 'Why the blank vote?'. They need to ask themselves the question.

Abbou: Indeed, if there is a blank vote, ask us why.

(Molenbeek focus group, conducted in
Molenbeek in October 2019)

Lara: I feel cornered a bit. I have the right to vote; I'm happy with that. But currently I don't know what party I would vote for as everyone makes the same mistakes. If I vote, it goes to a party that I didn't choose. I feel cornered. [...] I feel like my right has been violated.

(Yellow Vests focus group, conducted
in St-Gilles, in April 2019)

Walid: Ah no personally I voted for, I cast a blank vote, huh.

Abbou: [at the same time] Do you understand [@moderator of the focus group]? Like him [participant Walid], I prefer to vote blank.

Moderator: Did you cast a blank vote?

Abbou: I would cast a blank vote even if I was sent a fine, but I wouldn't pay it, I'm sorry.

Walid: They [politicians] just don't take enough initiatives, I think.

Abbou: All politicians do, is utter empty words. You see? In my opinion, politicians are people who just want to take money and put it in their pockets, that's all. I really think this is the truth and I no longer believe in what they have to say, in their word. They keep promising 'we're going to do this and then we're going to do something else', but it's all empty promises.

(Molenbeek focus group, conducted in
Molenbeek in October 2019)

Notwithstanding the highly critical stance concerning representatives, and perceived limitations to the current electoral system, focus group participants stressed that the intervention of politicians is still needed to solve problems. They explained that politicians are required to solve specific issues, as they have the means to do so on a larger scale. They argued that one cannot expect individual citizens to solve certain issues on their own. Participants used very specific issues to explain the need for politicians' attention, such as the decrease of purchasing power, unaffordable housing, pensions, healthcare, or the need for stronger measures to combat climate change. The following two excerpts are illustrative in this regard.

Melodie: I want to come back to what Sandrine was saying before, when you nevertheless omitted the question of asking, who, in the end, propose the alternative, should come up with solutions. Should it come from us [people] or from politicians? For me, it must clearly come from politicians because they are the ones who, in the end, have an overall vision of the spending budget, and we, well, we are nothing/have no say at all. I mean, precisely in relation to all these directives, how would I know what measures can be taken or enforced and at what governmental level measures can be enforced; the mayor of Liège does not have the same decision-making power as the minister. So, I don't know.

(Youth for climate focus group, conducted in St-Gilles, in April 2019)

Adil: In Mons [city] for example, I used to live there, there is no... Cycling paths are a rarity...

Walid: Even in Antwerp, eh, they have a lot of cycl–, uh, cyclists and all that. Therefore, politicians should, uh, should encourage more cycling paths or, I don't know, uh...?

(Molenbeek focus group, conducted in Molenbeek, in October 2019)

Imad: But they [politicians] are not all the same huh. Some do support us [people]. There is no-one, no-one to support us, but there is one deputy (or if there would be one deputy?). They do not listen... Are they [politicians] even there for us [people]? They do not react to us.
Yet, they are not all the same.
Some deputies have a heart and care [for the people]. Because they know the people who voted for some of them? You know, they grew up in popular neighbourhoods.... I know one deputy in France who now has a broken leg

because of... But, you know, they [politicians] don't really care.

(Blue-collar-worker focus group,
conducted in EU district, in February 2020)

Hence, what we find here is that, despite explicit resentment in some of the conversations, focus groups participants also do not dismiss representatives altogether. In some instances, the exchanges even illustrate that what resentful citizens actually might want is more and better representation; being heard more and better, through increased interaction between people and politicians, more transparency in the work carried out by politicians, and more outreach from their side:

Bilal: I would like to say something, it's... You know, it's not just in Belgium. It's the same thing almost everywhere: the lack of listening and the lack of reaction from... from politicians.

(Blue-collar-worker focus group, conducted
in EU district, in February 2020)

Adil: Politicians should come to the field, bring people together and talk.

(Molenbeek focus group, conducted
in Molenbeek, in October 2019)

Naima: But what if they came up with a political system that always requires a random number of citizens to sit around a table and discuss.

(Focus group in Dansaert
district, in October 2019)

Tony: So, uh... Well yes, so they are witnesses of experience,[7] not experts of experience. So basically, witnesses are citizens who go, who bear witness to their reality and the, the, the problems they encounter, uh, every day, and they form working groups, do discuss a variety of topics, like health care, and whatever else you can imagine. Then they meet politicians to present their demands, or rather, their

---

7   The participant discusses an initiative in francophone Belgium concerning the inclusion of people in situations of poverty in politics. He also explains how this initiative differs from the experts by experience in poverty service in Brussels.

proposals. Their proposals for improvement, uh, of politics in relation to people who are in precarious situations.

(Focus group with experts of experience in poverty, conducted in Brussels city in October 2019)

Sophie: Then you also have good examples. I mean, there are countries... The Scandinavian countries. They have long shown how transparency can be applied.

(Syndicat des Immenses focus group, conducted in Ixelles in December 2019)

Mehmet: You know, I would add a photo in relation to the politicians who are seated in the group. I actually want to know what they are talking about; what they are making decisions about.

Abbou: [interrupting him] Well, let's say, let's say they are mayors, and the politicians are there, working on their computers... But no; go out into the field, go see what's going on, walk around the neighborhoods...

Walid: [interrupting] Talk to people.

Abbou: [continuing] Talk to young people, talk to locals. You [@ moderators of the focus group] still made the effort to talk to us. Well then, why can't they, the politicians, do it then? Why can't they talk to us about the problems people experience? When there is no contact between local people and politicians, it is normal for people to vote blank.

(Molenbeek focus group, conducted in Molenbeek, in October 2019)

These observations in the focus groups tie in with the observations from the quantitative analysis, which shows that individuals who score higher on the political resentment scale tend to show higher support for democratic alternatives that imply the direct involvement of citizens, i.e., referenda and citizen fora (H4).

To summarize, we find that political resentment is a good predictor of dissatisfaction with democracy, populist attitudes, and voting blank or abstaining. However, this is not the complete picture. Resentful citizens have not lost (all) hope in democratic arrangements. Instead, they sometimes propose and support alternatives and solutions to the current shortcomings of (representative) democracy that increase citizen involvement in politics, without always or necessarily considering politicians as redundant. One possible explanation for this may be to say that resentful citizens' feelings of disappointment, anger and unfairness stem from their belief and high hopes in democracy (Celis et al., 2021), which they feel are not being met by the current system. Citizens who feel resentment towards the current democratic arrangement therefore do not always turn to solutions or alternatives that may be perceived as anti-democratic or as falling outside the realm of existing democratic institutions. Evidently, what we interpret as some remaining hope in existing institutions is also related to the fact that representative institutions (parliaments, governments, politicians) are the dominant set of institutions that structure the political and social imaginary of 'politics' across the citizenry. In other words, given that representative institutions are likely to be the political institutions that are most known to citizens, it is logical that they remain part of their reflections and discussions about politics.

An important caveat to this conclusion is that the survey did not include questions that tap into the possible support for anti-democratic alternatives (more authoritarian forms of governance for example), while recent survey research carried out in Belgium shows that preferences for authoritarian politics are on the rise (Noulet, 2022). Yet, such alternatives were not spontaneously chosen by participants in the focus groups. The solutions, or alternatives, that resentful citizens preferred remained within the democratic realm, but they put citizens more at centre stage than electoral politics. Referenda and citizen fora provide citizens with more direct impact in the decision-making process of specific topics. This support for alternatives that empower the citizenry ties in with disappointment in politicians and government, and with the feeling of not being heard, and sometimes being outright infantilized (as expressed in the focus group with participants to the Syndicat des Immenses). Similarly, they provide a response to the populist attitudes that are also related to a feeling of resentment. In addition to the (partial) shift in power that comes with these alternatives, their relative novelty might attract support as well. They present opportunities to break with the 'old' ways of representative democratic politics, such as voting. Support for alternatives that break with this system (by replacing it, or by adding more ways to participate in politics) could thus be a response at the affective level too, i.e., a way of responding to long-lasting and ubiquitous feelings of malaise and disappointment.

Linking empirical observations with democratic theory

Our contribution draws attention to the nuanced interplay between resentment and different types of political attitudes, and it offers routes to rethink democratic innovations to improve representative relationships as part of a democratic response to citizens' feelings of resentment. In particular, our discussion illustrates, for example, that some resentful citizens value collaboration and dialogue between citizens and representatives, and do not just reject them. This ties in with the normative ideals that recent democratic theory puts forward as solutions to foster responsiveness. We discuss these briefly here to suggest driving principles to innovate and improve the representative relationship.[8]

A first key concept is what Jane Mansbridge (2018) calls 'recursive communication' between representatives and the represented. Recursive communication requires 'iterative and interactive communication' between citizens and their representatives, in which they both inform each other about the problems and interests at stake, and, most importantly consider—'take in'—and respond to each other, in a way that is also mindful of the power-differentials between them. It can be understood as a deliberation in which both citizens and representatives engage: 'In the full ideal the representative would hear what the constituent says, take it in, consider it, and respond accordingly, while in turn the constituent would hear what the representative says, take it in, consider it, and respond on the basis of that consideration.' (Mansbridge, 2018, 299; see also Rosanvallon, 2011). Recursive communication would, at an individual level (i.e., in the interaction between citizens and their representatives) ensure citizens' input in the decision-making process. Yet, significantly, the interaction would not be limited to input 'from

---

8   For this discussion we draw on Celis and Childs 2020.

citizen to politician', but would also go in the other direction 'from politician to citizen'. Representatives should engage in a discussion of why a decision is fair and just in situations where the represented did not get what they initially wanted, and they should respond to any concerns or objections from citizens about the decisions made. In such discussions, representatives display what Dovi (2007) calls the 'virtue of fair-mindedness', which is about mediating and accommodating differences and disagreement amongst citizens, and ensuring the equal standing of all citizens, rather than representing only the interests of their constituents.

The analyses thus point towards the fact that resentment and dissatisfaction with the functioning of democracy potentially could be addressed by democratic alternatives that improve the relationship between elected representatives and the citizens they are to represent (see also Amara-Hammou, 2023). Feelings of disappointment with government decisions could be responded to with democratic alternatives that give more room to citizens' input in and power over what representatives discuss and do. A democratic innovation that would increase citizens' input could potentially address important dimensions of resentment. When citizens see that politicians do understand the issues they experience, have truly taken their perspectives, ideas and interests into consideration, and provide fair and just reasons for why they were unable to meet their demands (this time around), they might well be less disappointed, feel taken seriously (less infantilized) by politicians and consider that they have more power over those who govern them than in a system without the innovation.

In practice, this could take the shape of what Lisa Disch (2001) calls 'systemic reflexivity', which 'mobilizes both expressed and implicit objections from the represented' (Disch, 2022, p. 111). Reflexive political institutions ensure that these objections are registered, and moreover that a formal response is given to them. Reflexive political institutions enable citizens to see *and* judge a representative's efforts to be responsive. They position and empower citizens to hold representatives and representative institutions to account (see also Warren, 2019), yet they also enable citizens to know when their active participation is needed, and when, in contrast, they can trust their institutions to deal with their issues and conflicts. The latter is what Dovi (2007) calls 'critical trust', which is crucial, especially for vulnerable groups who lack the capacity or resources for extended active participation in representative processes—and, we would add, for deliberative, participatory and direct forms of decision-making.

Conclusion

In this chapter, we studied what resentful citizens identify as problematic in the current functioning of democracy, and what they are resentful about. We showed that political resentment is associated with lower levels of satisfaction with the way in which democracy works, and more populist attitudes. Disappointment in the electoral system, a perceived distance between citizens and politicians, and anger and feelings of unfairness regarding policies and processes explain these associations. Furthermore, we observed in the quantitative analysis that more resentful citizens show higher probabilities of voting blank or abstaining. The focus groups elaborate that resentful citizens often value the right to vote and believe that a system of political representation could work, but the lack of viable candidates makes them use blank voting or abstention to indicate their discontent.

This chapter further showed what resentful citizens' (anti-)democratic preferences are, and what alternative (democratic) institutional designs they prefer. We observed that more resentful citizens are more likely to support referenda and citizen fora. These democratic alternatives place more decision-making power in the hands of citizens. They offer a response to both the general, diffuse and long-lasting dissatisfaction with the traditional ways of 'doing politics', using classical channels of participation, and involving today's actors and institutions of representative democracy. We did not observe a widespread and outright rejection of (representative) democracy altogether.

Our findings also point to the fact that, rather than seeing 'resentment' as such as a problem or a threat to democracy, we should perhaps see it as a legitimate response to a malfunctioning democratic system and an embodiment of citizens' desire for political change. This challenges common assumptions about resentment as a largely 'negative' emotion. In other words, rather than locating the problem in the expression of resentment, our discussions rather hint at the fact that the problem or dysfunction lies with the lack of responses to these feelings by existing representative institutions.

Our contribution also includes a more speculative discussion on democratic innovations that seek to improve representative relationships between citizens and politicians. This is what resentful citizens hope for. Scholars argue that it is necessary to maintain what is left of the diffuse trust in the actors and institutions of representative democracy. Our interpretation of the problems that resentful citizens identify in existing representative democratic systems suggests that they could be addressed with democratic alternatives that create a recursive and reflexive relationship between citizens, and representatives and representative institutions.

Having said that, while there is potential for democratic innovations to attenuate citizens' political resentment, the feeling that the malaise has been enduring may challenge attempts to innovate in democratic politics. Even in the event of widespread use of referenda and citizen fora, collaborative decision-making, and strengthened accountability, it is likely that the formal institutions and actors involved will keep on generating negative assessments, disappointment and anger towards formal politics. When democratic innovations involve politicians and formal institutions, the anger, disillusion, distrust and impression that they have been doing a bad job for a long time can be expected to make citizens unwilling to invest time in participating in citizen fora, referenda, or collaborative policymaking efforts (given that citizens would still depend on, or need to work together with, the politicians that they resent). Such feelings are not an easy starting point for interaction. The association between political resentment and voting blank or abstaining illustrates this dynamic of withdrawal from (and at the same time signalling to) these institutions. This may be linked to the fact that democratic innovations, on their own, might not be able to respond to some of the root causes of political resentment, which lie perhaps less with procedures and actors than with other dimensions of social and political life. Democratic institutions are sometimes believed to perpetuate and crystallize socio-economic inequalities and systemic forms of social exclusion and discrimination, rather than to solve or attenuate them. Yet, notwithstanding the reduced potential of parliaments' own actions to increase trust (as it is foremost determined by dissatisfaction with the overall political system and external factors), scholars of representative democracy argue for democratic innovations to strengthen the public engagement of parliaments in order to maintain the little (diffuse) amount of trust that is still there (Norton, 2017; Judge and Leston-Bandeira, 2017).

Overall, it remains an empirical question how resentful citizens would react to the actual widespread implementation of democratic innovations and whether this would actually respond to feelings of injustice and anger across the citizenry. Democratic innovations might be insufficient to tackle the root causes of the problem, and perpetuate existing dysfunctions rather than opening avenues for fundamental change. While the results of our research indicate that it would be reasonable to expect a decline—or at least not an increase—of political resentment, it is unclear whether political resentment would decline across the board, or only among certain groups, depending on the strength of their resentment, its historical roots and origins, and how long-lived their resentment is.

References

Amara-Hammou, K. (2023). Theorizing representation from the perspective of the represented: How people in socio-economically difficult situations in Brussels understand representation. VUB: Unpublished PhD manuscript.

Bachman, V., & Sideway, J. (2016). 'Brexit Geopolitics.' *Geoforum*, 77, 47–50.

Béroud, S., Dufresne, A., Gobin, C., & Zune, M. (Eds.). (2022). *Sur le terrain avec les Gilets jaunes: Approche interdisciplinaire du mouvement en France et en Belgique*. Lyon: Presses universitaires de Lyon.

Bonikowski, B., & Gidron, N. (2016). 'The Populist Style in American Politics: Presidential Campaign Discourse, 1952–1996.' *Social Forces*, 94(4), 1593–1621.

Bonikowski, B. (2017). 'Ethno-nationalist populism and the mobilization of collective resentment.' *The British Journal of Sociology*, 68(1), 181–213.

Capelos, T., & Demertzis, N. (2018). 'Political Action and Resentful Affectivity in Critical Times.' *Humanity and Society*, 42(4), 410–433, https://www.doi.org/10.1177/0160597618802517

Celis, K., & Childs, S. 2020. *Feminist Democratic Representation.* Oxford: Oxford University Press.

Celis, K., Knops, L., Van Ingelgom, V., & Verhaegen, S. 2021. 'Resentment and coping with the democratic dilemma.' *Politics and Governance.* Special Issue: Reactionary Politics and Resentful Affect in Populist Times, 9(3), 237–247.

Christensen, H. S. 2020. 'How citizens evaluate participatory processes: a conjoint analysis.' *European Political Science Review*, 12, 239–253.

Cramer, K. (2016). *The Politics of Resentment: Rural Consciousness in Wisconsin and the Rise of Scott Walker.* Chicago: University of Chicago Press.

Creswell J. W. (2015). *A Concise Introduction to Mixed Methods Research.* Thousand Oaks, CA: Sage.

Dalton, R. J., & Welzel, C. (2014). *The Civic Culture Transformed: From Allegiant to Assertive Citizens.* Cambridge: Cambridge University Press.

Della Porta, D., & Felicetti, A. (2022). 'Innovating democracy against democratic stress in Europe: Social movements and democratic experiments.' *Representation*, 58(1), 67–84.

Dovi, S. (2007). 'Theorizing women's representation in the United States.' *Politics & Gender*, 3(3), 297–319.

Dovi, S. (2012). *The Good Representative.* John Wiley & Sons.

Michel, E., Feitosa, F., Lefevere, J., Pilet, J. B., Van Erkel, P., & Van Haute, E. (2023). 'Studying dimensions of representation: introducing the Belgian RepResent panel (2019–2021).' *European Political Science*, 1–19.

Fleury, C. (2020). *Ci-gît l'Amer: guérir du ressentiment.* Paris: Editions Gallimard.

Gerbaudo, P. (2017). *The Mask and the Flag: Populism, Citizenship, and Global Protest.* Oxford: Oxford University Press.

Hay, C. (2007). *Why We Hate Politics.* Cambridge: Polity Press.

Judge, D., & Leston-Bandeira, C. (2017). 'The Institutional Representation of Parliament.' *Political Studies*, 66(1), 154–72.

Kaltwasser, C. R., & Van Hauwaert, S. (2020). 'The populist citizen: Empirical evidence from Europe and Latin America.' *European Political Science Review*, 12, 1–18.

Klingemann, H.-D. (2013). 'Dissatisfied Democrats. Democratic Maturation in Old and New Democracies.' In R. J. Dalton & C. Welzel (eds.). *The Civic Culture Transformed: From Allegiant to Assertive Citizens* (pp. 116–157). Cambridge: Cambridge University Press.

Knops, L., & Petit, G. (2022). 'Indignation as Affective Transformation: an Affect-Theoretical Approach to the Belgian Yellow Vests Movement.' *Mobilization: An International Quarterly*, 27(2), 170–192.

Kostelka, F., & Blais, A. (2018). 'The Chicken and Egg Question: Satisfaction with Democracy and Voter Turnout.' *PS: Political Science & Politics*, 51(2), 370–376.

Kumlin, S. (2011). 'Dissatisfied Democrats, Policy Feedback and European Welfare States, 1976-2001.' In S. Zmerli, & M. Hooghe (eds.). *Political Trust. Why Context Matters* (pp. 163–185). Colchester: ECPR Press.

Lijphart, A. (1969). 'Consociational democracy.' *World Politics*, 21(2), 207–225.

Mansbridge, J. (2018). *Recursive Representation in Creating Political Presence: The New Politics of Democratic Representation*, Dario Castiglione and Johannes Pollak (eds.). Chicago: University of Chicago

Marcus, G. E. (2002). *The Sentimental Citizen: Emotion in Democratic Politics*. The Pennsylvania State University Press.

Mouffe, C. (2005). *On the Political*. Abingdon: Routledge.

Mouffe, C. (2018). 'Affects of Democracy, in Media, Conspiracies, and Propaganda in the Post-Cold War World.' *Critique and Humanism*, 49(1), 61–70.

Mudde, C. (2004). 'The Populist Zeitgeist.' *Government and Opposition*, 39(4), 541–563.

Norris P. (1999). *Critical Citizens: Global Support for Democratic Governance*. Oxford: Oxford University Press.

Norris, P. (2011). *Democratic Deficit. Critical Citizens Revisited*. New York: Cambridge University Press.

Norton, P. (2017). 'Speaking for Parliament.' *Parliamentary Affairs*, 70(2), 191–206.

Noulet, J.-F. (2022). 'Sondage RTBF/La Libre "Bye-Bye, la démocratie ?": un Belge sur quatre donnerait le pouvoir à un leader unique.' *RTBF*, https://www.rtbf.be/article/sondage-rtbfla-libre-bye-bye-la-democratie-un-belge-sur-quatre-donnerait-le-pouvoir-a-un-leader-unique-11100798

Pharr, S., & Putman, P. (eds.). (2000). *Disaffected Democracies: What's Troubling the Trilateral Countries?* Princeton: Princeton University Press.

Pilet J.-B., Talukder D., Sanhueza M. J., & Rangoni S. (2020). 'Do Citizens Perceive Elected Politicians, Experts and Citizens as Alternative or Complementary Policy-Makers? A Study of Belgian Citizens.' *Frontiers, Political Science*, 2, 567297.

Pilet, J.-B., Bol, D., Vittori, D., & Paulis, E. (2023), 'Public support for deliberative citizens' assemblies selected through sortition: Evidence from 15 countries.' *European Journal of Political Research*.

Rooduijn, M. (2018). 'What unites the voter bases of populist parties? Comparing the electorates of 15 populist parties.' *European Political Science Review*, 10(3), 351–368.

Rosanvallon, P. (2006). *La contre-démocratie, la politique à l'âge de la défiance.* Paris: Seuil.

Saward, M. (2020). *Making Representations: Claim, Counterclaim and the Politics of Acting for Others.* ECPR Press and Rowman and Littlefield International.

Slaby, J., & von Scheve, C. (eds.). (2019). *Affective Societies: Key Concepts.* Abingdon: Routledge.

Rosanvallon, P. (2011). *Democratic Legitimacy: Impartiality, Reflexivity, Proximity.* Princeton, NJ: Princeton University Press.

Trüdinger, E. V., & Bächtiger A. (2022). ,Attitudes vs. actions? Direct-democratic preferences and participation of populist citizens.' *West European Politics*, 1–15. https://www.doi.org/10.1080/01402382.2021.2023435

Van de Sande, M. (2020). They don't represent us? Synecdochal representation and the politics of occupy movements, *Constellations.* 2020(27), 397–411

Van Ingelgom, V. (2014). *Integrating Indifference. A Comparative, Qualitative, and Quantitative Approach to the Legitimacy of European Integration.* Colchester: ECPR Press.

Van Ingelgom, V. (2020). 'Focus groups: from data generation to analysis.' In Curini, L., Franzese, R.J., *Sage Handbook of Research Methods in Political Science and International Relations.* Sage.

Vieten, U. (2020). 'The "New Normal" and "Pandemic Populism": The COVID-19 Crisis and Anti-Hygienic Mobilisation of the Far-Right.' *Social Sciences* 9(16), 1–14, https://www.doi.org/10.3390/socsci9090165

Webster, S., & Albertson, B. (2022). 'Emotion and Politics: Noncognitive Psychological Biases in Public Opinion.' *Annu. Rev. Political Sci*

Appendix: models split by region

Table 10A.1 may be viewed online at https://doi.org/10.11647/OBP.0401#resources

11. Resentment, democracy and inequality

Concluding reflections

Louise Knops, Karen Celis &
Virginie Van Ingelgom

Multifaceted resentment

Belgium is a deeply divided country, and far from immune to the general trends of increased polarization, and declining levels of trust in representative democratic actors and institutions. At the outset of our study, we thus expected to find resentment. We did. This book documents a wealth and diversity of resentful feelings expressed by different groups of citizens towards politics: disappointment and frustration (van der Does et al., Chapter 5); feelings of being 'out of sync' with the pace of politics and the capitalist society (Knops et al., Chapter 8); shades of being unrepresented by existing political elites (De Mulder, Chapter 7); and a range of sometimes intense anger and hope associated with resentment (Bettarelli et al., Chapter 4). Resentment also comes in different levels: Feitosa et al. (Chapter 3) found there are substantially more respondents with high levels of resentment than respondents with low levels of resentment. Bettarelli et al. (Chapter 4) highlight that there are significantly more respondents who have high levels of anger about politics (about one third of Belgians), compared to citizens with high levels of hope (about 1 out of 10). De Mulder's study (Chapter 7)

    https://doi.org/10.11647/OBP.0401.11

reports that close to half of the citizens who participated in his study only feel slightly represented and about one third of Belgians citizens do not feel represented by anyone, which leads to 'disengaged' political resentment. Knops et al. (Chapter 9) discuss that, when asked about what democracy is, about one in eight respondents spontaneously says it is unfair, fake or cold.

The illustrations and expressions are therefore plentiful and ubiquitous across the Belgian population. The respondents included in our various studies are resentful about the actors, processes and institutions which are at the heart of the current functioning of our democracies: representatives and elections; the rules and outcomes of decision-making (Verhaegen et al., Chapter 10), and the temporalities along which representative democracy operates. Knops et al. (Chapter 9) even find that the word 'democracy' is sometimes associated with exactly the opposite of democracy: authoritarianism, unfairness, inequalities.

In the remainder of this concluding chapter, we discuss the findings presented in the book about what resentment is and what it does, politically speaking. We interrogate how the findings speak to each other and ask: what do these findings invite in terms of empirical and theoretical research and in terms of democratic (re)design? Our answers are organized around three themes: the 'tipping points' of resentment; the relationship between resentment and experiences of inequality; and pathways to reflect on 'affect-sensitive' democratic innovation. In a final section, we highlight some general findings about how to approach affect in future studies on politics, and the study of the crisis of representative democracy in particular.

Tipping points

At what 'point' should resentment be conceived as 'good' or 'bad', and crucially for whom, and in relation to what kinds of democratic values and ideals? Several chapters underscore that resentment should neither be seen as a 'bad' or a 'good' emotion, in absolute terms. More specifically, our findings highlight that resentment should not be seen exclusively through the lens of 'anti-democratic' behaviour or as an emotion that is opposed to democratic ideals and preferences (e.g.,

Chapter 1, Knops et al., Chapter 4, Bettarelli et. al. and Chapter 10, Verhaegen et al.). To the contrary, it can be seen as an essential fabric that drives citizens towards collective action and mobilization, and increases overall democratic vitality by expressing disagreement and contestation towards the existing state of affairs—both in terms of how democracy works (its processes, institutions and actors), and its outcomes. Resentment is also a democratic 'warning signal' for groups who are being marginalized, those who are made voiceless and invisible in the current political system. The voiceless demanding an equal say in decision-making, and expressing this in a resentful repertoire (involving different shades of moral anger and contentious practices) can serve as an engine of democratic renewal; being dissatisfied and critical, hoping and longing for change might, in that sense, have reinvigorating effects on democracies (Urbinati, 2006; Mouffe, 2018). In this sense, some of our findings serve to legitimize resentment as an affective citizen response to a democratic system perceived as unequal, deceitful or dysfunctional, and move away from stigmatizing accounts of the 'resentful citizen', often denigrated as a populist or anti-democratic phenomenon only.

Relatedly, expressions of resentment across society could then be seen as incentives or invitations for actors and institutions of democracy to re-align with core democratic ideals or to fundamentally transform. As our analyses show (e.g., Verhaegen et al., Chapter 10), this sometimes takes the form of demands for democratic reform at the institutional level, although, as we also show, this is unlikely to be sufficient if other systemic conditions are not addressed, such as the dependency of liberal democracies on the capitalist system which (re-)produces power-inequalities across society and offers the perfect terrain for resentment to grow.

Having said that, we should also be cautious not to consider resentment only for its potential contribution to democratic vitality and possible transformation. It should also be seen for its potentially more detrimental effects for democracies. Resentment can build up over time to a point where individuals are no longer able to identify culprits and responsibilities, and rather cultivate a generalized feeling of unfairness or injustice where the objects and causes of resentment have become blurred and homogenized. This is highly problematic for several reasons: resentful citizens may find it difficult to articulate precise political demands, and democratic solutions may not be readily available or identifiable based on these generalized feelings of injustice or unfairness (Fleury, 2020). Blurred or generalized feelings of resentment may also, ultimately, have a depoliticizing effect in the sense of merging different causes and culprits together, and distracting the attention from structural and systemic roots of resentment. Alternatively, it may also result in the scapegoating, stigmatizing and discriminating of differently situated others who become an easy target and outlet for this generalized feeling of resentment across the population. In that sense, while resentment may be a 'good' thing for democracy overall when it allows the voiceless to claim a higher stake in democracy or when it expresses a level of contestation with the existing system, it may also be 'bad' if and when it is steered in illiberal, anti-democratic or authoritarian directions (for a good overview, see Ilouz, 2022) to push 'others' to the margins of society. This is (in part) what we witness, for instance, in Hungary and Poland, but also in other Western democracies such as France or Belgium, where far-right, xenophobic, and ultra-conservative parties are enjoying unprecedented popularity, often bred on the back of widespread, diffuse feelings of resentment in parts of the population.

In the case of Belgium, our findings do not allow us to make conclusive claims about how many of the individuals who participated in our studies experience the kind of resentment which steers contestation and political engagement, and how many experience other more 'detrimental' types of resentment, which breeds anti-immigration sentiments, for example.

Ultimately, our findings question the binary categorization between what may count as 'good' or 'bad' resentment, and thus what may count as 'good' or 'bad' emotions, overall. Due to the fact that this is highly contingent upon 'who' resentment might be good or bad for, assessments about 'good' or 'bad' resentment can never be generalized. Yet, the high levels of resentment found among the population surveyed and interviewed for our studies, together with scholarship pointing to its anti-democratic potential (Fleury, 2020; Capelos and Demertzis, 2022), do suggest that there are reasons to be concerned for the future of democracies. This is particularly true as, at the time of writing the conclusion of this book, the far-right, xenophobic party Vlaams Belang has reached new records of popularity in the Flemish part of Belgium.[1]

More concretely, it calls upon scholars of politics and democracy to obtain a better understanding of what are the 'tipping points' when resentment may induce anti-democratic attitudes and behaviour; why; and, crucially, among which groups in society. Identifying 'tipping points' is also important to better understand moments of protest and mobilisation, and the reasons that may underlie citizens' rejection of and hate towards politics and political institutions. The idea of 'tipping point' is also important at the conceptual level because it introduces the idea that emotions should be seen from a more dynamic and relational perspective – such as resentment which breeds over time – rather than static states which can be measured and quantified.

The findings presented in our book point—to a certain extent—in this direction by documenting a wide scope of emotions and feelings which revolve around resentful affectivities; anger and hope (Bettarelli et al., Chapter 4), frustration, disappointment and indifference (van der Does et al., Chapter 5), different degrees and intensities of feeling 'unrepresented' (De Mulder, Chapter 7), a range of different feelings expressed vis-à-vis 'democracy' as an ideal and a system; emotions such as feeling ignored, disconnected, misunderstood; feeling betrayed, deceived, disillusioned; feeling discriminated, hopeless, powerless, resigned; exasperated (Knops et al., Chapter 9). However, further attention should be paid to the ways in which these feelings swing together and motivate different types of actions, political behaviour, preferences, and attitudes. For instance, we know little about the conditions that may precipitate certain types of tipping points, from frustration into resentment, or resentment into desperation and resignation; or from resentment into political mobilization and protest. Is it the intensity of emotions that matters? Or rather the type of emotions that are part of the resentment cluster? Is it linked to social and power positionalities, lived experiences and biographical trajectories? How do individual tipping points become collective across society? Of course, our findings do not allow us to answer all of these questions, but some of the contributions do offer some cues in this direction.

---

1   The manuscript was completed before the general election of 2024 in Belgium.

The contributions presented in the book inform the hypothesis that both the intensity and the kind of emotions play a role (De Mulder, Chapter 7; Bettarelli et al., Chapter 4). Other hypotheses may be formulated about the role of inequalities and the experience of socio-economic difficulties over time (van der Does et al., Chapter 5), but also about the importance of being cognisant of existing gaps and incongruence between citizens' and politicians' interests (Lefevere et al., Chapter 6). Both can be understood as 'knowledge' (experiential and factual) about the disconnect between societal needs and politics and raise important questions about the differentiated distribution of knowledge and information across society, and thus of power; of who has access to it, and who hasn't, of who experiences daily injustice from existing power systems and who does not; what type of knowledge and information is being channelled within different groups, and what role these dimensions play in reaching collective 'resentful' tipping points across society.

The idea of 'tipping points' also opens important questions about other types of spatial and temporal affective evolutions, such as a return of resentment after moments of mobilisation, the deepening of resentment into forms of resignation or desperation, or changes and evolutions in the objects of resentment over time. Does one cause of resentment lead to another? Given that resentment is an emotion that breeds over time, we may expect that one source of resentment feeds into another, creating an accumulated sense of frustration and disappointment. Similarly, we still know little about how resentment travels from one group to another, and why. Are certain events prone to further exacerbate resentment in society? When do we observe resentful contagion and resonance between differently situated social groups and what are the democratic and political implications of this contagion? These dimensions and questions go beyond the scope of what we were able to unpack and document in this book. They merit further conceptual and empirical attention to develop a more differentiated understanding of resentment, one that is mindful of the unequal distribution of resentment across society, and therefore of its differentiated political and democratic implications.

Inequality and lived experience

Some of the contributions gathered in this book provide empirical evidence about who are the resentful, sociologically and socio-economically speaking (Feitosa et al., Chapter 3; van der Does et al., Chapter 5; Lefevere et al, Chapter 6; De Mulder, Chapter 7). As discussed in the introduction, resentment is strongly related to both objective inequality and relative or 'felt' inequality caused by downgrading socio-economic realities and status. In addition, the unequal treatments and groups defined by socio-demographic markers are connected through different types of experience. Especially when approached in an intersectional manner, the intersections of mechanisms such as gender, age, class and race account for positions and experiences of being privileged or being excluded and marginalised; and relatedly, of who may be in objective situations of inequality compared to others, and perhaps have more 'objective' reasons to be resentful. Feitosa et al. (Chapter 3) indeed show that the identification of who experiences unequal treatment—which may give rise to resentment—cannot be captured by one identity marker, such as gender, educational levels, or regions of residence only.

Other contributors go a step further and suggest that, in addition to the importance of socio-demographic determinants, we should also pay close attention to the role played by the lived experiences of social inequality; in particular, the daily experiences of failed or insufficient public services and facilities (van der Does et al., Chapter 5), the long-term experiences of asynchronicity and dissonance created by the pace of neo-liberal capitalism (Knops et al., Chapter 8), the gradual experience of disillusionment by democratic systems that do not live up to citizens' expectations (Knops et al., Chapter 9). Overall, taking more subjective and experiential dimensions into account in studies of political resentment would allow for a better understanding of resentment in parts of the population who might otherwise be overlooked when focussing only on (intersecting) socio-economic features.

Integrating experience into analyses of resentment helps to make sense, for example, of the finding that resentment peaks around the age of 50 (Feitosa et al., Chapter 3), a finding which is consistent with the nature of resentment as an emotion which builds over time. The question then becomes; what kinds of experiences make citizens become resentful? Building from the literature discussed in the introduction, one could hypothesise that relative deprivation, and the subjective sense of entitlement versus loss of privilege and status might also well play a role. It could also be hypothesised that resentment grows, not only from the accumulated experiences (objective and/or subjective) of unfair and unjust treatment, but also from the factual knowledge about the incongruency between one's own interests and actual policies (Lefevere et al., Chapter 6). An alternative or additional explanation might be that different individuals, depending on their social position, and building on their experiences, may become more or less sensitive to the clash of temporalities imposed by capitalism on human societies (Knops et al., Chapter 8). Moreover, the daily experiences of failed or insufficient public services (van der Does et al., Chapter 5) invites one to consider seriously the role of public policies in the understanding of citizens' political resentment and thus, broadly speaking, in their relationships to democracy (Bussi, Dupuy & Van Ingelgom, 2022).

Future studies of situations and experiences of inequality along these lines would allow us to obtain a more sophisticated understanding of whether and how different types of experiences tie into different types of resentment, and what are the normative implications thereof: does resentment in the face of a subjective experience of inequality lead to similar or different resentful behaviours and preferences compared to resentment rooted in structural and historical forms of injustice and discrimination? How should these differences be integrated in our evaluations and study of resentment from a political analytical perspective?

Democratic transformation?

The findings we have summarized so far mostly relate to citizens' resentment per se, the shapes it may take and how it is expressed across society. They are important to provide a more sensitive and affective understanding of the growing disconnection between citizens and traditional political institutions. However, they should not be used to target or 'blame' citizens for structural problems in the existing organizations, values and actors of representative democracy. Rather, they should invite us to further investigate the structural and institutional causes of resentment and reflect on the political responses that may be designed in response to different types of resentment. Building from the discussions above, we contend that the type of responses that democratic systems can or should give to citizens' resentment highly depends on who expresses resentment in the first place, in response to what type of inequality, and to achieve what kind of broader political and normative objectives. Moreover, while all types of resentment may be important and interesting to study, it is also fair to expect that democratic societies should prioritize responses to specific types of resentment. The resentment expressed by groups facing structural and systemic inequalities (for example tied to (intersections of) age, class, race or gender) does not carry the same implications and normative load compared to the resentment expressed by groups who may feel relatively deprived, while still enjoying important privileges, and whose resentment may be rooted in the subjective experience of inequality or fear of status loss in the future.

Responding to expressions of resentment across democratic societies would entail several steps. On one level, it would entail reducing the sources of resentment, such as inequality, and tackling them at their (neoliberal capitalist) roots (Knops et al., Chapter 8). On another level, it would entail re-imagining democracy in ways that are responsive to citizens' desire for change, and desire for increased decision-making powers compared to the distribution of power within the existing institutions of representative democracy. Indeed, resentment can be responded to with a range of institutional reforms, such as citizens assemblies, referenda and different channels that increase citizen participation. Our findings show that citizens who feel resentment towards the current arrangements of democracy long for alternative solutions and ways of breaking with existing political cultures and practices that are considered as entirely disconnected from citizens' lives, experiences and needs (Verhaegen et al., Chapter 10).

In addition, and in contrast to accounts that suggest that it is no longer possible for existing democratic institutions—which are the target of citizens' resentment—to become the providers of solutions, our findings show that existing representative institutions are not entirely rejected. Even citizens who may have all the material and rational reasons to hate every part of the existing political system—for the structural and daily experiences of inequality and precarity—still demand that representatives would listen to them, and care more (van der Does et al., Chapter 5). Across different chapters, contributors to this book have found that resentful citizens express the demand that political actors and institutions should be better connected with and responsive to citizens' concerns and critiques (Knops et al., Chapter 9; Verhaegen et al., Chapter 10; van der Does et al., Chapter 5). In fact, the principles of representative democracy themselves are not necessarily or not always challenged by citizens we have labelled as 'resentful' (Celis et al., 2021). This may be due to the fact that the political imaginary of citizens in most liberal democracies is largely dominated by the institutions of representative democracy (its actors and procedures), which makes it hard for citizens to formulate or imagine demands outside this institutional arrangement. Yet, it does point towards the fundamental responsibility of existing institutions and decision-makers and the need to develop a holistic view of democratic reform and transformation (European Commission & Van Ingelgom, 2023).; Amara-Hammou 2023).

Beyond the matter of democratic design, strictly speaking and whether one would prioritize deliberative, participatory, direct or representative democracy, the response to resentment should entail the development of 'affect-sensitive' democratic innovations. In the wake of our findings on resentment and the growing recognition of the importance of emotions for democratic politics, democratic innovations and interventions should therefore also be 'affective'. This means for example that they should encourage political and 'pro'-democratic affectivities to shape democracy and democratic practice. What these affectivities are, and what types of democratic designs may encourage their emergence is beyond the scope of this book and remains an important task ahead. However, there are ideas and practices that we can build from. Wojciechowska (2019) for instance discusses the advantages of 'enclave deliberation'—a deliberative forum for previously disempowered groups only—as a democratic practice to foster equality with important affective effects such as increased interpersonal trust. Taking a feminist democratic perspective, Celis and Childs (2020; 2023) have suggested that we should redesign the process of representation to make it inclusive, responsive and egalitarian for all differently affected and situated citizens, including the most marginalized ones. Importantly this new design incentivises elected representatives to engage in 'democratic listening': the activity of 'the fair consideration' of their 'arguments stories, and perspectives' (Scudder, 2020). The intended effects include feeling recognized, included, empowered, connected, and cared for. Amara-Hammou (2023) suggests a democratic design rooted in the process of co-creation with and for marginalized communities (here focusing in particular on the local political level). This would ensure the integration of alternative forms of knowledge in political decision-making, and that elected representatives both bear the responsibility *for* but also *with* people to resolve concrete problems.

That being said, our findings also highlight that resentment does not always—or not only—result in demands for democratic reform and democratic innovations, and that citizens' resentment goes beyond technical or institutional fixes only. Placing all our hopes in institutional reform is therefore unlikely to be sufficient to respond to the deep-seated resentment citizens express towards democracy and politics overall. The multi-dimensional crisis—pandemic, climate, social, energy, war—we witness today might even keep fuelling political resentment, whatever the democratic institutional arrangements, in particular for as long as these institutions keep the unequal power structure of society practically untouched. Ample research has now documented the responsibility of existing democratic institutions in exacerbating inequalities and foreclosing the possibility to truly respond to, for example, ongoing climate and ecological transformations (e.g., Pickering et al., 2020). Furthermore, as well explained by Cynthia Fleury, there is something within the structure of resentment–and *ressentiment* in particular—which makes the response to resentment, what she calls 'reparation'—perhaps impossible. As she explains, resentment is a feeling that cannot be truly answered, because resentful citizens feel that no resolution will ever be able to match the level of the injustice or the inequality experienced.

Of course, our findings do not allow us to determine whether this is actually observed among the population that we surveyed and interviewed. Yet this idea does bring nuance and perspective to the temptation to 'respond' or 'solve' resentment through democratic designs and institutional innovations only. The tendency to try to 'solve' and provide 'solutions' fits with a technocratic framing of politics which may actually undermine, rather than reinforce, democracy. Other transformations, beyond political institutions and arrangements are therefore equally necessary. In this regard, the development of affective intelligence at all levels of society to increase citizens' capacity to build resilience and agency is key. Looking at the new emotions and emotional experiences linked to climate change, for example, Blanche Verlie (2021) suggests building collective emotional resilience and affective transformations as fundamental conditions for democratic societies and citizens to cope with the differentiated impacts of climate change and ecological crises: a logic that could be extended to many other domains and critical areas of change where societal responses may eventually come from collective mobilisation outside the scope of institutional innovation only.

To conclude

This book contributes to ongoing efforts that seek to consider emotions as an intrinsic and essential part of political attitudes, behaviour, and preferences, rather than seeing them as either separate from or detrimental to the proper dimensions of democratic politics. It also unsettles hard distinctions between 'rationality' and 'emotionality', or between 'positive emotions' and 'negative emotions'. The way we have approached resentment helps partly to undo these dichotomies (even though, admittedly, some of our contributions inevitably reproduce them to some extent). Resentment is not just an 'emotion'; it is also a 'rational' and legitimate reaction to objective and subjective experiences of unfairness, injustice, discriminations. It aligns with the feelings— whether substantiated or not—that representatives do not represent 'us'. It draws on both rational assessments and cognition evaluations of a harm or situation of material deprivation, and also comes across in spontaneous feelings.

Emotions are neither individual nor collective; they are both. Resentment is expressed by individuals and have collective implications which vary depending on who is expressing resentment, why and in the face of what type of inequality (whether experienced, perceived or feared). For these reasons, emotions can never be seen as either negative or positive, just by name or label. Resentment may be 'bad' at the individual level, by stirring up painful feelings of betrayal and bitter frustration, yet it may be 'good' at the collective level for its role in pushing people to express their anger publicly and mobilize politically. At the macro-level of political analysis, looking at where resentment lies is also 'good' in the sense of providing a powerful and sensitive indicator of existing socio-economic and political inequalities, of who may be experiencing them, who is allowed to denounce them publicly, and who may be prone to turn resentment into political engagement.

Overall, our study of resentment invites us, and future researchers, to keep interrogating these categories (emotion vs. reason, individual vs. collective, positive vs. negative), to better understand their implications, in terms of the normative backgrounds against which they are expressed and seek to denounce or contest. Admittedly, the contributions gathered in this book only scratch the surface of these considerations, but they do open pathways towards a more complex and multifaceted conceptual approach to resentment and emotions within political science.

The book opens up a number of important questions and paths for further research. In terms of democratic reform, first, our observations and analyses of resentment call for democratic renewals and transformations beyond the existing set of democratic innovations or arrangements. It calls for taking into account longer systemic patterns and trends, be they in terms of structural inequalities or in terms of the historical roots of resentment, and points towards to need to develop affective intelligence at all levels of politics and the citizenry. Second, in terms of political research, our attempts to study resentment as both a complex emotion and a political concept, and our efforts to bring together a broad range of methodologies and epistemologies to do so, has revealed the importance of not confining resentment to one approach, or to one of its facets only. Resentment is an emotion, but it is also the result of structural systemic conditions and repeated experiences; it is linked to important political concepts such as representation, congruence, trust, and relative deprivation. It plays a role both in mobilisation and political engagement, as well as in voting abstention. This multiplicity and multifaceted nature calls for a better integration of interdisciplinary —with necessary contributions from sociology, anthropology and social psychology, among others—and mixed-method research designs when approaching emotions and politics. Beyond resentment, and given the importance and explicitness of political emotions across the political spectrum—be it the fear and pride mobilized on the far right, the anxiety, guilt, and anger expressed by different flanks of ecological parties, the conservative affect that runs through the anti-woke narratives of right-wing parties—better understanding and studying these political emotions is a crucial task to grasp the complexity and polarized nature of politics today.

References

Amara-Hammou, K. (2023). Theorizing representation from the perspective of the represented: How people in socio-economically difficult situations in Brussels understand representation. VUB: Unpublished PhD manuscript.

Bussi, M., Dupuy, C., & Van Ingelgom, V. (2022). Does social policy change impact on politics? A review of policy feedbacks on citizens' political participation and attitudes towards politics. *Journal of European Social Policy*, 32(5), 607-618.

Capelos, T., & Demertzis, N. (2022). 'Sour grapes: ressentiment as the affective response of grievance politics.' *Innovation: The European Journal of Social Science Research*, 35(1), 107–129.

Celis, K. & Childs, S. (2020). *Feminist Democratic Representation*. New York: Oxford University Press.

Celis, K., & Childs, S. (2023). 'From Women's Presence to Feminist Representation.' *European Journal of Politics and Gender* (online first).

European Commission, Directorate-General for Research and Innovation, & Van Ingelgom, V. (2023). *Research on Deliberative and Participatory Practices in the EU*. Publications Office of the European Union.

Fleury, C. (2020). *Ci-git l'amer*. Paris: Gallimard.

Illouz, E. (2022). *Les émotions contre la démocratie*. Paris: Premier parallèle.

Pickering, J., Bäckstrand, K., & Schlosberg, D. (2020). Between environmental and ecological democracy: theory and practice at the democracy-environment nexus. Journal of Environmental Policy & Planning, 22(1), 1-15.

Scudder, M. (2020). 'The Ideal of Uptake in Democratic Deliberation.' *Political Studies*, 68(2), 504–522.

Verlie, B. (2021). *Learning to Live with Climate Change: From Anxiety to Transformation*. Taylor & Francis, London and New-York: Routledge.

Wojciechowska, M. (2019). 'Towards intersectional democratic innovations.' *Political Studies*, 67(4), 895–911.

Methodological appendix

All methodological information , including the information on which the Appendix is based,is compiled on the RepResent project website.[1] The different datasets and codebooks are available in DANS data easy deposit: the panel surveys[2] and the cross-sectional surveys.[3]

The voter panel surveys

The voter panel study consists of a pre- and post-electoral wave around the elections of 26 May 2019, a third wave about one year later (April 2020), and a final fourth wave. In the first, pre-electoral wave respondents were questioned between 5 April and 21 May 2019 (99% was interviewed before 6 May). The second, post-electoral, wave surveyed the *same* respondents immediately after the elections (between 28 May and 18 June 2019). Respondents were surveyed a third time one year after the elections (between 7 April and 27 April 2020), and a final fourth time two years after the elections (between 18 May 2021 and 4 June 2021). These surveys were conducted by Kantar TNS at the request of the Excellence of Science consortium RepResent.

The target population of the study are the inhabitants of Flanders, Wallonia, and the Brussels Region that were eligible to vote for the elections of 26 May 2019. The gross sample consisted of respondents that were recruited from diverse online panels (Kantar's own panel as well as panels from other online companies such as Dynata). The target was a net sample that would match the distribution on gender, age and

---

1   https://represent-project.be/
2   https://ssh.datastations.nl/dataset.xhtml?persistentId=doi:10.17026/dans-xf5-djem
3   https://ssh.datastations.nl/dataset.xhtml?persistentId=doi:10.17026/dans-zkg-rftw

     https://doi.org/10.11647/OBP.0401.12

education for the voting aged population in their respective regions. Due to non-response, the final samples differ from the target population distributions somewhat (see section 3).

The initial target was to have a net sample of 2500 respondents at the end of the second wave (1000 respondents in Flanders and Wallonia and 500 respondents in the Brussels Region). During the fieldwork, however, it was decided to oversample and continue the data collection even when the target was reached to be able to conduct a third and potentially fourth wave during the legislative term. For the third and fourth waves no target was set: the aim was simply to maximize responses.

Sample size wave 1

After concluding the fieldwork of wave 1, 7351 interviews were completed. Because the external panels do not report the number of emails sent out, it is impossible to calculate a response rate. Yet, such response rates are not comparable with traditional probability sampling designs anyhow, since respondents from maintained panels do not form a random sample of citizens.

Per region:

- Flanders: n=3298 interviews

- Wallonia: n=3025 interviews

- Brussels: n=1028 interviews

Sample size wave 2

Contacting the 7351 respondents from wave 1 ultimately led to 3909 completed interviews after the elections, which corresponds to a response rate of 53.2%.[4]

Per region:

- Flanders: n=1971 interviews = 59.8% response rate

- Wallonia: n=1429 interviews = 47.2% response rate

- Brussels: n=509 interviews = 49.5% response rate

---

4   Note that although 3917 respondents completed wave 2, we only retain
     respondents who completely finished both W1 and W2 in the sample, dropping
     eight responses.

Sample size wave 3

For the third wave, all 3406 respondents from Flanders and Wallonia who participated in both wave 1 and wave 2 were recontacted. This resulted in 1996 completed responses, which corresponds to a response rate of 58.6% compared to the second wave.[5] For the third wave we did not recontact respondents from Brussels, as this group was too small.

Per region:

- Flanders: n=1266 interviews = 64.2% response rate compared to the second wave

- Wallonia: n=730 interviews = 51.1% response rate compared to the second wave

Sample size wave 4

Finally, for wave 4 the 1996 Flemish and Walloon respondents that participated in wave 3 were contacted for a final questionnaire. In total, 1119 interviews were completed.

Per region:

- Flanders: n=721 interviews = 60.0% response rate compared to the third wave

- Wallonia: n=398 interviews = 54.5% response rate compared to the third wave

Waves 1–4

Tables A.1–A.4 may be viewed online at https://doi.org/10.11647/OBP.0401#resources

The cross-sectional surveys

Two additional cross-sectional surveys were carried out during the EoS RepResent project.

---

5   Again, respondents were matched between the three waves via a unique ID code. 38 respondents were omitted from the dataset in wave 3 because their age did not match with the previous waves (i.e., they were younger or more than two years older). Moreover, four Flemish respondents indicated to have moved to the region of Brussels between the second and third waves. As wave 3 only dealt with Flanders and Wallonia, these four respondents' answers for wave 3 were removed from the dataset (their answers for wave 1 and 2 were retained).

The first post-electoral cross-sectional survey consists of a questionnaire that was conducted shortly after the elections of 26 May 2019. The survey took place between 29 May and 30 June 2019. It was conducted by Kantar TNS at the request of the Excellence of Science consortium RepResent. The target population of the study are the inhabitants of Flanders and Wallonia (not the Brussels Region) that are eligible to vote for the elections of 26 May 2019. The gross sample consisted of respondents that were recruited from diverse online panels (Kantar's own panel as well as panels from other online companiessuch as Dynata). The target was a net sample that would match the distribution on gender, age and education for the voting aged population in their respective regions. Due to nonresponse, the final samples differ from the target population distributions somewhat (see section 3).

The target was to have a net sample of 2000 respondents (1000 respondents in Flanders and 1000 in Wallonia). Unlike the Voter Panel Study that was also conducted in the framework of RepResent, these respondents were not contacted for a second wave. In addition, respondents who are already part of the Voter Panel Study were not contacted for this cross-sectional survey.

Sample size

After concluding the fieldwork, 2036 interviews were realized. Because the external panels do not report the number of emails sent out, it is impossible to calculate a response rate.

Per region:

- Flanders: n=1012 interviews
- Wallonia: n=1024 interviews

Respondents were interviewed online. To this end, a CAWI questionnaire was programmed by the consortium on the Qualtrics platform. Respondents were invited to participate in the study via email by Kantar TNS. Several reminders were send by Kantar TNS to increase the response. At the start an extensive explanation was given to the respondents about the privacy rules and regulations concerning the processing of personal data. Only respondents that gave their consent proceeded with the surveys. The data collection was conducted in line with the General Data Protection Regulation (GDPR) and received ethical approval from the Ethics Committee for the Social Sciences and Humanities (EA SHW) of the University of Antwerp. The CAWI questionnaires could only be accessed via a computer or laptop. Because of the length and lay-out of the questionnaires we decided not to allow respondents to complete the survey on a mobile device (phone, tablet...). Mobile users therefore received a message in which they were requested to re-enter the questionnaire via a computer or laptop. The median duration of the online interviews was 16 minutes and 35 seconds.

Table A.5 Distribution in population and sample—Flanders.

Variable	Population	Survey	χ^2-test
Male	49,5%	52,4%	$\chi^2(1)=3,7$*[6]
Female	50,5%	47,3%	
Other	0,0%	0,3%	
Lower educated	27,0%	18,5%	$\chi^2(2)=38,1$**
Middle educated	41,6%	45,5%	
Higher educated	31,3%	36,1%	
18-29	17,7%	18,3%	$\chi^2(3)=0,5$
30-44	24,2%	23,6%	
45-65	34,5%	35,0%	
65+	23,6%	23,1%	
CD&V	12,1%	10,4%	$\chi^2(9)=201,3$**[7]
Groen	8,4%	8,6%	
N-VA	21,8%	24,7%	
Open VLD	11,5%	8,3%	
PVDA	4,8%	7,6%	
Sp.a	9,3%	10,3%	
Vlaams Belang	15,9%	20,1%	
Other party	1,7%	1,5%	
Blanc	4,2%	2,7%	
Did not vote	10,3%	3,2%	
Not allowed to vote	0,0%	0,2%	
Don't know	0,0%	2,6%	

The full description of the sample questionnaire of the cross-sectional survey can be found here: https://represent-project.be/wp-content/uploads/2020/05/Codebook_Cross_Section.pdf

---

6   χ^2-test was performed without the 'other' category.
7   χ^2-test was performed without the 'not allowed to vote' and 'don't know' categories.

The second cross-sectional survey was an online survey amongst a sample of N=2,035 adult (18 and older) respondents that live in the Flemish and Walloon regions of Belgium. The survey comprised an online (CAWI) survey, fielded in the first half of November 2021. The sample sizes for both regions are roughly equal at N=1,018 for Flanders, and N=1,017 for Wallonia.

The purpose of the survey was, in line with the broader RepResent project, to study political preferences and political resentment amongst Flemish and Walloon citizens. To this end, the topic covered in the survey include more typical political opinions and preferences, but also several questions targeted at surveying political resentment and democratic innovations such as citizen forums and referendums.

Ethical approval

The survey was developed by the RepResent consortium. The survey was implemented on the University of Antwerp's Qualtrics platform. Prior to the field work, the survey was granted ethical clearance by the University of Antwerp's ethical review board for the social and humane sciences (decision number SHW_21_94, preliminary approval 2 September 2021 / Definitive approval 4 November 2021).

Field work and context

The field work for the survey ran from 29 October 2021 to 14 November 2021, with most of the responses being collected in the beginning of the field work period (90% of the responses were recorded from 29 October to 4 November). In terms of context, this means that the field work occurred during the ongoing COVID-19 crisis: to this end, the survey contains several COVID-19 control questions near the end of the questionnaire.

Weights and representativeness

The aim of CS4 was to achieve a sample that matched the population of the Flemish and Walloon regions of Belgium on key socio-demographic indicators: age, gender and level of education. The survey was administered through online surveying (CAWI). The sample is a quota sample, with the aim being to achieve a sample whose distribution on age, gender, education and area of residence (province) matched the population distribution of citizens in the Flemish and Walloon region. The participants were recruited from the ongoing online panel Topix maintained by Kantar TNS and the Dynata online panel. Respondents were invited to participate in the survey, with the target being a net sample of at least N=2,000 respondents, split evenly over both regions. Respondents that did not agree to the informed consent form, that did not complete the survey in its entirety, were not part of the target population (18 years or older, living in Flemish / Walloon region), or whose answers did not meet the quality criteria, were removed. The quality of responses was assessed via two criteria: 1. No speeding through the survey, defined as having a response time of less than five minutes 2. No nonsensical responses on the open-ended questions on the 'Most important problem' and 'Which politician do you feel represented by'.[8] In the end, N=2,035 respondents are retained in the final sample.

One issue that was discovered after data cleaning was complete, is that several respondents straightlined question batteries, which indicates lower response quality. The dataset contains an additional weight variable that excludes respondents that straightlined key question batteries. The final sample consists of N=2,035 respondents. Although overall the deviations from the population distributions on age, gender and education are relatively minor, we do provide two weights that adjust the sample distributions to match the population distributions. Both weights were calculated using iterative proportional fitting (raking) using the *ipfraking* module in Stata.

- The first weight (weight_agesexedu) adjust the sampling distribution on age, gender and education to match those of the two regions. The N in the analysis is reduced to N=2,031 when using this weight (N=1,116 in Flanders / N=1,115 in Wallonia) because four respondents indicated 'other' as gender, and no population propensity for this gender category is available.

---

8   E.g., responses along the lines of 'fjkdfmqj', or copy-pasting part of the question in the answer box. This typically indicates a respondent who is rushing through the survey. So, all respondents who exhibited this behaviour were removed.

- The second weight (*weight_agesexedu_straight*) has the same function, but further limits the sample to only respondents that did not straightline more than half of the key question batteries in the survey (resentment, populism, cynicism, feeling represented). As such, the N is set to 1,761 (N=887 in Flanders / N = 874 in Wallonia) when using this weight.

The full cross-sectional survey dataset and the codebook can be found here.[9]

The focus groups dataset

A full overview of the focus group dataset and its participants is provided on the website of the RepResent project.[10]

The focus group data were collected between January 2019 and March 2021. The dataset gathers the transcripts of 28 focus groups (Amara-Hammou, et al., 2020) with a total of 150 participants ranging across different language groups and sociological backgrounds. The EOS RepResent Focus Group Dataset (FNRS-FWO n°G0F0218N[11]) originates from the intention of the RepResent project to study the linkage between citizens and representatives and answer questions such as: do people feel represented by their representatives? Do they believe that representatives are representing their concerns in the political arena?

To inquire citizens' experiences with, views about, and feelings towards political representation in an inductive and open manner, focus groups were organized around three guiding questions. More specific questions and variations were also asked depending on the particular context in which the focus groups were organized.

- What are the most important societal issues that Belgium is facing today?

- Who should take care of those issues?

---

9   https://ssh.datastations.nl/dataset.xhtml?persistentId=doi:10.17026/dans-zkg-rftw

10 https://represent-project.be/wp-content/uploads/2021/07/EOS_RepResent-Focus-Groups-Dataset.pdf
    This overview only gathers the first waves of the focus groups dataset.

11 Also with the help and cooperation of other projects, such as project FWO project G062917N (Prof. Eline Severs and Prof. Kris Deschouwer).

- How should they be resolved (i.e., political solutions)?

These three questions were asked in 28 focus groups carried out in the Brussels region. A short vignette activity was also organized during the focus groups. Participants were invited to look at a series of pictures that symbolised different forms of political participation (e.g., voting, protesting, charity work, citizen assemblies) and asked to comment on these and order them according to their potential and importance. On average, 6 people participated in each focus group. The average length of the focus groups was 2.5 hours. All focus groups were audio recorded–and, when participants agreed (written informed consent was required for participation), filmed. Based on these recordings, anonymized verbatim transcripts were produced. While all focus groups followed the same structure, the selection criteria and recruitment strategies aimed at reaching diversity in terms of participants and groups. Participants were selected along three main dimensions: a socio-political proxy, a socio-spatial proxy, and an experiential proxy linked to different experiences tied to the COVID-19 pandemic (for the focus groups carried out in 2020 and 2021). The goal of these selection criteria was to capture a diverse sample of citizens from whom resentful feelings might be expected and to examine how these feelings are linked to matters of political participation.

A first set of focus groups[12] examined the expression of democratic resentment and views on political representation in political spaces (i.e., socio-political proxy) with politicized and/or pre-identified groups (i.e., Yellow Vests, Youth for Climate, residents of Brussels in socio-economic difficulties, Experts du vécu, Syndicat des Immenses and blue-collar workers in the European Parliament—59 participants). Five focus groups were organized with social movements activists: three focus groups with Yellow Vests activists and two focus groups with Youth for Climate activists. A second set of focus groups included people originating from different social spaces and neighbourhoods (i.e., socio-spatial proxy), focusing on both mixed or less advantaged areas (i.e., 'Marolles' and Molenbeek–30 participants) and, to a lesser extent, on more advantaged areas of Brussels (i.e., 'Dansaert'–3 participants). Using these socio-political or sociospatial proxies and recruitment strategies led to the

---

12   A special thanks is due to Guillaume Petit for his work and coordination efforts in organizing these focus groups.

inclusion of participants with varying sociodemographic characteristics: (1) 64% of participants are male (36% female); (2) apart from 65+, respondents of all ages are relatively evenly represented; (3) about half of the participants obtained either no diploma or a diploma from secondary school, 14.3% were still in secondary school at the time. In total, 16 focus groups were organized in the first-two waves of focus group data collection.

A third set of focus groups[13] included people who had different experiences of the COVID-19 pandemic, depending on their professional occupation, among others, e.g., students or members of the cultural sector (58 participants, across 12 focus groups). This third set of focus groups were organized between December 2020 and March 2021. The recruitment included direct recruitment (students and cultural sector) as well the help of a firm (Bilendi) for the other targeted groups (e.g., anti-vaccine groups). Due to COVID-19 restrictions, the focus groups were all conducted online. The data comprises of 12 full transcripts in French (8) and Dutch (4) (with video/audio file with an average duration of 2 hours, min: 1h22; max 2h42). FGs gathered between 4 and 6 participants.

Table A.6 Overview of wave 1–3 of focus groups.

	Selection criterion	Type & number of groups	Total
Wave 1	Socio-political proxy	Yellow Vests (3), Youth for Climate (2), residents of Brussels in socio-economic difficulties (1), Experts du vécu (1), Syndicat des Immenses (1) and blue-collar workers in the EU (2)	10
Wave 2	Socio-spatial proxy	Molenbeek (3), Marolles (1), Dansaert (1), Douche Flux (1)	6
Wave 3	Experiential proxy (COVID-19)	Cultural sector (2), students (3), milddle-class (3), anti-vaccine (2), far-right voters (2)	12

---

13   A special thanks goes to Heidi Mercenier and François Randour for all their work and efforts in organizing these focus groups.

Across these three waves of focus group data collection, three types of recruitment strategies were used: (1) direct recruitment by the researcher on the field of study and (2) a mixed strategy, composed of direct and indirect recruitment via existing networks (i.e., pre-existing organization such as NGOs, foundations, etc.), (3) indirect recruitment via the recruiting firm Bilendi. The technical report of the study specifies which groups were recruited in what manner.

Index

About the Team

Alessandra Tosi was the managing editor for this book.

Lucy Barnes proof-read this manuscript; Rosalyn Sword indexed it.

Jeevanjot Kaur Nagpal designed the cover. The cover was produced in InDesign using the Fontin font.

Cameron Craig typeset the book in InDesign and produced the paperback and hardback editions. The main text font is Tex Gyre Pagella. The heading font is Californian FB.

Cameron also produced the PDF and HTML editions. The conversion was performed with open-source software and other tools freely available on our GitHub page at https://github.com/OpenBookPublishers.

Jeremy Bowman created the EPUB.

This book was peer-reviewed by two referees. Experts in their field, these readers give their time freely to help ensure the academic rigour of our books. We are grateful for their generous and invaluable contributions.

This book need not end here...

Share

All our books — including the one you have just read — are free to access online so that students, researchers and members of the public who can't afford a printed edition will have access to the same ideas. This title will be accessed online by hundreds of readers each month across the globe: why not share the link so that someone you know is one of them?

This book and additional content is available at:
https://doi.org/10.11647/OBP.0401

Donate

Open Book Publishers is an award-winning, scholar-led, not-for-profit press making knowledge freely available one book at a time. We don't charge authors to publish with us: instead, our work is supported by our library members and by donations from people who believe that research shouldn't be locked behind paywalls.

Why not join them in freeing knowledge by supporting us:
https://www.openbookpublishers.com/support-us

Follow @OpenBookPublish

Read more at the Open Book Publishers BLOG

You may also be interested in:

Democracy and Power
The Delhi Lectures
Noam Chomsky

https://doi.org/10.11647/obp.0050

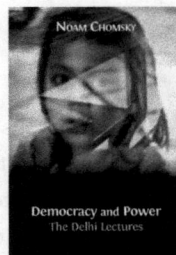

Peace and Democratic Society
Amartya Sen (Ed.)

https://doi.org/10.11647/obp.0014

Thinking Blue / Writing Red
Marxism and the (Post)Human
Stephen Tumino

https://doi.org/10.11647/obp.0324

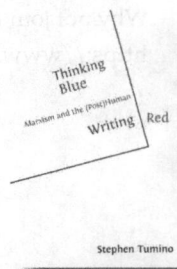